THE ROUGH GUIDE

Macs & OS X

by
Peter Buckley and Duncan Clark

ROUGH GUIDES

www.roughguides.com

Credits

The Rough Guide to Macs & OS X

Text, Layout & Design:
Peter Buckley & Duncan Clark
Proofreading: Michelle Bhatia
Production: Julia Bovis & Katherine Owers

Rough Guides Reference

Series editor: Mark Ellingham
Editors: Peter Buckley, Duncan Clark,
Matthew Milton, Joe Staines
Director: Andrew Lockett

Acknowledgements

All pictures of Macs and iPods courtesy of Apple Computer

Publishing Information

This first edition published October 2005 by
Rough Guides Ltd, 80 Strand, London WC2R 0RL
345 Hudson St, 4th Floor, New York 10014, USA
Email: mail@roughguides.com

Distributed by the Penguin Group:
Penguin Books Ltd, 80 Strand, London WC2R 0RL
Penguin Putnam, Inc., 375 Hudson Street, NY 10014, USA
Penguin Group (Australia), 250 Camberwell Road, Camberwell, Victoria 3124, Australia
Penguin Books Canada Ltd, 10 Alcorn Avenue, Toronto, Ontario, Canada M4V 1E4
Penguin Group (New Zealand), Cnr Rosedale and Airborne Roads, Albany, Auckland, New Zealand

Printed in Italy by LegoPrint S.p.A

Typeset in Minion and Myriad to an original design by Peter Buckley & Duncan Clark

A catalogue record for this book is available from the British Library

ISBN 13: 978-1-84353-553-9
ISBN 10: 1-84353-553-X

1   3   5   7   9   8   6   4   2

Contents

contents

PICTURES

VIDEO

SECURITY & MAINTENANCE

MACOLOGY

About this book

Macs aren't perfect. But with their elegant design and ergonomic OS X operating system, they come much closer to a futuristic digital Utopia than the ugly, virus-infested Windows alternative. Indeed, on the whole, modern Macs are a joy to use. We wouldn't have written and designed this book using them if we didn't think so. In fact, we wouldn't have written this book at all.

If you're reading this, however, you probably don't need much convincing. Chances are you're either a Mac user already, or you're sick of PCs and are thinking of defecting. Either way, *The Rough Guide to Macs & OS X* has something for you. It covers everything from buying and upgrading Macs, via making music, editing pictures and creating DVDs, to online security and customizing your system with extra software.

We've avoided the patronizing walk-throughs common to much computer publishing ("This is a mouse – try clicking the button!"), so as to pack in more of the stuff that you'll actually find useful and interesting. As well as background information and scores of tips and tricks, we've included plenty of links to websites and downloadable goodies, plus the occasional bit of wider context – such as the weird world of Apple obsession covered in Chapter 38.

This book focuses on OS X version 10.4 – aka "Tiger" – and covers all its major new features, such as Dashboard and Spotlight. If you purchased your Mac before summer 2005, and you haven't upgraded, then you'll have an older version. In that case, a few of the things we describe will be missing, or different, on your Mac, but the vast majority of what you read will still apply.

Finally, a couple of things to note. Prices are stated in $US and £UK (real prices, not conversions), though in the case of software downloads you'll often see only one currency listed. That's because you'll pay in this currency regardless of where you are in the world, either by credit card or a safe online payment service such as PayPal (www.paypal.com). And if you find yourself confounded by some strange hieroglyphics – the likes of ⌘ ⌥ ⌫ – these are simply instructions for keyboard shortcuts. To find out how to interpret them, see p.48.

Frequently asked questions

Macs & PCs

What's a Mac?

A Mac is one of a series of personal computers produced by a company called Apple. Macs – which take their name from the McIntosh, an apple variety grown in northern USA – have been around for more than two decades, though today's slick-looking models don't look or work much like the machine released to much fanfare back in January 1984.

Macs come in various shapes and sizes: laptops and desktops aimed at both the consumer and professional markets. Despite their varied portability and firepower, however, all Macs work in the same way, since they all run the software operating system OS X (more on this overleaf).

What's a PC?

PC stands for personal computer, so in that broad sense a Mac is a kind of PC. But in everyday use, the term "PC" means something far more specific than just any old personal computer. It refers to a particular type of machine capable of running Microsoft's Windows operating system (not to be confused with Microsoft's Office programs, such as Word and Excel, which are available for both Macs and PCs).

In this more standard sense, PC is short for "IBM PC compatible", reflecting the fact that modern-day PCs are based on a model released by IBM back in 1981. Today, however, PCs – unlike Macs – are made by countless different companies; you can even purchase the various components and build your own. For more on PCs, see *The Rough Guide to PCs & Windows*.

How many Mac users are there?

Apple is an amazingly visible and influential company – especially in this era of iPod adulation. But Macs account for only a very small percentage of the world's personal computers. Figures vary, but most current estimates give Macs a 2–3 percent market share globally, and 4–5 percent in the US and Europe. Some studies claim to show that Macs score better when you measure the "installed base" of computers actually in use; but there are also figures that suggest the opposite.

Which is better, a Mac or a PC?

Macs and PCs both have their die-hard devotees, so be careful posing this question or you might find yourself on the receiving end of an impassioned rant. In truth, both camps make some fair points.

Operating systems

Every modern computer features an operating system, or OS: the underlying software that acts as a bridge between the hardware (the physical bits), the application software (programs such as word processors or image editors) and the user (you). On current Macs, the operating system is OS X. On PCs, it's usually Windows, though it may also be Linux or various others. For more on OS X, see p.7.

The main argument in favour of PCs is that you get better value in terms of sheer bang per buck. That is, if you take a Mac and a PC with the same price tag, the Mac will be slower at accomplishing most tasks. Why the price difference? It's partly because Apple use high quality components and throw in lots of good software, but competition between PC manufacturers also has a lot to do with it. Apple's design budget must also be factored in: everything from the computers to the boxes they come in are produced with almost obsessive attention to detail. You might also make the case that, since whole industries (such as publishing) are effectively locked in to Mac use by industry-wide convention, Apple's pricing of high-spec computers strikes a balance between winning new consumer users on the one hand and maximizing the revenue from commercial sales on the other.

Intel, Wintel, MacIntel...

The defining feature of a "PC", as opposed to a Mac, is that its central processor, or CPU, is a member of the x86 family. This type of processor was first produced by Intel, who still dominate the market. Since most PCs combine these Intel-style processors with the Windows operating system, they're commonly referred to as "Wintel" machines.

Since 1997, Macs have used the PowerPC family of processors (which includes the G3, G4 and G5), manufactured by IBM. But in mid-2005, Apple announced that they were switching over to the PC-style x86 processors in 2006–07. Supposedly, the reason is that IBM failed to keep up with its own development "roadmap", but many commentators have suggested other reasons (such as Apple wanting to score bargain iPod chips from Intel). Whatever the reason, it's goodbye G5.

Intel Macs, already dubbed "MacIntel" or "Mactel", are likely to offer higher speeds at lower costs. The first models to be released are expected to be Mac laptops with Pentium M processors. These should appear some time in 2006, with desktops following afterwards. The complete Mac line is due to be Intel-based by the end of 2007.

Another advantage of PCs is there's a broader selection of hardware peripherals to choose from. For example, if you want to buy a webcam (see p.163) for a PC, you can choose from a huge range of models and prices; the only choice for Mac users is Apple's own iSight (see p.163). This is probably the best webcam ever made, but it doesn't come cheap. Similarly, PC users claim to have a broader selection of software applications at their disposal.

So why choose a Mac?

Despite the above points, Macs have a whole lot going for them. For a start, since the core hardware and software components are designed by the same company, the whole package "just works" to a much greater extent than with PCs. In the course of a Mac's lifetime, you're far less likely to run into hardware conflicts, inexplicable malfunctions and the like.

Even if you do have problems, you may find a Mac easier to troubleshoot. Millions of people will have exactly the same Mac model as you (unlike with PCs, where each producer combines a slightly different selection of hardware components). This means that, when you run into trouble, someone else has probably come across precisely the same annoyance – and posted a solution on the Web.

Another advantage of Macs – and one that's becoming more important year on year – is that they're far less susceptible to online woes such as viruses and spyware (see p.264). This is less to do with the way Macs are designed, and more to do with the fact that malicious programmers tend to focus their misdeeds on Windows. To date, there's never been a serious virus outbreak on Macs.

Then there are aesthetics to consider. Apple was the first company to make computers that are actually pleasant to look at, and it remains almost impossible to find a PC with even the slightest

A design thang

Jonathan Ive has frequently been credited with having reinvigorated Apple's fortunes with his clean, streamlined designs. The 1997 iMac was his, as was the iPod and G4 Cube.

Born in London in 1967, Ive studied art and design in Newcastle and then set up his own design company, Tangerine. In 1992, he presented his new laptop design to Apple and they liked it so much they offered him a job. Today he is the company's Senior Vice President of Industrial Design.

But life wasn't always so glamorous for Mr Ive. The story goes that only a few days before his big break with Apple, Ive was presenting a new design to the bathroom-suite company Ideal Standard. The location was Hull, the item was a toilet, and the design was rejected. It was Comic Relief's Red Nose day, and, as if to add insult to injury, the company's head of marketing sat through the presentation wearing a plastic hooter.

visual appeal. And when it comes to computers, beauty isn't always skin deep. Macs score highly on build quality, as well as other not-so-obvious things such as laptop battery life.

As for software, PC users may have more available, but a huge percentage of it is ugly, unreliable and, potentially, full of spyware. In truth, nearly every major application is available for OS X, as well as tens of thousands of other programs, plug-ins, widgets and utilities, many of them downloadable via the Apple site.

But probably the single most persuasive reason for buying a Mac is the operating system, OS X…

OS X

What's OS X?

As already explained, every personal computer has an operating system, or OS. This is the software responsible for controlling the physical hardware of the machine. It also provides the "platform" on which other programs run, and features a set of tools to help you browse, copy and delete files, and choose which application to open them into. Modern operating systems typically come bundled with a wide range of extra programs, from Web browsers (see p.143) to simple word processors (see p.117).

The operating system found on Macs is called, logically enough, Mac OS (at least that's been the name since 1996; before then it was just called "System"). The current generation of Mac OS is the tenth, hence the term OS X – pronounced "ten" not "ex". The first edition of OS X was released in 2001, replacing OS 9.

OS X on a PC?

Mac OS has always been available for use on Macs and Macs alone. But the 2005 announcement that Apple is preparing OS X for a new generation of Macs based on PC-style processors (see p.5) has raised the prospect of being able to run OS X on PCs. Apple have no professed intention of allowing this to happen, so although a number of PC manufacturers – including Dell – have suggested they might be interested in offering "Mac PCs", this looks unlikely in the immediate future. In the longer term, it seems perfectly plausible that Apple will find the opportunity to eat into Microsoft's monopoly too tempting to resist. But until then, the only PC versions of OS X are likely to be the illegal "cracked" copies that will doubtless be circulated on the Net before the new OS X is even released.

Why X not 10?

There are a couple of reasons why Apple chose "OS X" over "OS 10". First, while many previous updates to the Mac system had been relatively minor (OS 8 doesn't look or feel very different to OS 9, for example) OS X was a total redesign. The "X" helped Apple make the difference as apparent as possible.

The second reason is that OS X is based on another operating system called UNIX, and there's a long traditional of UNIX-based systems having names ending in X – Linux, Minix and Xenix being just a few examples.

Which is better, OS X or Windows?

Modern versions of both Mac OS and Windows are incomparably better than their predecessors. Both systems are relatively stable, and both feature a host of useful features. As to which is better, it's largely down to personal preference, though many people who are experienced with both systems (including the authors of this book) find OS X *much* nicer to work with.

Comparing the two systems available at the time of writing, OS 10.4 ("Tiger") feels much more intuitive, flexible, elegant and powerful than Windows XP. This is partly down to some excellent "surface" features, such as the Dock, but it's also because of how and when it was developed. At its base is the security, stability and power of the venerable UNIX system, but the interface (the "look and feel") was designed pretty much from scratch only a few years ago, and has been energetically improved every year since.

By comparison, Windows, with its global monopoly clearly established, has been substantially improved only once every few years, with each new version feeling like an unhappy compromise between real invention and a fear of changing too much.

What's UNIX?

UNIX is a powerful multi-user operating system known for being stable and secure. First developed in the late 1960s by staff at AT&T, it's now available in many different versions – some free, others commercial. Initially used primarily in academic and scientific contexts, UNIX later became popular for Internet-related tasks, but wasn't used on personal computers until the advent of Linux (a free, open-source UNIX-based system) in the early 1990s. UNIX finally entered the consumer market mainstream when Apple chose to use BSD – the UNIX version developed at Berkeley university – as the basis of Mac OS X. Technically, OS X is not actually "a UNIX system", as it isn't certified to meet the Single UNIX Specification, but that's pretty-much detail. Anyone who knows UNIX can roughly find their way around OS X's technical back-end – via the Terminal utility – and Macs can even run UNIX applications, though only once the applications have been "recompiled".

"OS X 10.4.2 Tiger". Eh?

Every year or so Apple release a new edition of the Mac operating system, complete with new features and other improvements. These new versions are not radically different enough to be branded "OS 11" or "OS XI". Instead, they're considered new versions of OS X and are numbered accordingly: v10.1, v10.2, and so on. The latest edition is given away with new Macs, and is also available to buy as an upgrade for existing Macs (see p.34).

Beside these major new versions, Apple also releases interim upgrades to each version to fix problems, improve security and perhaps add a feature or two. These interim upgrades add another decimal point to the number. If you installed OS X v10.4, your Mac's Software Update tool (see p.46) may flash up offering you v10.4.2. A few months down the line, you'll get v10.4.3, and so on.

As well as a number, the last three versions of OS X – v.10.2, 10.3 and 10.4 – have been named after a type of big cat: Jaguar, Panther and Tiger respectively. Leopard, aka OS X v10.5, is expected in early 2006. This is presumably intended primarily to help market them: "Tiger Unleashed" certainly has more of a ring to it than "10.4 Unleashed". It also gives Mac users a shorthand that's more friendly and memorable than a number with one decimal place.

The choice of giant felines stems from the fact that OS X version 10.0 and 10.1 were codenamed Cheetah and Puma in Apple HQ during their development. Such code-naming is quite normal in the world of software: Windows XP was code-named "Whistler", for example, and the follow-up is known as "Longhorn".

Can I install OS X on my old Mac?

Possibly, but it may not be worth it. Turn to p.34 for more information on upgrading your operating system.

OS Wars

For a superb in-depth and balanced comparison of OS X Tiger and Windows XP, visit:

XvsXP www.xvsxp.com

The site examines and rates nearly every element of the two operating systems. The overall scores at the time of writing are: 800 for OS X and 665 for XP home.

2

Thinking of switching?

Will I find a Mac difficult to get used to?

If you're used to Windows, switching to a Mac is inevitably a touch confusing for a while, though most converts find the transition to be relatively painless – not least because Mac OS X is a very user-friendly and intuitive system. Furthermore, unless you're quite technically savvy anyway (in which case you won't struggle at all), most of your computer skills are related to specific applications, rather than the system itself. These applications don't vary much: using, say, Microsoft Word on a Mac really isn't very different from using Microsoft Word on a PC.

If you're terrible with computers, and it took you years to master your PC, then the changeover will undoubtedly be a tad more confusing. But work your way through this book and you'll probably end up far more clued-up and skilled on your Mac than you ever were on your PC.

Will my PC documents, data, emails and applications work on a Mac?

Not long ago, Macs and PCs spoke very different languages, but these days compatibility is not much of an issue for the average home user. That said, don't assume that everything on your PC can be effortlessly migrated to your new Mac.

What's easy is copying all your documents, photos, emails, contacts and so on onto the Mac. The question is whether you'll actually be able to open them. Many common file types won't pose any problems – photos, PDFs, simple text files, and so on. But other types of files require you to install the appropriate application. For example, if you want to open and edit Microsoft Excel documents, you'll need to install Excel.

Unfortunately, you can't actually install PC programs on Macs (at least not without the hassle and expense of running a Windows emulator package: see box). So you'd have to acquire the Mac version of the application in question – assuming it even exists and that the two platform-specific versions are perfectly compatible. Furthermore, buying the Mac version of an application is a pain if you've already paid for the PC version.

In certain cases, files can be opened on a Mac but only after a certain amount of fiddling around. For example, you might want to move all your old emails from Outlook Express (on the PC) to Apple Mail (the Mac equivalent). This can be done but only via a faffy process involving IMAP mail (see p.72).

For more on actually "migrating" your emails, files and more from a PC to a Mac, see p.71.

Windows emulators

If you want to run Windows programs on a Mac, or connect to Windows-only hardware or networks, you'll need a PC emulator. These let you run a fully functional version of Windows within the OS X environment. It's slower than a "real" PC, but usable enough for most tasks. There are various emulators on the market (see www.macwindows.com), but the most popular is Microsoft's own Virtual PC, which even puts a Windows Start menu in the OS X Dock. If you already own a copy of Windows, you can buy Virtual PC for $129; otherwise it's $219, or $499 as part of Microsoft Office Pro. Read more at mactopia.com

Are Macs OK for Microsoft Word?

First, let's get a few things absolutely clear, since this is a common point of confusion. Word – and the Office "suite" that it is a part of – is separate from Windows, despite the fact that both are made by Microsoft, and despite the fact that some new PCs are sold with Word or Office pre-installed.

Word is available for both Macs and PCs, and though the Mac version looks a tiny bit different from the PC version, they're essentially the same. A Mac with Word installed *can* open, edit and resave a Word doc created on a PC – and vice versa.

Currently, new Macs ship with a trial version of the whole Office suite (including Word), which works for a couple of weeks. After that, you can pay online to turn the trial version into a full version. Alternatively, acquire Word or Office from elsewhere.

What about my music files?

Music files in the MP3 format, as well as any AAC files created or purchased using the PC version of iTunes, will work fine on a Mac. The other popular format – WMA (Windows Media Audio) – may be more problematic. WMA files you created yourself by "ripping" CDs should be OK. But if you purchased them from a legal download service you may find they are protected by Digital Rights Management (DRM), which could stop them playing on the Mac. There is usually a way around this (see p.72), but it's not ideal.

Will my printer and peripherals work?

Most printers are compatible with Macs. Indeed, in most cases you can just plug in a printer and it will work straight off (OS X comes preloaded with around one gigabyte's worth of printer drivers).

Note, though, that Macs don't have a parallel socket – the long sockets with teeth and screws used to attach older printers – so you'll need a printer with a USB connection.

Other PC peripherals that should work fine with a new Mac include monitors, external hard drives and keydrives (also known as thumb drives and USB flash drives). Most scanners and digital cameras are also compatible, though it's worth checking with the manufacturer (or doing a bit of research via Google) to make sure, especially if the device is more than a few years old.

However, there are also many peripherals that won't work on Macs – at least not without advanced technical tweaking way beyond the skills of most people. This includes webcams and Wi-Fi adapters, many MP3 players and gaming devices, as well as some older scanners, cameras and printers.

For a full list of devices that OS X can handle without any driver installation, see:

OS X Upgrade www.apple.com/macosx/upgrade

My friends use PCs. Does that matter?

Switching to a Mac won't affect your ability to email, share pictures and instant message with your PC-using friends and family. One thing to note, however: video conferencing with a webcam (see p.162) will only work if the PC users are prepared to install AOL Instant Messenger.

What about my work?

If you're wondering whether a Mac would be suitable for work as well as home use, think about which applications you use at your place of employment. If it's mainly Word, Excel, PowerPoint and other standard office programs, you shouldn't have many problems, assuming you install Microsoft Office on the Mac. Occasionally there might be annoyances – a document written in a PC typeface, for example, might look different on a Mac – but you won't often run into more serious problems.

For any other applications, however – from corporate systems to graphics packages – it might be more difficult, or simply impossible, to do the work on a Mac. And, in the case of laptops, you may not be able to attach your Mac laptop to certain office networks. So be sure to enquire with whoever runs the computer system at your workplace before splashing out.

What's with the one-button mouse?

One thing that infuriates many PC users when they try out a Mac is that the mouse (or trackpad on a laptop) only has one button. This is part of Apple's desire to keep their computers approachable and easy to use, but don't worry if you think you'll miss your right button. Holding down the **Control** button while you click does exactly the same thing as pressing the right button. And if you don't like that solution, you can plug in any two-button USB mouse and it will work just as it does on a PC.

Can a Mac and a PC share files, Internet and printers in a home network?

Absolutely – and unless your PC is ancient, it shouldn't be difficult to set up. For more information on networking and sharing files and Internet, turn to p.63. For printer sharing, see p.138.

Buying & upgrading

Where to buy, when to buy

The obvious place to buy a new Mac is from the Apple Store via either the phone or the Web. The main advantage of this option is that you get to customize the computer with a different hard drive size, Bluetooth and other such options (see p.28).

Apple Store UK www.apple.com/ukstore • 0800-039-1010
Apple Store US www.apple.com/store • 1-800-MY-APPLE

Other dealers typically won't let you customize the Mac – at least not to the same extent – but their prices might be fractionally lower than Apple's. Also, different sellers may throw in different extras, so it's worth shopping around. The easiest way to do this is using a price-comparison agent such as, in the US:

Froogle www.froogle.com
Shopper.com www.shopper.com
Shopping.com www.shopping.com

…and in the UK:

Kelkoo www.kelkoo.co.uk
PriceRunner www.pricerunner.com
Shopping.com uk.shopping.com

Tip: At the time of going to press, the Apple Store will lower their price on Macs and other Apple products by up to ten percent to match lower prices found elsewhere. Note this doesn't apply to educational buying, and the compared prices don't include delivery, sales tax (in the US), and other extras. For more details, call the regular Apple Store number.

where to buy, when to buy

In the US, you can keep track of ▶
the various offers, discounts and
rebates available on all types
of Macs at the buyers' guides at
www.macreviewzone.com
and dealmac.com

Buying abroad

Many prospective UK Mac owners stumble across the US Apple Store website and notice a significant difference in price – especially when the pound is strong against the dollar. The obvious question is: should I wait and get a friend to bring me back a Mac from the US? Many people have done just this and made savings, though if you're considering it, you should bear in mind the following: though you're unlikely to get fined, it's technically illegal unless you declare it; the prices you see on the US Apple Store don't include sales tax, which adds up to 7.25 percent; and a US Apple warranty will only work in the UK for laptops, not desktops.

One problem with buying over the Internet or phone – including from Apple themselves – is that you can usually expect around a week's wait for delivery. Some online retailers tend to be quicker, including the best known of all:

Amazon US www.amazon.com
Amazon UK www.amazon.co.uk

But if you want the Mac the same day, your only choice is to visit a "real" store. In the US – and in London, Birmingham and Manchester in the UK – that might mean heading straight to one of Apple's own retail stores. For a list, see:

Apple Retail Stores www.apple.com/retail

Or to locate other approved Mac dealers, follow the "Where to buy" links from:

Apple Hardware US www.apple.com/hardware
Apple Hardware UK www.apple.com/uk/hardware

Pre-owned Macs

Refurbished Macs

Apple, and a few other retailers, offer refurbished Macs. These are either end-of-line models or up-to-date ones which have been returned for some reason. They come "as new" – checked, repackaged and with a full standard warranty – but they are reduced in price by up to 45 percent (though it's usually more like 15 percent). The only problem is availability: the products are in such hot demand that, in the UK, you can only see Apple's selection on Wednesdays, from 10am onwards (get there early).

Apple Store UK Refurbished
http://promo.euro.apple.com/promo/refurb/uk

In the US, supply is also limited, though you can at least check whether anything is on offer throughout the week. Follow the

Special Deals link from the Apple Store website (www.apple.com/store) or, for the most up-to-date information about availability, call 1-800-MY-APPLE. Alternatively, check with your local Apple retailer to see whether they offer refurbished or returned Macs.

Used Macs

Buying a used Mac is much like buying any other piece of used electronic equipment: you might find a bargain but you might land yourself an overpriced bookend. That said, the standard Apple warranty is, in practice at least, transferable, so if you buy one that is less than a year old (and with the documentation to prove it) you should be able to get it repaired for free if anything goes wrong early on. Obviously, that will rely on the type of damage being covered by the warranty. It will also rely – except in the case of laptops, which are covered internationally – on the Mac having been purchased in the country where you want to get it repaired.

If you do buy a used Mac, make sure you see it in action before parting with any cash (except if you're shopping on eBay: see box), but remember that this won't tell you everything. Like all computers, Macs can develop hidden hardware problems that lead them to cut out unexpectedly. Or a particular component – the FireWire port, say – might be broken. In the case of laptops, also think about battery life, which diminishes over time. If an iBook or PowerBook battery has had heavy use, it may soon need replacing – which will add substantially to the cost: see p.279.

Also consider that older models won't necessarily support more recent accessories or software, and that older Macs will run slowly if you upgrade to the most recent version of OS X.

Finally, before buying any used Mac, investigate to see whether a new version is rumoured to be coming out in a few weeks' time (see

see p.279.

Macs on eBay

Though it's better to see any used item before you buy it, the online auction site eBay does cover your back to a degree. You can ask the seller as many questions as you want via email before you commit to a bid – something you may not feel able to do when responding to a classified ad. And by selling on eBay, the vendor enters into a legally-binding contract that they will supply a product in exactly the condition they have described. So even if you're one of the tiny minority who get scammed, you may be able to recover your cash. The only problem is that there's such demand for Macs on eBay that you're unlikely to save much cash compared to buying new.

eBay UK computers.ebay.co.uk
eBay US computers.ebay.com

below). If so, you might be better off waiting, because when the new Mac comes out, older used models are suddenly less expensive and more widely available on the second-hand market.

To buy or to wait?

When shopping for any piece of computer equipment, there's always the tricky question of whether to buy the current model, which may have been around for a few months, or hang on for the next version, which may be both better and less expensive. In the case of Macs, the dilemma is even worse than normal, both because they're expensive and because Apple are famously secretive about their plans to release new or upgraded versions of their hardware.

Unless you have a friend who works in Apple HQ – and an opportunity to get them drunk – you're unlikely to hear anything specific from the horse's mouth about new Mac models until the day they appear. So, unless a new one came out recently, there's always the possibility that your new purchase will be out of date within a few weeks. About the best you can do is check out some sites where rumours of new models are discussed. But don't believe everything you read...

Apple Insider www.appleinsider.com
Mac Rumors www.macrumors.com

Wait for an Intel Mac?

As this book goes to press, Mac sales, especially laptops, are expected to dip a little as savvy buyers wait for new-generation Macs powered by Intel processors (see p.5). It's definitely worth getting the latest rumours on this before buying any G4- or G5-based Mac, new or used.

Which model, which specs

Once you've decided to purchase a Mac, then comes the hard bit: picking which model to plump for and choosing a set of specifications suited to your needs and budget. The following few pages may help: we've avoided giving detailed information on the specs of each Mac model, since it would probably be out of date before this book even rolled off the press. Instead, we've focused on the general issues and options that you need to consider before you buy.

The first decision you need to make is whether to go for a laptop (notebook) or a desktop. If you need to work on the move, then the decision is already made, but many people also buy laptops for home use, as they're so easy to move between rooms and hide away when not in use. Indeed, in May 2005 total US laptop sales even overtook those of desktops. Perhaps the most attractive thing about a laptop is wireless Internet, which lets you browse the Web, email and chat anywhere in the house or garden.

But mobility doesn't come free. For a Mac laptop and Mac desktop with roughly comparable specs, expect to pay around 50 percent more for the laptop. And, of course, the most powerful Mac laptop will be much less powerful than the top-of-the-range desktop.

Tip: In general, Macs aimed at the professional market are labelled "Power" and are housed in anodized aluminium cases, while consumer and education models, whose names are usually prefixed with an "i" or "e", are cased in durable white plastic.

Mac laptops: PowerBook or iBook?

Since 1999, Apple have produced two laptop families: iBooks, aimed primarily at the consumer and education market, and PowerBooks, aimed mainly at professionals. Appearance-wise, the two families follow the wider Apple tendency: plastic for consumers; metal for pros.

PowerBook

Not all the differences between the iBook and PowerBook are set in stone. For example, PowerBooks come with built-in Bluetooth (see p.31) and large hard drives, but if you shop at the Apple store you can add both these features to an iBook at the time of purchase. However, other differences are more fundamental. The main advantages of the current PowerBooks are:

▶ **Horsepower** At any one time, the main processors offered in PowerBooks are faster than those in iBooks. PowerBooks also have faster internal data connections (bus speed), use faster RAM and can hold more of it. All in all, this adds up a to a zippier laptop, especially when using processor-intensive applications.

▶ **Size** The PowerBook range offers bigger screen sizes and thinner bodies.

▶ **Video connections** PowerBooks offer many ways to connect to external screens: DVI and ADC, besides the S-Video, Composite and VGA capabilities of iBooks. Furthermore, they allow "screen spanning" (using two monitors simultaneously as if they were one big screen) and "clamshell mode" (running a PowerBook closed, with an external keyboard, mouse and monitor). Note, however, that it is possible, unofficially, to achieve monitor spanning and clamshell on an iBook (see box overleaf).

▲

The wide screens on the PowerBook 15" (pictured) and 17" models are great for working with video, images and page layouts.

▶ **Line-in** PowerBooks feature an audio line-in jack, so that you can record directly from an external sound source; iBooks, by comparison require an external audio interface (see p.202) to record sound.

▶ **Other ports and slots** PowerBooks support faster Ethernet and FireWire ports (non-essential for most home users), and, except for the 12" model, feature a PCMCIA ("PC Card") slot for devices such as 3G data cards (see p.62). They also have one USB port on each side (as opposed to two on the left-hand side on an iBook) – useful when connecting an external mouse, for example.

iBook advantages

The above features make quite a big difference for professional-level video, sound and image work, but most home users won't notice much benefit – unless you get into video editing. For the rest, an iBook should deliver more than enough power (indeed, much of this book has been edited and typeset on an iBook G4). And, though iBooks may not be quite as fast as PowerBooks, they do have some advantages of their own, in addition to being much less expensive:

▶ **Wireless range** iBooks have excellent wireless reception – better than most PCs and also better than the PowerBook, since the plastic body disturbs the signal less than the aluminium.

▶ **Impact resistance** iBooks are not completely indestructible, but they're much closer to being so than most computers

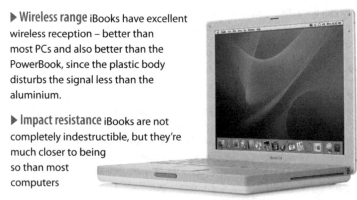

Screen spanning

iBooks, iMacs and eMacs cannot by default handle screen-spanning: the use of a second screen to "extend" the built-in display. They can connect to an external display, but it simply "mirrors" what's on the built-in screen rather than allowing you to use a higher resolution setting and "arrange" the two screens as if they were two parts of one huge monitor. It is possible, however, to circumvent this limitation using a free down-loadable utility called Screen Spanning Doctor (available from www.macparts.de). The program is not supported by Apple, and may damage computers that aren't on the list of compatible machines. Hence its use may invalidate your warranty. But that hasn't stopped it being very popular online – especially among iBook users.

thanks to their polycarbonate plastic shell – made from "the same high-grade material used in bulletproof glass", according to Apple. This durability is one of the reasons iBooks are popular with the education market.

▶ **Heat and noise** PowerBooks are more susceptible to getting uncomfortably hot than iBooks. And though PowerBooks are extremely quiet compared with many PC laptops, iBooks are practically silent.

▶ **Battery life** Fully charged, an iBook battery will run for slightly longer than that of a PowerBook. At the time of writing, iBooks keep going for up to six hours and PowerBooks go for either five hours (12") or four and a half (15"/17"). For more on maximizing your laptop's battery life, see p.279.

Our conclusion? Unless you plan to do serious video or sound editing, you'll get far better value with the iBook. But be sure to chock up the RAM (see p.30).

> **Tip:** Both PowerBooks and iBooks perform far better with extra RAM (see p.30). So factor in this extra cost when choosing between them.

Mac desktops: mini, e, i & Power?

Mac desktop computers currently fall into two families: Mac mini, iMac, eMac and Power Mac. As with laptops, some of the differences – AirPort, hard drive size, etc – can be cancelled out by customizing the machine when you buy (see p.28), but others – from shape and size to internal firepower – cannot. Here's a quick briefing on the main pros and cons of each of the four types of desktop Macs available at the time of going to press.

> **Tip:** As we explain on p.278, it's possible to use one Mac as an external hard drive to another Mac. This is particularly useful for Mac mini owners. For example, you could take your Mac mini from home and open its files on a desktop Mac at work.

Mac mini

Released to much acclaim in January 2005, the Mac mini is designed primarily for PC users wanting an inexpensive way to

which model, which specs

The Mac mini doesn't leave much room for upgrades, but third-party extras make it possible to keep expanding. This MicroNet miniMate sits snugly under a mini, providing 400GB of disk space, 4 USB ports and 3 FireWire ports.

▼

Tip: The iMac's "i" is said to have originally stood for Internet, while the "e" in eMac reflects the fact that this model was originally sold only in the education market.

switch to a Mac. The mini comes without monitor, keyboard or mouse, the idea being that you use the ones you already have for your PC. Simply replace the PC's beige box with the diminutive Mac (6.5" x 6.5" x 2") and switch on.

Any monitor – DVI or VGA – should work fine with a Mac mini, though the keyboard and mouse need to be the type that connect with USB rather than PS/2 (the old-school round-ended connectors). If you do have a PS/2 keyboard and/or mouse, you can pick up an adaptor for around $15/£10, or buy new ones. For the keyboard, at least, it's worth considering an Apple model ($29/£19 at the time of writing), partly so you don't have a Windows key in place of a command (⌘) key, and partly because an Apple keyboard comes with two USB ports handily positioned on the back.

But the mini isn't only for PC users thinking of switching. It's also the single least-expensive way to get a Mac – even if you have to buy a monitor. And it's by far the least expensive way to get a portable Mac – it's even lighter than a laptop to carry around, so can easily be taken, say, from home to work. (That said, you have to factor in a pretty bulky power adapter.)

As for processing speed, the mini isn't exactly a powerhouse, so it's not ideal for video editing or gaming. But it's more than capable of holding its own for the vast majority of tasks – especially if you get extra RAM when you buy.

eMac and iMac

If you fancy something with a bit more kick, a DVD burner ("SuperDrive") or a built-in screen, you can choose from the two straight-out-of-the-box Mac models: the economical eMac and the slicker, more powerful flatscreen iMac.

The first iMac, released in 1998, was one of the most radical

redefinitions of the personal computer in history. The machine may have lacked power and upgradability, but its slick design and out-of-the-box user-friendliness was a real breakthrough. In 2002, Apple completely revised the iMac to add a flat screen, and introduced the eMac – essentially a bigger, faster version of the first iMac – as a less expensive option, primarily for the education market. Both eMac and iMac have been improved substantially since then.

The iMac is almost like a large, powerful laptop on a stand. It has a narrow "footprint" and is lighter to carry around than the eMac (left). For another iMac pic, see p.3.

So which to choose? Aesthetics aside, the iMac is an altogether more powerful computer, partly due to its higher-end processor. (At the time of writing, the iMac features a G5 processor, and the eMac has a G4, though it remains to be seen how these two models will develop during the transition to Intel processors, due to be completed by 2007.) The iMac also benefits from higher RAM capacity, faster RAM type and much zippier bus speeds (internal data connections).

Once you also factor the wider, higher-res screens available on the iMac, it's clear that this model is far better equipped than the eMac for multimedia work such as video, music and picture editing. It also scores highly as a DVD player, thanks to its wide screens and lower weight, making it easier to move between rooms.

But if value is what you're after, the eMac is hard to beat. It may have been designed as an "education computer", but it's more than capable of performing everything that the average home computer would do – albeit slightly slower than the iMac. If you want an all-in-one machine mainly to use for Internet, iTunes, Word, and digital photos, perhaps with the occasional bit of amateur video and sound editing, then this is the best-value choice by far.

The Power Mac G5.

Power Mac

The Power Mac is Apple's top-end desktop. It's often referred to as just the "G5" (or "G4" for the older models), after its PowerPC G5 processor, though this is set to change with the arrival of Intel processors some time in 2006–07.

The main advantage of a Power Mac is its sheer speed, which it achieves courtesy of one or two high-speed 64-bit CPUs, super-fast bus connections and a massive RAM capacity (up to eight gigabytes at the time of going to press). Unlike other Macs, it also features a "tower"-style case, which leaves room for multiple hard drives as well as PCI and AGP slots to host (among other things) professional-level video cards capable of powering up to two enormous screens. And there are scores of ports (from Bluetooth antenna to optical audio) to boot, including some handily stationed on the front of the case.

Do you really need this kind of power and expandability? If you plan to do professional-level graphics, video or sound editing, or supercomputer-style number crunching, then perhaps you do – in which case the Power Mac is a matchless computer. If not, it's both overpriced (note that no monitor is included in the advertised prices) and overweight (clocking in at nine times heavier than an 12" iBook).

Which specs?

Once you've chosen which type of Mac to buy, you need to pick a specific model. And, if you buy the computer via the Apple store (see p.17), you'll be offered various customization options at the time of purchase. The factors you may need to grapple with include the following:

▶ **Processor** The processor, or CPU, is the brain of a computer: the bit that actually does the computing. This is a key factor in determining a Mac's potential speed, but don't think that it's the only one – getting a slightly slower-processor model and spending the extra money on plenty of RAM (see p.30) will often result in a faster machine.

▶ **Screen size** A bigger, wider screen is always nice to have. It comes into its own for watching DVDs and working with professional-level applications in which the "palettes" of options take up quite a lot of screen real-estate even before you open a file. Note, however, that the dimensions of a screen in pixels are more important than its physical size. At the time of writing, for example, there are two iBook screen sizes, but they both have the same number of pixels. That means you can't actually fit any extra information on the bigger screen: it's just that each pixel is slightly larger.

▶ **Combo Drive** or **SuperDrive** All Macs come with either a Combo Drive (which will playback CDs and DVDs and burn recordable CDs) or a SuperDrive (which will do the same but also burn DVDs). Burning DVDs is useful for distributing your home videos to friends and family, and also for backing up data. But if backing up is your main aim, you could consider spending the extra money on an external hard drive instead.

▶ **Hard drive capacity** The hard drive is a computer's storage cupboard where all your documents, music, applications and other files live. There are different types of hard drive but, when customizing a Mac, the only thing you

How many gigs?

When choosing a hard drive size, the first thing to consider is that a decent chunk of the space will be used up even before you've saved your first file. One reason for this is that hard drives, once formatted and in use, always offer around 7 percent less space than advertised. Another is that OS X and the applications that come with a Mac take up a few gigabytes themselves. So a "60GB" hard drive, for example, only really offers around 50GB of empty space. In that space, you'll be saving all your files, including the following:

▶ Music Allow around 1GB per 200 songs in iTunes. Or, for making your own music at CD quality, 1GB equals around 90 minutes.

▶ Video Unedited footage imported from a DV camera (see p. 249) takes up around 1GB per 5 minutes of footage.

▶ Photos Depending on the camera and setting, you'd fit around 1000 pictures in 1GB.

▶ Documents Text documents such as spreadsheets and Word docs with no pictures are relatively tiny. Almost not worth factoring in.

▶ Extra software Allow around 1GB for each major software suite (eg Microsoft Office or Adobe CS). Smaller applications take up much less room.

can choose is the drive's capacity, measured in gigabytes (GB). See the box above for more on choosing how large a hard drive you need.

▶ Memory or RAM When you open an application or document, the relevant files are pulled from the hard drive into the RAM (Random Access Memory) so that the processor can quickly access them. So the more RAM the system has, the more files and programs it can handle at the same time. RAM makes an enormous difference to performance – even more than the processor in terms of the price-to-power ratio – so be sure to choose a model that allows room in your budget to add some extra. However, unless you're buying a Mac mini, consider adding the RAM yourself, as Apple will rarely be offering the best price (see p.37).

▶ **AirPort Extreme** If your Mac model of choice doesn't come with AirPort Extreme built-in (ie it's "AirPort-ready") you could pay extra to add this feature. AirPort (Apple's name for Wi-Fi) allows you to connect to other computers and the Internet, over a range of up to a couple of hundred feet, depending on the number and type of walls in the way. Note, though, that you'll also need a wireless router (see p.64) to connect to the Internet wirelessly. As with RAM, it's easy to add an AirPort Extreme card yourself (see p.38) on all models expect the Mac mini.

▶ **Bluetooth** This short-range wireless technology is used for connecting to nearby Bluetooth-enabled keyboards, mice and printers. It also lets your Mac talk to your mobile phone, either to sync contacts and calendars (see p.136) or connect to the Internet (see p.62). It's possible to add Bluetooth to a Mac at any time using an inexpensive third-party USB Bluetooth module (which you can also move between computers). But only by adding Bluetooth at the time of purchase will it be built into your Mac.

▶ **Keyboard and mouse** All Macs apart from minis and laptops come with the standard Apple keyboard and mouse. A wireless set means less desktop clutter and greater portability, but on the other hand doesn't feature the handy USB ports that reside on the back of the wired keyboard.

▶ **AppleCare** All Macs come with Apple's standard one-year hardware warranty (international on laptops; country of purchase on desktops) and 90 days of phone support (for Apple applications, OS X and hardware issues). The AppleCare scheme bumps up both streams of support to three years. So is it worth it? If you're terrible with computers and likely to make extensive use of the phone support, then perhaps. Otherwise, it's probably not good value: there's lots of technical support available for free online (see p.283), and though it's gutting to have any piece of equipment go wrong soon after the warranty period, Macs are known for being comparatively reliable.

Finally, you'll be offered lots of accessories, many of which are discussed elsewhere in this book. AirPort or AirPort Express (see p.64), .Mac (see overleaf) and iSight (see p.163), for example.

Megs & gigs

The basic unit of computer data is the "bit", which represents either a zero or a one in the RAM or hard drive. Roughly speaking, eight bits make one "byte" – the space required to describe a single character of text.

▶ **1 KB** (kilobyte) = 1000 bytes

▶ **1 MB** (megabyte) = 1000 kilobytes

▶ **1 GB** (gigabyte) = 1000 megabytes.

Mathematically-minded readers may be interested to know that all these figures are actually approximations of the number two raised to different powers. A gigabyte, for example, is two bytes to the power of thirty, which equals 1,073,741,824 bytes.

.Mac & SpyMac

One of the accessories that Apple may try to sell you when you buy a Mac is a subscription to .Mac (pronounced "dot Mac"). This suite of Internet-based services grew out of an earlier free service called iTools. A subscription costs $99/£69 per year, which buys you:

▶ **Email** An email account accessible online and via a mail program. You'll get an address in the form yourname@mac.com

▶ **iDisk** An online storage area for backing up and transferring files. At the time of writing you get 250MB, shared between your email and iDisk.

▶ **HomePage** An online tool for creating your own website from pre-made templates. The webpages live in your iDisk and are accessible via your own web address, which takes the form homepage.mac.com/yourname

▶ **Backup** An application for automatically backing up key files to your iDisk or external media such as hard drives, CDs and DVDs.

▶ **Sync** With a .Mac account, it's possible to synchronize your contacts, calendars and bookmarks across more than one Mac.

None of this is essential. Free email addresses and online storage space are easy to come by (see p.152 and p.274), and you can build your own websites (see p.167), and do your own backups (see p.269), without any special tools. True, there's no alternative to the Sync tool, but that's only really useful if you have multiple Macs.

Despite all this, .Mac remains attractive due to its sheer ease of use and seamless integration with OS X. Before signing up, however, check out alternatives such as SpyMac, which offers a 3GB mailbox as well as 250MB of online storage for only $40 per year.

.Mac www.mac.com
SpyMac www.spymac.com

Upgrading

If your Mac hardware or operating system is past its best, or you want to expand your set-up to store more files or add extra firepower, you'll be in the market for an upgrade. This section takes a look at what kind of upgrades are possible, and which ones are actually worth the time and money.

Upgrade to OS X

As we've already discussed (see p.9), OS X was a quantum leap for Macs. Though a few die-hard supporters of the previous systems remain, the vast majority of people who have switched from OS 9 (or earlier) to OS X will testify that there's really no comparison. Apart from the fact that OS 9 doesn't support most of the recent Mac applications, it's also much less intuitive, far less fully featured, and *much* less stable. On pre-OS X Macs, when one application crashes, it's highly likely that the whole system will freeze up and you'll have to restart. Applications crash in OS X from time to time, but the system as a whole almost never goes down.

Is my Mac up to OS X?

Though OS X is a vast improvement over previous versions, it's not necessarily sensible or possible to install it on an old Mac. First,

> **Tip:** Certain old-style beige-box G3 Macs won't run the latest version of OS X but will run v10.2 Jaguar, which can be easily picked up via eBay or Amazon.

Classic mode

All versions of OS X up to and including v10.4 (Tiger), feature "Classic" mode, which essentially allows you to run OS 9 within OS X. Double-click any old-style Mac application and Classic will automatically fire up, complete with old-style Menu bar and Apple menu. You can run Classic and native OS X applications at the same time, and switch between them in the normal ways.

you'll need to work out whether your old Mac is up to Apple's specified minimum requirements. For version 10.4 (Tiger), these are: G3/G4/G5 processor; FireWire port; 256MB of RAM (physical, not virtual); 3GB of available hard drive space; and a drive that can read DVDs, as the operating system ships on DVD rather than CD.

Even if your machine matches these requirements, however, consider its speed: OS X can be frustratingly slow on anything less than a G4. And if you want to run many applications simultaneously, 512MB of RAM is a more realistic minimum.

If you do decide to upgrade an old Mac to any version of OS X up to 10.4 Tiger, you shouldn't have any problems running your old documents and applications due to the existence of Classic mode (see box). However, this feature is expected to disappear in OS X v10.5 – "Leopard" – due for release in 2006.

Upgrade OS X versions

There's been a new release of OS X roughly once per year since its appearance in 2001. The new versions are shipped with new Macs, but users wishing to upgrade have to buy the new edition – typically for around $130/£80. Many users have split this cost between groups of friends, since so far there's been no practical enforcement

of the single-user license (unlike, say, with Microsoft Windows). But installing a copy on more than one Mac is illegal – unless you buy the "Family Pack", which you can run on up to five computers within one household.

Installing an upgrade is easy and usually takes less than an hour. Unless you're unlucky, you won't have to reinstall any of your applications, and none of your documents and data should be affected (That said, it's worth backing up first: see p.269). Furthermore, the new version shouldn't slow down your system since, unlike most operating systems, OS X has actually got *faster* with each release.

Speed increases are very welcome, especially on earlier Macs, but for most people the main reason for upgrading to a new edition of OS X is to get new features. Each new version adds a few significant new tools as well as hundreds of minor improvements. The most important additions have included the following.

▶ **v10.2 Jaguar** added the Address Book (see p.134), iChat (see p.161) and Universal Access (see p.49).

▶ **v10.3 Panther** added faxing tools (see p.137), FileVault (see p.260), Exposé (see p.97) and greater Windows compatibility (see p.11).

▶ **v10.4 Tiger** added Spotlight (see p.90), Dashboard (see p.100), Safari RSS (see p.143) and Automator (see p.112).

If money's no object, then, every new OS X version is worth having. Otherwise, consider upgrading every second version, as you'll get more features for your money.

At the time of writing, the current version of OS X is 10.4 (Tiger), but v10.5 (Leopard) is due to arrive in early 2006 so you might want to think twice before upgrading to Tiger in late 2005. However, if you currently use Classic mode for running pre-OS X applications, Tiger may be your best bet, as Leopard is expected to drop this feature. See the rumours sites for more on future editions (see p.284) or, for a comparison of the versions released so far, see:

OS X Versions www.apple.com/macosx/upgrade/compare.html

Tip: Certain old-style beige-box G3 Macs won't run the latest version of OS X but will run v10.2 Jaguar. You could buy a used copy via eBay or Amazon.

Upgrade Mac hardware

Macs, like all computers, can be upgraded in two ways: by getting under the hood and adding or replacing internal components; or by hooking up external peripherals. Sometimes you can achieve the same effect by either means.

The number of internal operations that you can perform on your Mac without voiding the warranty varies widely between different models. In short, you can easily add RAM and an AirPort card – if you don't have one already – to all recent Macs except the mini (see box). But only with the iMac G5 or the Power Mac G3/G4/G5 can you also add or replace hard drives, DVD drives, expansion cards and more.

Opening a Mac mini

Unlike other Macs, the mini doesn't theoretically have any DIY upgrade potential. However, many users have opened their Mac mini (usually to swap the RAM chip for a bigger one) using two thin putty knives to pries off the case. Apple has given mixed messages about whether or not this will invalidate your warranty. If you don't damage anything, the answer is probably no; if you do, the answer may be yes. For more advice, see the Mac mini sites listed on p.285.

For tasks that Apple considers manageable for punters, you should be able to get easy-to-follow PDF instructions on the Apple site. Visit www.apple.com/support and follow the link for your model. Alternatively go straight to Apple's online DIY centre:

Apple DIY www.apple.com/support/diy
Apple DIY UK www.apple.com/uk/support/diy

You may also find the following site useful as a source of info as well as for buying parts (UK only):

MacUpgrades www.macupgrades.co.uk

If you decide the upgrade you want is beyond your capabilities, any authorized Apple dealer should be happy to take over. But, depending on the job and your particular set up, you may find that it's cheaper to opt for an external add-on. The following is a quick look at the most common upgrade jobs.

RAM

Adding extra RAM to any personal computer can make an enormous difference to performance. Applications will start and run more quickly, and when you're dealing with large files or performing many tasks at once, the improvements will be particularly marked. One of the best places to buy trustworthy RAM is the Crucial Memory website, which features a handy tool for picking exactly the right chips for your system.

▲
RAM is usually sold in modules of 256MB, 512MB or 1GB. Desktop computers use DIMM chips, while laptops use SODIMMs.

Crucial US www.crucial.com
Crucial UK www.crucial.com/uk

When choosing how much RAM to buy, bear in mind that, annoyingly, your Mac won't necessarily have an empty RAM slot – so you may have to remove, say, an existing 128MB or 256MB chip to make way for the new chip that you've purchased.

Hard drive

If you run out of hard drive space, first try clearing out old files (see p.45). If that doesn't have any effect, the best solution in most cases is to buy some kind of external hard drive to connect to your Mac via a FireWire or USB2 cable. Not only is this solution foolproof and comparatively inexpensive, but an external hard drive is also a very useful thing to have around – for backing up (see p.269) and transferring files between machines (see p.66).

Tip: When handling internal computer components – such as RAM chips – be aware that a small static electric shock from your hand could be enough to fry your newly acquired piece of kit. To avoid this, touch something unpainted and grounded (eg a tap or plumbing pipe) before touching any components and avoid placing parts on carpets.

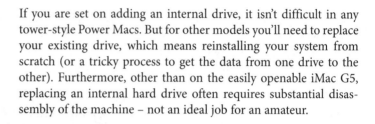

Processor upgrades

With most Macs, there's no easy way to upgrade the processor. But it is possible in some models, such as G3 and G4 towers and cubes. For more information, browse CPU upgrades under the "Hardware Reviews" section of: www.macreviewzone.com

If you are set on adding an internal drive, it isn't difficult in any tower-style Power Macs. But for other models you'll need to replace your existing drive, which means reinstalling your system from scratch (or a tricky process to get the data from one drive to the other). Furthermore, other than on the easily openable iMac G5, replacing an internal hard drive often requires substantial disassembly of the machine – not an ideal job for an amateur.

SuperDrive

Again, unless you have a Power Mac or an iMac G5, you can't easily add a SuperDrive (DVD burner) to your machine. It can be done, but unless you're happy to invest substantial time or money, you might be better off considering an external DVD burner, such as those made by:

Lacie www.lacie.com

AirPort or AirPort Extreme card

Except on a Mac mini (see p.25), it's very easy, if a touch fiddly, to add an AirPort card to any recent Mac that's lacking one. First, trawl the support section of the Apple website to work out whether your Mac requires an old-school AirPort card or a newer AirPort Extreme card. Then locate the AirPort slot (it's behind the CD tray on an eMac, and under the keyboard on a iBook or PowerBook), drop in the card and attach the tiny antenna cable. Switch on and you're ready to connect to a wireless network (see p.64).

For more details on upgrading your Mac, try the model-specific websites listed on p.285. And for advice on importing data from an old Mac or PC, see p.71.

Setting up

Welcome
to OS X

If you're new to OS X, you'll need to get used to an interface slightly different from the one you're familiar with from Windows or "classic" Mac systems. If you're completely new to Macs, you'll also need to get acquainted with an Apple-style mouse and keyboard. This chapter takes you through from switching on for the first time, via the basics of the OS X environment, to speeding up with Mac keyboard shortcuts.

Your first time...

When you fire up your Mac for the first time, you'll be prompted to enter various bits of information. It's largely self-explanatory, though a couple of things are worth noting:

▶ **Details** If you don't have Internet and email details or other info to hand you can ignore these stages and set it all up later (see p.57 and p.154).

▶ **Registering** If you don't want to register with Apple, or you have trouble entering your country information, click ⌘Q to quit the process.

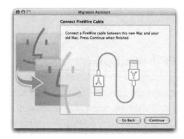

▲
When you first switch on your Mac, you'll be offered the services of the Migration Assistant tool, which allows you to hook up to an existing Mac and have everything transferred automatically. But the old machine needs to have OS X v10.1 or later, and you'll need a standard 6-pin to 6-pin FireWire cable. For more on migrating data from old Macs and PCs, see p.70.

The OS X environment

1 ▶ Apple menu This menu is always there, whichever application you are using; it holds log out and shut down options, System Preferences, and more. To customize the menu, see p.109.

> **Tip:** To find out about your Mac's hardware, click **About This Mac** in the **Apple** menu for the basic specs, and then hit **More Info…** for the full techie version.

2 ▶ The desktop Similar to the desktop of a Windows PC, this is a place for storing your currently used docs, downloads, etc. The desktop can also be located as a folder within your named **home** folder. To customize the desktop, see p.105.

3 ▶ Finder window Double-click any folder to reveal its contents in one of these. For much more on Finder windows, see p.85.

4 ▶ The Dock Home of quick links to applications, folders, minimized windows and the Trash, the Dock is also used for switching between open applications. For much more about the Dock, turn to p.75.

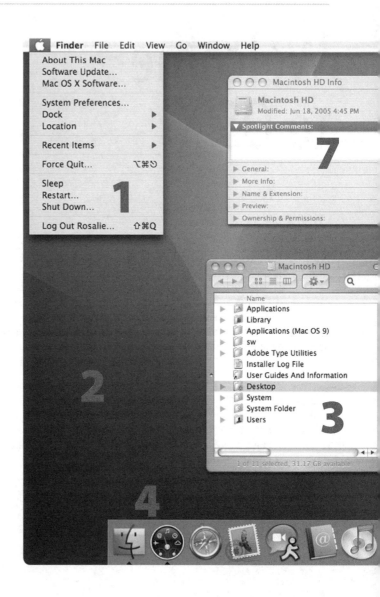

◀ *Running along the top of the OS X screen is the menu bar, which holds application menu headers and, depending on how you set it up, status indicators, a clock, the current user's name (see p.51) and a Spotlight (see p.90) button.*

5 ▶ Macintosh HD The default name for your Mac's hard drive. If you imagine that everything in your Mac lives within a family tree of folders, this is the folder at the top.

6 ▶ System Preferences The home of scores of options and settings – a bit like the Windows Control Panel. Accessed via the Apple menu.

> **Tip:** If an item is greyed-out in System Preferences, you don't have privileges to access it (see p.56).

7 ▶ Info panel To see details about any file or folder, select it, hit ⌘I and one of these panels will appear. As well as giving info, these are used for changing icons (see p.110) and the application used to open a file (see p.82).

> **Tip:** If you're really confused, you could try the feature-stripped version of OS X: **Simple Finder** (see p.53).

Other basic concepts

Finder

Finder is the application at the centre of the Mac user experience, allowing you to find, copy and delete files, organize them into folders, launch applications, switch between tasks, connect to servers… and much more.

Finder doesn't seem like an application *as such*, since it's inseparable from OS X as a whole. Yet Finder is an application nonetheless, complete with all the prerequisite parts, such as menus, Preferences and an icon (the long-standing Mac smiley face, which is permanently welded to the Dock). Unlike most applications, it doesn't feature a "quit" option, but if Finder ever misbehaves or freezes up, you can relaunch it (see p.275).

Whenever Finder or another application needs your input or approval, it will display a "dialog box" (just like in Windows). If a button is highlighted in blue, it can be activated by hitting the Enter key instead of clicking. You can also often activate a button by holding down the ⌘ key while hitting the first letter of the word displayed on the button.

▼

Home

Your "home" folder is the place where all your documents and other files (including the items on your desktop and various files related to your use of applications) are stored. If there is more than one account set up on a Mac, each user has their own home folder. The various home folders live within **Macintosh HD/Users**.

Applications

Applications, or programs, are pieces of software for anything from writing a letter to composing a piece of music. An application can live anywhere on your system, but usually they reside in the **Applications** folder. For more on applications, see p.94.

Trash

When you delete a file, it isn't really deleted: it's sent to the Trash, where it stays until the Trash is emptied. To do this: choose **Empty Trash** from the **Finder** menu, or click and hold the Trash icon on the Dock. Alternatively, use this shortcut: ⌘ ⇧ ⌫

Tip: Even when you empty the Trash, the file may remain on your drive, from where it could potentially be recovered (see p.280). If you really want to delete the Trash's contents for good, select **Secure Empty Trash** from the **Finder** menu.

◀ *The Trash icon changes to let you know at a glance whether it contains "owt" or "nowt".*

Drives and discs

When you connect an external hard drive to your Mac (or other "volumes" such as digital cameras, key drives and so on) they'll appear on the desktop and in your Finder Sidebars with a white disk-drive icon, ready for you to open them up and add, copy and remove files.

CDs and DVDs also appear on the desktop and in Sidebars when inserted. If blank they are labelled CD-R, DVD-RW, etc, and you can drag files onto them. When you're ready to write the disc, select it on a Finder Sidebar and press **Burn**.

When you've finished using an external drive or a CD or DVD, you need to eject it – don't just unplug a drive or you might damage it. To eject a drive, either press the eject icon next to its name in the Sidebar of any Finder window, or drag the drive or disc to the Trash, which will morph into an eject icon the moment you start dragging.

Software Update

Tip: Software Update has its own panel in **System Preferences**. Here you can stop OS X checking for updates automatically, and make various other changes.

Apple ongoingly updates OS X and their various applications to make them more stable and secure or to add extra features. Whenever you're connected to the Internet, you can click **Software Update** in the Apple menu to check for the latest updates and have OS X install them for you. Even if you don't, OS X will, by default, automatically check for updates every few weeks.

When you check for updates, you can choose which items to install and which to ignore. Unless you have a specific reason not to (such as a grindingly slow Internet connection), install everything. And, at the very least, accept anything related to security. With regards to online threats of all kinds, keeping your operating system up to date is more important than installing third-party virus software.

Mac Help

Mac OS X comes with a reasonably comprehensive, if slightly slow, Help tool, so if you get stuck or want to know how to do something, select **Mac Help** in Finder's **Help** menu – or use the shortcut ⌘⇧?

Shut down, sleep, log out

Tip: OS X offers a good range of power-management features, which you'll find under the **Energy Saver** panel of **System Preferences**. Here you can schedule your computer to switch on and off at the same time each day, set how long it should wait before entering Sleep mode and, if you have a laptop, alter the settings for battery use.

To switch off your Mac, select **Shut Down** from the Apple menu. Alternatively, just leave it on, and within a few minutes it will go into a low-energy "Sleep" mode, ready to be quickly awoken next time you need it. If you have an iBook or PowerBook, simply shutting the "lid" has the same effect – and you can safely carry a Mac laptop around in Sleep mode.

If more than one user account is set up on the Mac, you could also **Log Out** from the Apple menu to return to the screen where the next user can log in.

Keyboard & mouse

Various settings for the keyboard and mouse (or laptop trackpad) – for example the double-click speed of the mouse and the repeat time on the keyboard – can be found in the **Keyboard & Mouse** pane of **System Preferences** (in the Apple menu). But, especially if you're new to Macs, the following tips are far more important:

Context menus

If you're used to using the Windows right-click menu you might have been shocked to discover that your shiny new Mac mouse has only one button (see p.14). Don't despair: you can get exactly the same kind of "context" menu of options in OS X by clicking items while holding down the **Control** key (also known as ^ or **Ctrl**), found in the bottom corners of the keyboard. Alternatively, plug in any two-button USB mouse.

Keyboard shortcuts

Throughout this book you'll come across hotkeys or shortcuts: special combinations of keys that allow you to quickly perform a function in a particular application or across your system without using your mouse to trawl through menus and icons. It's worth taking the time to get used to shortcuts: they greatly increase your computing efficiency (as well as reducing your chances of developing repetitive strain injury).

Tip: If you have a Bluetooth mouse and keyboard, the relevant **System Preferences** panel can also be reached from the Bluetooth icon on the menu bar.

Tip: If you have a PC mouse with more than one button, or a scroll wheel, don't put it out to grass just because you have a new Mac – it will work and you'll even get the context menu from the right-click.

Tip: If you let your mouse hover over an item, button, or command, a small label pops up to tell you a little bit more about what you're about to click.

Tip: Many keyboard shortcuts are listed to the right of commands in application menus. They're usually represented using the same symbol system used in this book.

PC shortcuts

If you're coming to Macs from a PC background, you'll find that the ⌘ (Command) key is the equivalent to the Control key in Windows. So while **Ctrl-X** is "cut" on a PC, **⌘X** does the same on a Mac.

Tip: If you connect a PC keyboard to a Mac, the **Windows** key becomes the ⌘ key.

Tip: The various keys in a keyboard combination don't need to be hit simultaneously. The instruction **⌘C**, for instance, means "hit **C** while holding down ⌘" – just as you'd create a capital letter by hitting a letter key while holding down **Shift** (⇧).

Most shortcuts revolve around a handful of keys found in the bottom corner of the main section of the keyboard. If the Apple world is less confusing than the PC world in general, these keys are an exception, since each can be referred to with various names and symbols:

⌘ = ⌃ = Apple = Command
⌥ = Alt = Option
^ = Control = Ctrl
⇧ = Shift

In this book, we've stuck to the symbols when describing keyboard shortcuts (eg **⌘V** or **⌘⌥S**) but you might come across the above names when reading elsewhere. One other key symbol we use is:

⌫ = **Backspace** (not delete!)

Many applications feature their own panel for setting shortcuts (in Word, for example, look in the **Tools** menu under **Customize**). OS X system shortcuts can be set in **System Preferences** within the **Keyboard & Mouse** panel. Here you can also apply shortcuts to particular menu commands to work in all applications.

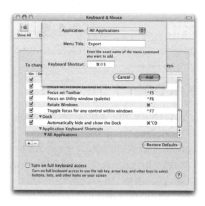

Universal Access

If you have any difficulty seeing, hearing or using the mouse and keyboard, you may find that OS X's impressively comprehensive set of accessibility features make your Mac easier to use. You'll find them within the **Universal Access** panel of **System Preferences**, which you can open from the Apple menu. The most important accessibility features include:

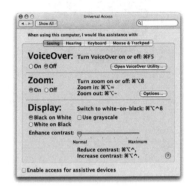

▶ VoiceOver Provides spoken feedback to help you navigate between items, windows and applications with the keyboard.

▶ Zoom Once activated, the shortcuts ⌘⌥= and ⌘⌥- zoom in and out on any area of the screen, following the mouse pointer around. Things don't become clearer (higher-resolution) as you zoom in: they just get bigger.

▶ Display Lets you switch your screen to **Grayscale** (like a "black and white" movie) or **White on Black** (like a film negative). To toggle between the modes, hit ⌘⌥^8.

▶ Enhance Contrast Increases the starkness of the difference between dark and light. The shortcuts ⌘⌥^. and ⌘⌥^, have the same effect.

▶ Flash A visual alternative to the alert sound.

▶ Sticky Keys Allows you to enter key combinations in sequence rather than simultaneously.

▶ Mouse Keys Turn on this feature to control the mouse pointer using the numeric keypad section of your keyboard. On an iBook or PowerBook, you'll need to hold down the **fn** key to access the numeric keypad.

▶ Cursor Size Makes the mouse pointer larger.

In addition, you might wish to activate the OS X Speech Recognition features (see p.182).

User accounts

If more than one person uses – or will use – your Mac, consider setting up separate user accounts. This way, each person has their own personal set-up, complete with their own folders, iTunes Library, desktop background, custom settings and so on. It's almost as if each user has their own computer – except, of course, only one person can use the Mac at any one time.

When you first got your Mac out of the box and set it up with OS X, you will have been prompted to enter a name, "short name" and password (and also to pick a twee little image from a selection including a butterfly, snowflake and billiard ball). Whether you realized it or not, you were setting yourself up with an account – and, more specifically, an account with "administrative" powers.

Every Mac has at least one administrator – a person who has power to make system-wide changes, install updates and applications, and generally be fully autonomous. When you add other users, you can choose whether to make them administrators (if you trust them not to do anything stupid) or standard users (great for technophobes and kids).

Tip: The way that Accounts work in Macs – with home folders, access privileges and so on – is entirely inherited from UNIX (see p.8). Multi-user capabilities were one of the key aims during UNIX's early development back in the 1960s.

Tip: It is possible to remove administrator privileges from the user who originally set up the Mac – but only if another user has been given admin status, since there must be at least one administrator at any one time.

Manage accounts

All the settings for user accounts can be accessed via the **Accounts** pane of System Preferences. Here, you can add and remove accounts – if you're an administrator – using the standard "+" and "–" buttons. You can also make changes to…

Name, short name and password

When you enter a name into a new account, a short name will automatically be generated, but you can override this and pick anything you like. The short name is, in short, the name that will appear on your home folder (see p.44), and though you can change your name at any time, you can't easily change your short name.

If you do really want to change your short name for an account that already exists, the easiest option is to create a new account with the correct name, copy all your files across and then delete the previous account; for instructions, visit www.apple.com/support and search for

Tip: Only those with administrative powers can make changes to all user accounts, and even then they will have to enter their password to do so.

Tip: By default, your account password will also be the password for your "Keychain", which exists to save you remembering lots of other passwords. See p.262 for more on Keychains.

Forgot your account password?

If you forget your password, ask any user with administrative privileges to log in, open **Accounts** from **System Preferences** and let you reset your password. If there are no other administrators set up, try this:

▶ **Turn off** your computer, and insert your Mac OS X Install CD (which should have come with your Mac (or Tiger upgrade).

▶ **Press C** while you turn on the Mac and keep it held down until the Apple logo appears.

▶ **Choose Reset Password** from the Installer menu and choose your username – NOT "System Administrator". Then follow the prompts.

This shouldn't affect your Keychain or any other passwords.

106824. There are some other workarounds, but they're for technically advanced users only.

Next you have to choose whether or not to pick a password. You don't have to use one if you don't want to. Not having a password makes it quicker to log in, but it means anyone with physical access to the Mac will be able to instantly access your files. If you do choose to use a password, a nonsensical concoction of letters and numbers is theoretically best for security (press the key-icon button to rate a password for crackability), but on a day-to-day level, unless you're dealing with anything top secret, it's more important to pick something that's quick and easy to type – and difficult to forget.

Picture

If the default pics don't appeal – for some strange reason you don't have yourself down as a dog or a baseball – hit **Edit** and load something else. Either press **Choose** to browse for a pic on your Mac, or drag an image directly into the Edit window from a folder, from a webpage, or from iPhoto. Then use the slider to zoom in and drag the pic around to select the area you want to use.

> **Tip:** The picture you choose for your account also finds its way into your Address Book card and iChat profile – it will be seen by messaging buddies, so don't choose anything too embarrassing.

> **Tip:** If you have an iSight (see p.163) connected to your Mac, the Edit window also gives you the option of grabbing a snap of yourself there and then.

Parental Controls

This area lets you restrict the applications and features available in the account used by a child – or anyone else for that matter. The panel gives you direct access to the Parental Control features of

Safari (see p.143), iChat (see p.161) and Mail (see p.154), but you can also disable some or all applications by clicking the "Finder & System" **Configure...** button. The same button also lets you implement **Simple Finder** mode: a very child-friendly intro-duction to OS X (nice

big icons, simplified menus, etc). Once you have made any of these changes, the affected account is labelled "Managed".

Tip: Before you initiate **Simple Finder**, make sure you have selected only the applications you want the user to have access to or you could end up with all your applications being duplicated into the user's **My Applica-tions** folder – a potentially big waste of disk space.

Login Items

This panel lists the programs or files that will launch automatically every time you log in or switch on. To add and remove Login Items, use the standard "+" and "–" buttons. If you like, use the check boxes to tell OS X to hide applications once they've been launched. This simply saves you from facing a screen full of windows each time you log in.

Tip: If there are techie-look-ing items in your Login items, leave them be – they probably relate to a specific applica-tion feature that runs in the background.

Logging in & out

OS X offers various options for how your Mac handles the accounts – what happens when you switch on the machine, for example, and how to switch between accounts once someone is logged-in. Open **Accounts** from **System Preference** and click **Login Options**.

If you are the only user on a machine and you're not worried about people seeing your data in the event of the computer being stolen or otherwise accessed (see p.264), set OS X to automatically log in to your account. Otherwise, click **Display Login Window** and choose whether you'd like the Mac to request both the **Name and Password** of whoever is logging on, or present a **List of users**, in which case you just click your name and enter your password. The latter is convenient, though fractionally less secure.

Fast User Switching

Also within the Login Options pane you can enable Fast User Switching – and you probably should. This useful function allows one user to log on without the current user first logging off. Any documents, applications or webpages that the current user has open stay active "in the background": hidden from view and password-protected (assuming the account does have a password). When you switch back, it will be as if you never logged out.

When the function is activated, the current user's name (or a generic icon) appears in the menu bar, next to the clock. Click here to reveal a menu that lets you switch between users – complete with a cool cubic pirouette. It can take a few seconds to log in a user this way, but switching between users who are already logged in is almost instant.

Tip: Fast User Switching provides a convenient way for everyone to, in effect, use the machine at the same time – but this can take its toll on system resources. If there are ten accounts running in the background, each with many open applications and documents, your Mac may run much more slowly.

Tip: Users can access the **Accounts Preferences** panel from the Fast User Switching menu on the menu bar, though if they are not authorized to make changes, they will find all the options greyed-out.

Private & shared folders

Each user set up on the system has a home folder, pre-loaded with sub-folders labelled **Documents**, **Music**, **Pictures**, **Movies**, etc. You can use, ignore or add to these folders as you see fit – though it's better not to delete or rename them (especially the **Library**).

The various home folders reside in the Users folder within the top level of the hard drive, which is probably labelled **Macintosh HD**. When you're logged-in, your home folder bears a little house icon, but other users' homes look like standard folders, and the items in them won't be accessible. Note, though, that anyone with a bit of know-how can access your files – unless you follow the instructions described in the Privacy & Passwords chapter (see p.259).

Sharing files

If you *do* want to pass files or folders between users, you have a few options. The easiest is to drop them either into the **Macintosh HD/Users/Shared** folder or the **Public** folder within your home folder – both of which any user on the machine can access. Alternatively, if you want to give a file to another user without putting it some-

Libraries

In OS X, **Library** folders hold all manner of system- and application-related files, from fonts to widgets. You've probably noticed that there's one in the top level of your hard drive as well as in your home folder. The purpose of this arrangement is to allow new functions or features to be installed either for one or all user accounts. When you choose a typeface in a word processor, for example, the fonts on offer consist of all the ones in your home **Library** folder and all the ones in the top-level **Library** – but not those in the Libraries of other users. The same goes for widgets, screensavers and many other items.

Tip: If you regularly access either the **Shared** user folder, or a particular **Drop Box**, drag its icon onto your Finder-window Sidebar (see p.87) or Dock (see p.75) for quick access.

More to share…

You can share your screensavers (see p.107), widgets (see p.101) and fonts (see p.125) with other users by dragging them from their folders in your personal **Library** to the corresponding folders in the top-level **Library**.

where public, find the relevant person's home folder (within **Macintosh HD/Users**), open their **Public** folder and put the file into their **Drop Box** – a special folder that anyone can put things into but not view the contents of.

A final option, worth considering if you need to set up a more complex sharing arrangement, is to use permissions (see below).

Sharing music & photos

If you choose **Share My Library** in iTunes or iPhoto preferences, other users of the Mac will be able to play or view (but not change or delete) your songs and photos. This is very useful, though if you want more than one user to really "share" a single iTunes Library, with both parties able to add tracks, create playlists, etc, the only option is to employ a techie workaround using permissions. It's beyond the scope of this book to go into the details, but if you're determined, search online for more information.

Ownership & permissions

OS X, like other UNIX-based systems, provides a "permissions" set up that allows complete control over the access to files and folders by the various users of the computer. By default, the user who creates a file is considered the **Owner** and only they have access to it. But users with administrative powers can change these settings by selecting a file or folder, pressing ⌘I and looking under the **Ownership & Permissions** pane. Here, you can specify access – read, write, both, or none – for specific users (under "groups") or for all users (under "others").

Permissions settings can be very useful, but unless you're quite technically minded and you have a specific reason to make use of them, this is one area of OS X that's best left alone.

Connecting to the Internet

8

All Macs come ready to connect to the Internet, but you first need an account with an Internet Service Provider (ISP). If you've just upgraded from an old PC to a Mac, you should be able to continue using your previous ISP account – as we explain below. If you don't already have an ISP account, or you have one but it's not up to scratch, then it's time to choose another one – and preferably a broadband account.

This chapter takes a quick look at installing an existing connection or choosing a new one – and covers getting online when you're out and about with your iBook or PowerBook. For much more detailed information about everything Internet-related, get *The Rough Guide to The Internet*.

Set up an existing account

It's usually very simple to set up an existing ISP account on a new Mac, but the procedure depends on whether you've got an old-school dial-up connection, standard broadband, or broadband with a wireless router. If you're not sure whether you have a dial-up or

Tip: Some ISPs, such as AOL, may require you to install their own special software instead of simply plugging in your account details. If so, follow their instructions – but also consider switching ISPs.

broadband connection, it's easy to tell: if you can use the telephone and be on the Internet at the same time you have broadband; if not, you have dial-up.

Dial-up

Tip: Some dial-up accounts require you to input more data than just the phone number, username and password. You might also need the details for a proxy server, DNS servers and more. You should be able to recover this info either from your old computer or ISP.

Setting up a dial-up ISP account basically just means plugging in a few details, the essentials being the phone number, user name and password. If you don't know these details, but they're set up on your old PC, boot the PC, look for **Network Connections** or **Dial-up networking**, find the relevant ISP account, right-click it and choose **Properties**. This will give you the phone number, username and any other details except the password; if you don't know the password, phone the ISP.

Internet Connect

Once you have all the relevant details, you'll need to plug them into the Mac. Open Internet Connect from **Applications** (or via the phone icon near the clock) and click on the **Internal Modem** button. Key in the details and press connect.

If that worked, you should now be able to connect and disconnect via the phone icon in the menu bar – or by using Internet Connect. If it didn't work, you'll find more options in the **Network** panel of **System Preferences**. Choose **Internal Modem** in the **Show** menu and explore the settings.

Broadband

If you've got a cable or ADSL account already set up, and your broadband modem or router has an Ethernet socket on it (like a fatter version of a phone jack), then no configuration should be needed – just plug an Ethernet cable from the modem to the Mac and you'll be online. However, some ADSL modems connect by USB (especially in the UK), and they *don't* have an Ethernet socket. If so, you'll need to set-up the modem on the Mac. Dig out the CD and instructions that came with your modem; if you can't find them, try getting online by any other means and downloading the relevant driver software from the website of the modem manufacturer. If the modem doesn't appear to be compatible with OS X, phone your ISP for advice.

Wireless

If your Mac was sold with built-in AirPort capability, then it's easy to get online via an existing wireless network. Make sure you're in range of the base station, and click the fan-shaped AirPort icon in the menu bar to reveal networks in range.

If your Mac lacks wireless capabilities, then you'll need to buy and install either an AirPort or AirPort Extreme card, depending on the age of the computer. Any Apple stockist should be able to tell you which you need.

Tip: Don't connect a USB modem to your Mac before you install the software that came with the modem. This is a common cause of problems. If you can't get your USB modem to work, try disconnecting it, uninstalling the software, restarting the Mac, installing the software and only then reattaching the modem.

Tip: If you don't seem to be able to connect to a password-protected wireless network, try sticking a $ sign before the password (without a space). Depending on the type of password used, this is sometimes essential.

Tip: A Mac sold as "AirPort Ready" or "AirPort Extreme Ready" does *not* have wireless built in. This simply means the Mac is ready to have an AirPort or AirPort Extreme card added.

Sharing an Internet connection

Even if you don't have a router, it's possible to share your Internet connection between two computers, allowing both machines to be online at the same time. To find out how, see p.65.

Choose a new ISP account

If you're choosing a new ISP account, the first decision is whether to go for dial-up or broadband. Broadband, where it's available, is usually around 50 percent more expensive, but it offers three main advantages:

▶ **Speed** Broadband provides a faster ("higher-bandwidth ") connection. That means webpages load faster, file downloads happen quicker, and video and music can be streamed more easily. It also makes broadband more suitable for setting up a home network and sharing the connection between more than one computer (see p.63).

▶ **A freed-up phoneline** Unlike dial-up, broadband lets you make and receive calls while online – even when it works through the phoneline. (One exception to this rule is satellite broadband, which sometimes requires an outgoing dial-up connection.)

▶ **Always-on access** With dial-up, each time you connect to the Net you'll need to spend around 30 seconds actually "dialling-up". But broadband is usually "always on", so when your Mac is switched on, you're online.

Once you've picked a type of Internet connection, you need to pick an ISP. The best approach is to ask around, read Internet magazine reviews and see which companies others recommend. If someone swears by an ISP, and they seem to know what they're talking about, give it a go. That's just about the best research you can do. However, there's lots of information available on the Web – so if you can already get online, you could try consulting one of these sites:

ADSL Guide www.adslguide.org.uk (UK)
ISP Check www.ispcheck.com (US)
ISP Review www.ispreview.co.uk (UK)
The List www.thelist.com (US)

Modems and routers

When you sign up for broadband, the ISP will usually provide a suitable cable or DSL modem. They may also offer you a router (or perhaps a combined router/modem) to enable you to share the connection between more than one computer. Any router – including wireless routers – should be fine for Macs, PCs or a mixture of both. For more on sharing an Internet connection, see p.63.

Once you've picked an ISP and contacted them via the phone or Internet, they should send you everything you need. If it's a dial-up account, that's probably just a few details, which you can key into your Mac as described on p.58. If it's broadband, you may need to deal with a few more complex settings. If you get stuck, try searching for the name of your modem or router at:

Apple Discussions discussions.apple.com

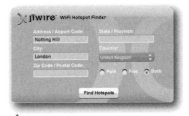

▲
To locate hotspots, try the JiWire hotspot directory widget, free from www.jiwire.com/macosxtiger.htm

Connecting on the move

At home, iBooks and PowerBooks can connect to the Internet in all the same ways as other computers. But laptops are designed for moving around, and being on the road shouldn't stop you getting online. There are five main ways to connect an iBook or PowerBook while out and about:

▶ **Wi-Fi hotspots** A Mac with AirPort capabilities (see p.31) can connect at wireless "hotspots", commonly found in cafés, hotels, airports and elsewhere. Some hotspots are free, but often you'll have to pay – either directly or via an online sign-up process.

▶ **Phone sockets** If you have a dial-up ISP account (and many broadband ISPs provide a dial-up "backup" number), you may be able to get online wherever you can find a phone socket. If you're far from home, use Internet Connect as described on p.58 and add the national or international phone number. But before shelling out on dialling long distance, check with your ISP to see if they have a local number in your location.

▶ **Via another computer** If you're at a friend's house and you want to share their Internet connection, run an Ethernet cable between the two machines and quickly set up Connection Sharing (see p.63). Obviously, if they have a wireless set up, you should be able to use AirPort instead.

Network finders

The AirPort menu bar entry does a pretty good job of showing you which wireless networks are within range, but for something with more bells and whistles, showing you password protection and signal strength before you try and connect, try iStumbler (www.istumbler.com). Or to check for wireless networks without even opening your bag, investigate Kensington's handheld WiFi Finder (www. kensington.com).

▶ **Via a mobile phone** For maximum mobility, try connecting your iBook or PowerBook via a cell phone. The basic requirements are a data-compatible phone – ideally one with a fast connection such as GPRS – and a way to connect it to the computer. The best solution is to use Bluetooth wireless technology, which is built into many modern phones.

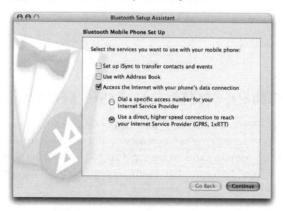

Tip: If you're connecting via a mobile phone, why not download your numbers into Address Book while you're at it (see p.136).

If your Mac doesn't have Bluetooth, you can add it with an inexpensive USB adapter. To get the connection going, click on **Bluetooth** in **System Preferences**, hit **Devices** and then **Set up new device...** and follow the prompts. If the set-up seems to work, but you can't get online, contact your phone provider to make sure your tariff allows data calls.

▶ **Via a card phone** If you have a PowerBook (which, unlike the iBook, has the necessary slot), you could buy a high-speed PCMCIA card phone – such as the Vodafone 3G Card (pictured). That way you can get a fast Internet connection anywhere you can get phone reception. Such cards are usually not expensive to buy, but you'll be hit with monthly, hourly or per-meg usages fees. Ask in any phone shop for more details.

More than one computer

Connecting two or more computers together enables them to share files, printers and an Internet connection. And these days it's very easy to do – even with a mixture of Macs and PCs. Don't be put off by the jargon: a "network" or "LAN" is simply two or more connected computers. As this chapter explains, the computers can be connected either directly, or via a central hub called a router. And the computer and router can communicate either via cables or wirelessly.

The first thing to do when setting up a home network is work out whether you need any extra hardware. That depends on whether you want a typical router-based network or a money-saving computer-to-computer network…

Router-based networks

Traditionally, a network requires a router – a physical device that acts as the junction between the various computers. In a typical set-up, the router is attached to the Internet via a broadband modem

> **Tip:** If you're trying to network a PC and a Mac but the PC doesn't have an Ethernet socket or Wi-Fi, you'll need to add one of these things to the PC with either an Ethernet or wireless adapter. These are relatively inexpensive and usually not difficult to fit.

Top to bottom: AirPort Extreme, AirPort Express and a non-Apple wireless router (by Linksys).

Buying a router

Apple produces two routers – AirPort Extreme and AirPort Express – both of which are wireless, nicely designed, fully featured and very easy to set up. However, any router should work with both PCs and Macs, so if you're on a budget you might want to investigate the wider market, dominated by Netgear, Linksys, Belkin and D-Link.

When looking around at the alternatives, the first decision to make is whether you want one with or without wireless capability. The latter cost slightly more, but not much, and they can save you money overall as you won't have to buy any Ethernet cables. And wireless routers give you the best of both worlds, as they typically have ports for connecting with cables, too.

Next, you need to decide whether you need a router with a modem built in: if you already have a cable or DSL modem with an Ethernet socket, then a standard router should be fine. If not – for example, if you have a USB ADSL modem – then it's neater and cheaper to choose a router with a built-in ADSL modem.

Other things to consider when choosing a router from Apple or any other company include:

▶ **AirTunes** Currently only available on the AirPort Express, AirTunes allows you to connect the router to a hi-fi and stream music wirelessly from iTunes and, with a little know how, other applications (see p.180).

▶ **Ethernet ports** Does it have Ethernet sockets as well as wireless capabilities? If so, how many?

▶ **External aerial socket** This is useful if you ever want to expand the range of your network beyond the couple of hundreds yards (depending on walls in the way) that a standard router will give you.

▶ **Firewall** A decent in-built firewall improves your network security.

▶ **USB port** A USB port, as found on the AirPort Express, allows you to connect a printer to the router – very useful if you use a laptop.

▶ **Wireless speed** Don't go for anything slower than AirPort Extreme (802.11g).

(sometimes these two devices are combined in one unit) and each computer connects to the router, either with wires or, in the case of a wireless router, via Wi-Fi (AirPort).

Setting up a router can be as easy as plugging it in, switching it on and following a few on-screen instructions. Or it can be as unpleasant as a trip to the dentist – especially with a non-Apple router, and even more so if you're configuring a broadband connection at the same time. It's beyond the scope of this book to go into the details; follow the instructions that came with your unit and Internet account, and if you get stuck phone your ISP or look online for help (see p.288).

Computer-to-computer networks

Having a router for your home network is definitely the ideal option. But if you'd rather not spend any money buying one, or you want to quickly create an impromptu network – for example to share files between two laptops – you could opt instead for a computer-to-computer (or peer-to-peer) network.

In this arrangement, the two machines connect directly with one another. One of them connects to the Internet in the normal way, and its operating system (OS X or Windows) takes care of sharing the connection with the other computer (in effect acting as a "software router"). Again, you can do this with either a standard Ethernet cable or wirelessly.

Peer-to-peer networks work fine, though they're not great for more than two computers, and they can be inconvenient, as the computer that distributes the connection has to be switched on and connected to the Net in order for the other(s) to get online.

AirPort & Wi-Fi

On Macs, wireless capability is branded as AirPort. But the underlying technology is Wi-Fi – just as with wireless PCs. That means that Macs and PCs can connect to the same networks, and to each other.

Wi-Fi, also known by the less user-friendly name 802.11, is actually a family of slightly different standards, all of which work with each other. The most common standard today is 802.11g, also known as "AirPort Extreme" and "54g". This allows faster data transfer than the earlier 802.11b (aka "non-Extreme" AirPort).

Wireless security

Most wireless routers will let you activate a WEP or WPA password. Do this, or anyone within a few hundred feet will be able to access your network. Note that in some cases you may need to prefix the password with a dollar sign (eg $secret) when connecting your Mac to the network.

Tip: If you're making a wired computer-to-computer network with two Macs, you could use a FireWire cable instead of a standard Ethernet cable.

Tip: By default, your Mac will be called something like "Peter_Buckleys_Computer". Feel free to change it to something shorter and more user friendly in **Sharing**, within **System Preferences**.

Setting up

Setting up a computer-to-computer network is simple. First, connect the two computers together using a standard Ethernet network cable. Or, if it's to be a wireless network, hit the AirPort menu on the Mac's menu bar, choose **Create Network...** and pick a name (and a password if you want extra security). Then go to the other computer and select the new network.

Another stage is required before you can share an Internet connection. First, choose which computer will connect directly to the Internet and get online in the usual way. If that machine is a Mac, open **Sharing** from **System Preferences** and choose the **Internet** tab; pick your connection type (AirPort, Ethernet, etc) and click **Start**. Alternatively, if you want a PC to connect to the Internet and share the signal with a Mac, get the PC online in the usual way and then launch the **Network Setup Wizard** or **Internet Connection Sharing Wizard**. You'll find this in the windows **Start** menu under **More Programs/Accessories/Communications**.

Sharing files

Sharing files between networked OS X Macs is usually very simple. First, on each Mac that you want to share files between, open **System Preferences**, hit **Sharing** and check the **Personal File Sharing** box. You should then be able to browse for **Public** and **Shared** folders on each machine via **Network** (in any Finder window, or in the **Go** menu).

For more complete file sharing, however, you'll need to log in to one Mac via the other. Re-open the **Sharing** pane of **System Preferences** and you should see some small text at the bottom giving the computer's network address. Enter this address on the other Mac by selecting **Go to Server...** from the **Go** menu (or pressing ⌘K).

If you log in as a "guest" you'll only be able to access shared folders, so choose "registered user" and enter the name and password of whoever's files you want to

share. The relevant home folder should appear on your desktop – and also in the Sidebar in your Finder windows.

File sharing with PCs

In theory, sharing files between PCs and Macs on the same network should be almost as easy as sharing between Macs, though it doesn't always work out like that.

First, on the Mac, open **System Preferences**, select **Sharing** and switch on **Windows Sharing**. On the PC, run the **Home Networking Wizard** (which you'll find in the Start menu under **Programs/Accessories/Communications**) and then select folders you want to share, right-click them, select **Sharing and security** and check **Share these files on the network**.

You should then be able to browse for shared files via **Network** (on the Mac) or **My Network Places** on a PC. However, if you want full access to the Mac files on the PC, you'll need to log in as a user. To do this, go back to the **Sharing** preferences on the Mac, select **Windows Sharing** and make a note of the address supplied at the bottom of the pane. Open My Computer (or any other Explorer window) on the PC, enter the Mac's address in the Address Bar and press Enter. When prompted, enter the user name and password of the Mac user account you want access, and press **OK**.

Xgrid

Fancy turning your network into a super computer? OS X's Xgrid function allows you to combine the computational power of all the Macs you have connected together. See:

Xgrid www.apple.com/macosx/features/xgrid

Tip: If you're struggling to access your Mac's files from a PC on the network, try turning on **FTP Access** in the Mac's **System Preferences/Sharing** pane and entering the supplied FTP address on the PC. This sometimes works when Windows Sharing won't.

Help!

To find out more about home networking, or if you're struggling to get yours up and running, try the following sites:

www.atpm.com/network
www.macwindows.com
www.practicallynetworked.com

Importing files & programs

There's something deeply pleasing about switching on a brand new computer – free from corrupt files, badly labelled documents, old software and other debris from years of use. But most people will want to import at least some data – applications, files, emails, bookmarks and the like – from their old computer. The process depends on the computer you're importing from…

From a Mac with OS X

Importing data – including files, applications, emails, preferences and settings – from a Mac with OS X (version 10.1 or later) is a breeze. All you'll need is a standard FireWire cable, which you can pick up in any computer store. Plug the cable between the two machines and, on the new Mac, open **Migration Assistant** from **Applications/Utilities**. You'll be asked to restart the old Mac while holding down the **T** key. This boots the old Mac in what's known as "Target Mode" (see p.278), in effect treating it as an external hard drive to the newer Mac.

The Migration Assistant will offer you a bunch of options about what you want to transfer. Importing **Applications** automatically imports the **Library** folders, which contain emails, fonts and other system- or application-related files. Finally, hit the **Migrate** button and things should start moving over (this can take a while).

If something isn't working properly after you've used Migration Assistant, repair permissions with Disk Utility (see p.278). If that doesn't help, try manually installing the problematic application.

Tip: If you used FileVault on the old Mac, turn this off before starting Migration Assistant, or you won't be able to import your account.

Manually copying files between computers

There are four main ways to move files between computers:

▶ **On a hard drive or key drive** Portable hard drives and keydrives, which plug in via FireWire or USB, are perhaps the easiest way to move (and backup) data. Once connected, the drive's icon will appear on the desktop (Mac) or in My Computer (PC), ready for you to drag files onto it. When you're done, eject the drive, connect it to the destination machine and drag the files to wherever you want them.

▶ **On an iPod** You can use an iPod as a portable hard drive. Just plug in the Pod, open **iTunes Preferences** (in the **iTunes** or **Edit** menu), check the **Enable FireWire Disk Use** box, and the iPod will appear as a drive on the desktop or in My Computer. If there's no room on the iPod, you could temporarily delete the music from it using iPod Software Updater (download it from Apple if you can't find it). Next time you connect to iTunes, the music will be copied back across.

▶ **On CDs & DVDs** If the machine you want to copy files from has a CD or DVD writer, you can burn data CDs with files and use that to move them to the destination computer. To learn about burning CDs, follow the instructions that came with your computer or CD writer.

▶ **Via a network** If the computer you want to copy files from has Wi-Fi (AirPort), an Ethernet port or a FireWire port, you can quickly network it together with the destination machine and copy the files across directly. See p.66 for instructions.

Tip: When copying files between a Mac and PC using any kind of external drive (including an iPod), the drive will need to be formatted on the PC. The reason is that OS X can recognize Windows-formatted drives but PCs can't recognize Mac-formatted drives.

From an older Mac

You can manually copy data from an old Mac using any of the standard techniques (see box on p.69). Besides any documents, photos, music and movie files, you need to think about moving…

Applications

Some applications can simply be copied over – take the relevant folder or file from **Applications** (on the old Mac) and drop them into **Applications (Mac OS 9)** in the top level of your new Mac's hard drive. If some applications won't work, you may need to reinstall them from the original CD or downloaded installer file.

Email

> **Tip:** If you only need a few key emails on your new Mac, why not just forward them to yourself? This is quicker and easier than importing mail boxes.

First, you need to get the emails from the old Mac to the new one. If you use Netscape or Eudora, you should be able to export (or simply drag) mailboxes out of the program. Copy the resulting files to the Desktop of your new Mac. If you're using Outlook Express, this won't work; instead, find your "Identity" folder (buried in your hard drive) and copy this folder to your new Mac's desktop.

Next, open Mail (or whichever email program you intend to use on the new Mac) and choose **File/Import…**. Follow the prompts, directing the program to your freshly imported folders on the desktop when necessary. If you can't get any of this to work, you could try transferring your mail via IMAP (see p.72).

Contacts

Open whichever program you use for contacts on the old Mac and look for an **Export…** option – it will usually be in the **File** menu.

If offered a choice, export them in the vCard or LDIF format. Move the resulting files to your new Mac, open **Address Book** from **Applications**, choose **Import...** from the **File** menu, and point the program to the relevant location.

Bookmarks

Open Internet Explorer on the old Mac, choose **Organize Favorites** from the **Favorites** menu, and then choose **Export Favorites** from the **File** menu. Move the resulting file to the new Mac, open **Safari**, press **Import Bookmarks...** from the File menu, and pick the relevant file.

Import scripts

If you're having problems importing data into Mail or Address Book, try the relevant scripts under the AppleScript menu (see p.114).

From a PC

Again, you can copy files from a PC using any of the usual techniques (see p.69) or using a special transfer system such as Move2Mac (see right). Besides everything in My Documents, you may consider moving the following:

Program files

Don't bother. Macs can only handle Windows programs using an emulator (see p.11) and even then you'll need to install them from CD or installer files, not by just dragging the files across.

Outlook data

The easiest way forward is to spend $10 on Outlook2Mac (www.littlemachines.com), a little application that exports mail, contacts and calendars from Outlook (*not* Outlook Express) into formats that can be imported into Address Book, iCal and Mail or Entourage.

▲

Move2Mac ($50) combines software and a cable (either USB or parallel-to-USB) for moving files, contacts and bookmarks (but not mail) from PC to Mac. You might find it handy if the PC lacks a CD burner or an Ethernet port, and you don't have a portable hard drive. See: www.detto.com/move2mac

Non-Outlook email

If you use Outlook Express, there's currently no easy way to import your messages, but you could try IMAP (see box). Most other mail programs let you export your mailboxes – look in the **File** menu or drag the mailboxes and email folders directly from the application window to the PC's desktop. Then move the resulting files to your Mac, launch your new mail program, choose **Import** from the **File** menu and follow the prompts.

Address Book & bookmarks

Create a folder on the PC's desktop. Then open Outlook Express, choose **Tools/Address Book** and then press **Select All** in the **Edit** menu. Drag the addresses to the folder you just created, then move that folder to your Mac, open Address Book and press **File/Import**. Alternatively, try the **Import Address** AppleScript (see p.14).

For bookmarks, open Internet Explorer, choose **Import and Export** from the File menu to export your "Favorites" as an HTML file. Move them over to the Mac, launch Safari, choose **Import** from the **File** menu, and select the relevant file.

Music

If you have music on your PC, copy the files to your Mac and drag them directly into iTunes. If some tracks won't import, the files may have DRM protection. To get around this, return to the PC and try burning the tracks to CD; then rip the CD into iTunes (see p.186). If this doesn't work, or you're worried about the negative effect on sound quality that will result from burning and ripping the tracks, look online for a program to strip off DRM protection. Be aware, though, that in some cases using these may not be legal.

IMAP mail transfers

If you can't export your mail in a format that your new Mac mail program can recognize, you could try setting up your email on the old machine via IMAP and moving your mail via a mail server. Your ISP may allow you to do this for free. For more details, search Google for **Apple 106778** or **Microsoft Q311129**.

Tip: If you want to export bookmarks from Firefox, you'll need to choose **Manage Bookmarks** from the **Bookmarks** menu before you can choose **File/Export**.

OS X tips
& tricks

The Dock

The icon-laden strip that sits (by default) at the bottom of your screen is the Dock, a useful one-stop shop for accessing frequently used applications, files and folders, and for controlling applications and windows currently in use. If you're coming to Macs from a PC background, you'll find the Dock a bit like a combination of the Start Menu and Taskbar in Windows. But it's far more versatile, and there's more to it than immediately meets the eye.

The Dock is split into two sections. On the left are frequently used applications. If an application is running, you'll see a small triangle below its icon; if it's not running, clicking on the icon will launch it. On the right are icons for frequently used files and folders, and the Trash (see p.45). These two portions of the Dock are separated by a thin line called the Dock Separator.

It's important to understand that applications, files and folders don't actually live on the Dock. Rather, the icons are "shortcuts" to files and folders that reside elsewhere on your Mac (or to pages on the World Wide Web). Deleting something from the Dock *does not* delete the file or folder it points to. Equally, if you drag an item onto the Dock you are not making a copy of the file or folder, so *don't* then go and delete the original.

Tip: By default the Dock displays the applications that Apple thought you might like to be there. If you find yourself lumbered with Dock icons you never use, simply drag them off the Dock and they disappear in a puff of smoke.

Dock Preferences

The **Dock** pane of **System Preferences** lets you make a few changes to the way the Dock looks and works. For quick access to these options, use the **Dock** submenu of the Apple menu, or **Control-Click** the Separator to reveal a context menu.

Mess around with the **Position on screen**, **Magnification**, **Minimize using**, **Animate opening...** and **Dock Size** settings to see what you like. And don't worry about leaving room for future additions: the Dock will automatically scale down as you add extra items.

For more Dock customizations, try the interface tweaking tools listed on p.109.

listed on p.109.

Tip: To slide the Dock discreetly off screen when your mouse pointer has moved away, turn on **Hiding**.

Tip: Drag the Separator up or down to scale the Dock and its icons. Hold ⇧ down before you click and you can drag the Dock between the right, left and bottom edges of the screen.

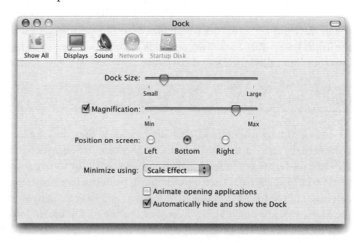

Add application icons

You will no doubt be keen to see your favourite applications permanently stationed on the Dock. Open your **Applications** folder (see p.94), pick a program and drag its icon to the left-hand side of the Dock, dropping it between two others. Once there, icons can be dragged around into any order you like.

◀ Once an application is in the Dock, clicking and holding its icon reveals a menu of application-specific options, including a shortcut for making that program open when you are logged in at start-up.

Add files & folders

Similarly, you can add (and remove) shortcuts to any file or folder on your computer to the right-hand section of the Dock. This is great for items you need to access frequently – perhaps your home folder, or a document you're currently working on.

The best thing about these Dock shortcuts when used with folders is what happens when one is clicked and held – it unfurls to reveal the folder's contents on a menu, complete with submenus for sub-folders. This feature really comes into its own when used, for example, with your iTunes Music folder, providing you with a quick and easy way to browse your music, find a song, and start it playing in iTunes.

"Live" minimizing

The right-hand portion of the Dock is also used to keep track of any minimized windows (see p.97); click one to bring it back to life. These minimized items aren't just icons, but "live" miniaturized versions of the expanded windows. So if you minimize, for instance, a video window – such as a playing DVD or streaming QuickTime movie – the action will keep on rolling in miniature form.

Dock tips & tricks

▶ **Extra menu items** Click and hold an application to reveal its context menu, then hit ⌥ to see additional options, such as **Force Quit** (see p.275).

▶ **Show in Finder** Hold ⌘ while clicking any Dock item to reveal the original item in a Finder window.

▶ **Toggle Dock hiding** ⌘⌥D toggles between hiding and showing the dock.

▶ **Hide current application** Clicking an application icon while holding ⌥ will switch to that application and hide the current one.

▶ **Hide others** Hold ⌘⌥ and click on an application's icon to hide all other applications.

The Dock in context

In the mid-1980s, Steve Jobs, co-founder of Apple, was for a while extricated from the company after one too many run-ins with CEO John Sculley and the board of directors. During his time in the wilderness, Jobs set up a computer firm called NeXT, which produced the operating system that later developed into OS X, after Apple purchased NeXT in 1996.

The Dock is one of the most obvious remnants of NeXT in OS X – though the version Mac users know today is a far more shiny and fancy affair than the old, non-animated NeXT equivalent. And its usability has doubtless helped win many new Mac converts.

Certain features of the Dock have cropped up elsewhere. For example, preview versions of the latest edition of Microsoft Windows (code-named Longhorn) have icons that enlarge when hovered over. And Google even developed a version of their search engine, GoogleX, with a Dock-style tool for choosing between different types of search. Interestingly, it was only live on Google Labs for a day or so, though it can still be found at: www.thejosher.com/googlex

12

Files & folders

Whenever you save a piece of work on your Mac – whether it's a letter you've created, a photo you've downloaded, a spreadsheet, a movie or a piece of software – it is saved as one or more files. There are tens of thousands of files on your Mac even before you add any yourself. So to keep everything tidy, files are organized into folders.

This chapter provides tips on working with files and folders: how to browse, find, open, move, copy, arrange, delete and compress them. With this knowledge your Mac will be a tidier, more efficient and much less confusing place.

The basics

Folders, also known as directories, are usually represented by an icon that looks like a paper folder – either plain or featuring a graphic that says a little more about the folder's contents. Double-clicking any folder icon displays its contents in a Finder window.

Current Work

Applications

Most files, by contrast, look like pieces of paper with a folded corner – though this isn't a golden rule. Usually, the icon reflects the application that OS X will try to use to open the file if you double-click it (which is something you can choose, as we explain on p.90).

my document

PDF

my pdf

Creating files & folders

To create a new folder, make sure you're in Finder (by clicking the desktop) and then either choose the appropriate option from the **File** menu or use the shortcut ⌘⇧N. Alternatively, press the cog-style **Action** button in any Finder window. The folder will appear with the highlighted label "untitled folder", ready for you to type in a name for it, followed by **Enter**.

To create a file, you need to open an application, create some work and save it. Unlike Windows, OS X doesn't offer you a way to create a new blank file directly from Finder.

Renaming files & folders

You can rename any file or folder by clicking its text label and typing the new name. Alternatively, select a file, hit **Enter** and start typing. Note, though, that you shouldn't change the name of your home folder or any system or application files – it's bound to cause problems.

Deleting files & folders

To send a file or folder to the Trash (see p.45), either drag it to the Trash icon on the Dock or select it and press ⌘⌫.

Selecting multiple files & folders

To select more than one file or folder, hold the ⌘ key while clicking items. Or, to select a range of "adjacent" items, hold ⇧ as you click the first and last in the range. You can then hold down the ⌘ key and remove individual items from the selection. A final option is to drag over multiple files, starting in some blank space.

Special folders

As well as regular folders, the Finder file menu lets you create a couple of special folder types:

▶ **Burn Folders**
Use these for collecting files and folders that you want to burn to CD or DVD. When you're ready to write the disc, open the folder and hit the **Burn** button. Note that when you drag a file or folder into a Burn Folder you don't move the original but create an alias (see p.89) that points to the original.

▶ **Smart Folders**
These are essentially saved searches (see p.90). Their contents are determined by a set of parameters that you define in advance, and they stay up to date in real time as new or edited items meet the Smart Folder's criteria. To create one quickly, press ⌘⌥N (or press **Save** when you're searching Finder).

Opening files

The obvious way to open a file is by double-clicking it. Assuming you have an application that can handle the file, things will spring into life. OS X will take a guess at which application you want to use to open the document, and set things in motion.

Pick the application

Most of the time this works fine, but very often more than one application is capable of opening the same file. For example, you could open a digital photograph in Preview, iPhoto, iMovie and various other applications.

To open a file in a different application to the one that OS X seems to favour, you can:

▶ **Control-click the file** and browse the **Open With…** option in the menu.

▶ **Drag the file** directly to the icon of the application you want to use – either on the Dock or elsewhere.

▶ **Launch the application** you want to use and press **File/Open**.

If, however, you *always* want to open a particular file with a particular application, **Control-click** the file, select **Other…**, choose the application you want to use, and check the **Always Open With** box.

Change the default application

You can also set the default application for a particular type of file – for example, if you wanted all PDFs to open into Abode Reader (see p.139), rather than Preview, when double-clicked. To do this, you'd select any PDF and click ⌘I (or choose **Get Info** from the **File** menu) to bring up the file's Info panel. From the **Open With** section,

Tip: If you want to open an application or file you have used recently, it can be accessed quickly from the **Recent Items** submenu of the **Apple** menu.

Tip: To find out how to change the icon of any file or folder, see p.110.

This JPEG file would open into Preview if double-clicked. A quick way to open it in iPhoto instead is to drag it to iPhoto's icon.

choose the application you want to associate with the file type and then hit **Change All....** All the icons of that file type should change to reflect the new setting (as shown).

petersfile.pdf   petersfile.pdf

Files with blank icons

Files with blank icons are not associated with any particular program. When double-clicked, they'll elicit a dialog box with a **Choose application** button. If you have a hunch that a blank file contains an image, say, try a couple of image programs from the list. If that fails, select the file, press ⌘I and check the file extension (see box). If there's already an extension specified, search online to find out more about what it implies; if there isn't one, try adding one that relates to the type of file you suspect you might be dealing with.

Tip: If you drag a file over various application icons in the Dock, you can tell at a glance which applications will at least try to open the file by seeing whether each icon changes colour as the file hovers over it.

File extensions

Every file has a file extension on the end of its name – a special identification tag, a little like a surname. In OS X, file extensions are frequently hidden to keep things tidy, though they can be revealed. To see the extension for an individual file, select it, press ⌘I and look at the name at the top of the info panel; to show extensions for all files on your Mac, choose **Preferences** from Finder's **Finder** menu and click **Advanced**, then tick the **Show all file extensions** box.

Even if file extensions are hidden, you can change the extension of a file simply by single-clicking its text label and adding the extension you want after a dot. This is occasionally useful if a file comes through in the wrong format after being transferred from another computer by email or some other means.

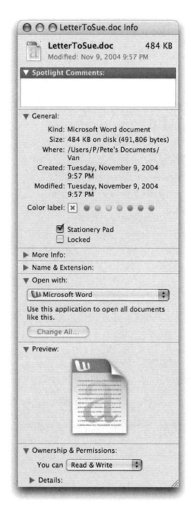

Using the Info panel

To find out more information about any file or folder, open its Info panel by selecting it and hitting ⌘I or choosing **Get Info...** from the Finder's **File** menu. As well as filling you in on various bits of information, Info panels let you make all sorts of changes to a file. The most useful options include:

▶ **The icon** You can click here and paste in a picture. See p.110 for more on customizing icons.

▶ **Spotlight Comments** By adding information or descriptive phrases to this panel, you can improve the efficiency of your Spotlight searches. See p.90 for more on spotlight.

▶ **Stationery Pad** Check this box if you want to temporarily treat a file as a kind of template. When you double-click a stationery file, you actually open an untitled copy of the document, which you can edit and save without affecting the original.

▶ **Locking files** When a file or folder is locked, a padlock appears on its icon and it becomes "read only" – you can't edit or delete the file until the document has been unlocked.

▶ **More Info** Lists the metadata that Spotlight can use when searching for the file (see p.90).

▶ **Name & Extension** Lets you see and change the extension of the file (see p.82) and choose whether it should be displayed in Finder.

▶ **Open with** As we've just seen, you can use this panel to change the default application for a specific file, or for all files of the same type.

▶ **Ownership & Permissions** This panel lets you control which users on the Mac will be able to access the files or folders, as described on p.56.

Browsing files & folders

Though you can search for files (see p.90), you'll probably spend more of your time browsing for them using Finder. To open a Finder window, double-click any folder or drive, or use the ever-useful shortcut ⌘N.

Once you have a Finder window open, the most obvious way to navigate around is to double-click items within it. But there are various other tricks to browsing files and folders:

▶ **Back and forward** Use the back and forward buttons on the Finder window toolbar to move between previous views – just like browsing the Web.

▶ **Going up** Very often you'll want to move "up" a level: go to the folder that contains the folder you're currently viewing. Either use ⌘↑ or, even better, **Control-click** the title at the top of the window to go "up" as many levels as you like (see illustration). This also works in applications: click the document title at the top of a window to see the containing folders.

▶ **Select and open** Instead or selecting files and folders with your mouse and double-clicking to open them, try using the keyboard. With a Finder window open, you can jump to a file or folder by simply typing the first few letters of its name, or using the ↑ and ↓ keys. To open the selected file or folder, press ⌘↓.

▶ **New windows** To open a folder in a new window simply hold down the ⌘ key as you double-click it. Hold down ⌘⌥ if you want the current window to shut as the new one opens.

▶ **Ready, steady...** Finder's **Go** menu features links to various useful places – plus a submenu of recently visited folders. Also, get used to the menu's shortcuts, such as: ⌘⇧C (to see all the drives and discs in your computer) and ⌘⇧H (your home folder).

Tip: To set what you see when you press ⌘N to open a new Finder window, open the **General** pane of **Finder Preferences**.

Tip: You can also move back and forward in Finder using the shortcuts ⌘[and ⌘].

Control-click the title of a window to see a dropdown of the folders containing the folder you're using.

Change your view

Tip: To switch views using the keyboard, hit ⌘1 for icons, ⌘2 for lists, and ⌘3 for columns. To open view options, use ⌘J.

OS X provides a number of options for letting you change the way things look when you're browsing through your files and folders. Most obviously, each Finder window offers you three view options, which you can select from the trio of grouped buttons on the toolbar, or from the **View** menu. And you can tweak the settings for each view using **View Options**, also found in the **View** menu

Icons view

In its default state, this view is a bit annoying and untidy, but open **View Options** and it comes into its own: you can set the icon size and have Finder automatically align items to a grid – or keep them organized by name, date modified, size or type. You can even change the background colour. As with the other two views, you can either apply your changes to the window you're currently viewing or to every window you open from now on.

List view

The great advantage of the list view is that it allows you to view all sorts of information about your files – and sort them accordingly. **View Options** lets you choose which columns appear in the window, and then you can click on the top of any column to sort by that "field".

The other useful feature of this view are the little triangles that appear next to each folder. Click these to "expand" and "collapse" the folder in question. Alternatively, select a folder and use the shortcuts ⌘→ and ⌘←.

Columns view

This view gives you a bit more perspective: when you click a folder its contents are displayed in the next column, and so on ad infinitum. It's often very useful for dragging files from one location to another, but the real beauty of this view is that when you select a file rather than a folder, a new "preview" column will appear. If it's a music or video file, you can play the track or watch a thumbnail of the footage without even leaving the finder window.

The Sidebar

The Sidebar that appears by default in all Finder windows is one of the most simple, yet useful, features of OS X. The top section displays your Mac's drives, discs and network browser, while the bottom section provides handy shortcuts to files and folders of your choice – a bit like the right-hand section of the Dock (see p.75).

Drag any file or folder onto the Sidebar and it will be easily accessible not only from any Finder window but also – less obviously – from the **Where** dropdown menu when you press **Save As** in any application (see right).

To remove an icon from the Sidebar, simply drag it off – this *won't* delete the original file or folder. To change the width of the bar, or to close it, drag the grey separator between it and the rest of the window.

Tip: To change which items appear in the top half of the Sidebar, open **Preferences** from the **Finder** menu, and choose from the various options under **Sidebar**.

Tip: If you have to perform a repetitive task involving copying and moving folders, explore Automator and Folder Actions (see p.112).

Tip: To cancel a drag that's in progress, hit **Escape**. This works in most applications – not just files in Finder.

Tip: If, when dragging an item, you hold it over the icon of a folder or drive (including those on the Sidebar of a Finder window), the folder or drive will open up in a new window. This is very useful, as it means you can always drag to wherever you like, even without having multiple windows open: drag the item to **Macintosh HD** and drill down from there. Hitting **space** while hovering over a folder makes it open instantly.

Tip: You can open a folder in to a new window by holding ⌘ while you double-click it. This can be handy when moving files around.

Housekeeping in Finder

It pays to keep all your files and folders as neatly organized as possible. Here's the least you need to know…

Moving & copying

In most cases, if you drag a file or folder from one location on your Mac's hard drive to another, it will simply be moved. However, if you drag something to a separate drive or server, or into some applications, it will be copied. And if you try to drag a whole drive, or drag a file onto a blank CD, you'll drag an alias (see box) rather than a copy. Your mouse pointer will display a green plus if the item is going to be copied, and a black arrow if an alias will be created.

RG to Macs and OS X
3 items

RG to Macs and OS X

If the default choice doesn't suit your purposes, hold down a key while you drag:

⌥	drag a copy (also works for text in most applications)
⌥⌘	drag an alias
⌘	move instead of copy; copy instead of alias

Of course, dragging isn't the only way to move and copy files in OS X. You can also:

▶ **Duplicate** Select one or more files or folders and press ⌘**D**. A copy will appear next to the original.

▶ **Copy and paste** You can copy and paste (though not cut) files and folders, just as you would text in a document. Select something, hit **Copy** in the **Edit** menu (or ⌘**C**); open the folder or drive where you want to put it and press **Paste** (or ⌘**V**).

Aliases

An alias, or "shortcut", is a file that exists simply to point to another file, folder or drive. There's less reason to manually create aliases in OS X than there used to be, since it's so convenient to drop shortcuts on the Dock (see p.75) and Sidebar (see p.87). Still, it can sometimes be useful – if you fancy having access to your home folder via the desktop, say.

To create an alias, select a file, folder or drive and hit ⌘L, or choose **Make Alias** from the **File** menu. Alternatively, drag the file while holding down ⌥⌘. If you want to delete a shortcut, you can do so safely: no harm will be done to the original file or folder.

Tip: You can set Finder to always open folders into a new window from the **General** pane of Finder's **Preferences**, though this does tend to make things a little cluttered as more and more windows appear.

Tip: Many of the options and functions mentioned on these pages can also be accessed from the **Action** button (the one with the cog graphic on a Finder window toolbar). Its contents relate to whatever's selected in the window or, if nothing is, the whole folder that you are viewing.

Labels

The Labels feature lets you mark up any file or folder as one of six colours, which can be useful for staying organized if you're working with lots of files and folder. In one project folder you might mark your unfinished documents in red, say, and finished ones in green. To pick a colour label, select one or more items, and choose from the **Label** section of the **File** menu – or in the context menu when you **Control-click**.

If you like, you can edit the names of the labels – from "red", for example, to "unfinished" – in Finder's **Preferences**, which you can open from the **Finder** menu. That way, when you're using Finder's list view (see p.86), you can add Labels as a column and see your customized names.

Searching with Spotlight

One of the most significant features to be introduced in OS X Tiger was the Spotlight search tool. Spotlight searches fast – and not only for file and folder names, and the contents of text documents, but also for so-called metadata: information *about* the files. Metadata includes everything from the exposure time of a digital photo via the album tag of an MP3 file to the recipient of an email.

Note, though, that not every application is supported. Spotlight will find emails in Mail but not Entourage, for example. But you can make many applications Spotlight compatible with a plug-in from:

Spotlight Plug-ins www.apple.com/downloads/macosx/spotlight

Search for everything

To perform a complete system search, click the magnifying glass icon in the top-right of the screen or hit ⌘**Space**. Type in whatever you want to search for and a list of top results will appear. Click a result to open it, or hit **Show All** (or the **Enter** key) to open the results in a Spotlight window, where you can refine and group them…

Tip: Spotlight works by "indexing" your hard drive, a bit like the way that a search engine indexes the Web. Creating an index can take a few hours, so Spotlight may not work on a drive that's only just been added.

Tip: To go straight to a Spotlight window, hit ⌥⌘**Space**.

When the results are grouped by ▶ *Kind, look on the blue strip for various view options. When images are present, hit the* ▶ *icon for a slideshow.*

◀ *Use the right-hand panel to refine your search results according to location, date modified, etc.*

▲
Click the "i" button for more information about any single result.

Searching in Finder for files & folders

If you want to find files and folders while ignoring emails, meta-data and other results, use the Spotlight search box found in every Finder window – double-click any folder or drive and you'll see it in the top-right of the window (if it's missing, see p.106). Alternatively, choose **Find** from the **File** menu – or hit ⌘F.

In most cases you'll just want to type your search terms and specify the location you want to search. The grey locations strip will, by default, include options for your whole computer, your home folder and, perhaps, the folder you were viewing when you clicked ⌘F. To choose a different location, click **Other...**

To hone your search results, use the dropdown menus to add extra criteria (if necessary, add extra parameters with the "+" button). For oodles of choices, select **Other** from the first dropdown and you'll be offered criteria ranging from tempo and lyricist to exposure mode. Choose **Author**, for example, and you can search for all the files on your machine created by a particular person. None of this will work flawlessly, as not every application adds all the relevant metadata. But it can be hugely useful nonetheless.

Smart folders

You can save a Finder search as a Smart Folder (see p.81). The folder will automatically update as you add, edit or delete files on your Mac, allowing you to quickly reach fresh results without re-searching.

Essential search tips
▶ You can search for more than one word, including incomplete words. So Beet Conc, say, would find Beethoven's *Violin Concerto* in your iTunes Library.
▶ Type ! before a word to exclude it from the search. For example, Beet !Conc would find all your Beethoven recordings except concertos.
▶ In the **Spotlight** pane of **System Preferences** you can: stop Spotlight finding any particular type of file; change the order in which results are displayed (by dragging items up and down in the list); and set new search shortcuts.
▶ You can stop Spotlight searching a particular location (for security or performance reasons) in the **Privacy** pane of Spotlight preferences.
▶ To quickly search within a specific folder or drive, open it in Finder, hit ⌘F and then choose its name from the locations bar at the top.
▶ To see some of the metadata that a file contains, select it, hit ⌘I and look under the **More Info** section.

Compressed files

When you download software or other large files from the Web, you'll often find they arrive "zipped" or "stuffed" – saved in a special compressed format that your Mac has to decompress before you can do anything with the contents. This kind of compression serves two purposes. First, it reduces the overall size of files in order to make them quicker to transfer by email or over the Web, and to make them more space efficient on a hard drive, CD or any other media. Second, it allows you to bundle any number of separate files into a single "archive", again making them much more convenient to transfer over the Internet.

Opening compressed formats

There are many different compressed file formats. Your Mac can open most of the ones you'll come across – .zip, .dmg, .gz, .tar and .bz2 – without any extra software. Simply double-click the file and a new "unzipped" version will appear next to the original. However, at some stage you'll inevitably be sent a StuffIt (.sit or .sitx) file, in which case you'll need a free application called StuffIt Expander to open it up.

StuffIt Expander www.stuffit.com (free)

Creating compressed files

If you're sending files by email or trying to save disk space by far the easiest way to compress them is to make a ZIP file: select one or more files and folders, **Control-click** and choose **Create Archive of…** from the context menu. If for any reason you want to create a DMG file, follow the directions on p.261, perhaps without adding a password.

StuffIt versus ZIP

StuffIt was once the most widely used compression format on Macs, and StuffIt Expander was included in OS X up to version 10.3. Compared with ZIP files, StuffIt archives are better at squashing data to the smallest possible size. However, StuffIt is now on the way out because: OS X can handle so many compressed formats itself; PC users can open ZIP files without downloading StuffIt Expander; and Mac users can create ZIP and DMG files with OS X. To create StuffIt files, you need to spend $49 on a special StuffIt application.

How lossless compression works

When a file is zipped up, or stuffed, the computer looks for repeating patterns that it can represent more concisely. Let's say that you've saved a document containing this text:

```
every land, every sea and every sky:
    here, there and everywhere
```

The compression program would notice that "here", "every" and "and" occur more than once, so would assign each of these collections of letters a more concise symbol. For example:

```
every = !, and = *, here = ^
```

Then it could write the same sentence as:

```
! l*, ! sea * ! sky: ^, t^ * !w^
```

In reality, of course, it's not quite this simple, and the computer would use numbers rather than symbols. But the basic principle is the same.

Images, music & video compression

The type of file compression discussed so far is known as *lossless* compression, meaning that the data that comes out when the file is unzipped or unstuffed will be identical to what you put in. This is distinct from the *lossy* compression widely used for shrinking sound, image and video files.

With lossy compression, the computer applies ingenious methods of picking out which bits of data our eyes and ears notice least, and discards them. Unlike lossless compression, this is a one-way process – you can't take a compressed music or image file and turn it back into the uncompressed original.

For more on compressing music, images and video, see p.188, p.168 and p.255 respectively.

Text as code

Sound, video and image files can withstand minor degradation through lossy file compression. But you could never perform the same techniques on a text or number documents. The reason is that words and numbers are really types of "code", so a minor change can completely alter the meaning.

13 Applications

An application is a piece of software that helps you perform a particular task or set of tasks. It might be something that came with OS X – such as iTunes – or something you installed yourself, such as Photoshop. If you're coming to Macs from a PC background, you might be used to calling applications "programs" – there's no difference between the two.

By default, all your applications live, logically enough, in a folder called **Applications**, which you'll find at the top of the folder tree in your hard drive. However, this is just a tidy and convenient storage place – you can put an application wherever you like on your Mac.

Within the **Applications** folder you'll also find another folder called **Utilities**. A utility is an application for techie tasks such as setting something up or diagnosing a problem. For quick access to your **Utilities** folder, press ⌘⇧U.

Launching & quitting

As we've seen (see p.77), if you regularly use a particular application, you can drag its icon onto the Dock for quick access; likewise you could drag a shortcut to an individual application onto your desktop (see p.89). But what if you want quick access to your whole **Applications** folder? A few other possibilities:

▶ **Via the keyboard** When in Finder, hit ⌘⇧A to jump to **Applications**.

▶ **Via the Dock** If you drag your whole **Applications** folder to the right-hand side of the Dock, you can click and hold to view its contents (see far left). The only problem is that OS can be sluggish at displaying the menu.

▶ **Via the Apple menu** Using a customization program (see p.109), you could add individual applications – or your whole **Applications** folder – to the Apple menu.

Tip: To quickly exit an application, press ⌘Q. Conveniently, the keys for save (⌘S) and close window (⌘W) live nearby. So when you've finished working in a particular application you can save and shut up shop with only the slightest movement of the thumb and middle finder.

The application menu

Once an application is up and running, you'll find all its menus at the top of the screen. The first one displays the name of the application and contains everything relating to it "as a whole": information about it; preferences for it; and options for quitting (closing) and hiding it.

The application menu also includes **Services**. Many Mac users ignore this feature of OS X, but it can be very useful, providing quick access to various tools and utilities. Let's say you're listening to a track in iTunes and you want to quickly look up the artist via Google. Simply highlight the name of the artist and click **Services/Search With Google**. Or if you're typing something in a program with no spell-check feature, select **Services/TextEdit/New Window Containing Selection** and the text will appear in TextEdit, where you can quickly check the spelling.

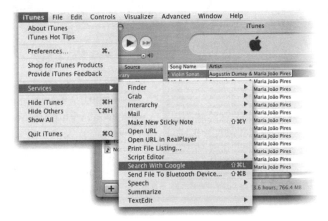

Switching apps & windows

If you're working in multiple applications and windows simultaneously, you may find yourself rooting around for a particular pane like a pig looking for truffles. Thankfully, there are a couple of tricks that make it much easier to quickly access the application, window or file that you're looking for...

The king of shortcuts: ⌘→|

If there's one single keyboard shortcut that will transform the way you use your Mac, it's ⌘→| (**Command-Tab**). Hold down the ⌘ key, hit the →| key and a bar will appear displaying all the applications you currently have open. Keeping holding down ⌘ and you can cycle between the applications with repeated clicks of →|. When you get to the application you want to access, release the keys.

Tip: While cycling through applications with ⌘→|, hit **Q** to quit a highlighted program or **H** to hide one. This is a great way to quickly close lots of programs or clear the decks.

To cycle through the applications in the opposite direction, add ⇧ (**Shift**). Alternatively, keep holding down ⌘ and select one of the icons with your mouse.

To cycle between open windows in a specific application, swap →| for ` (the key next to **Z**). Again, add shift to cycle through in the opposite direction. Note that this shortcut won't work in all applications, and it will ignore minimized windows.

Exposé

OS X v10.3 introduced a flashy new feature called Exposé – a quick way to "expose" open windows and the desktop with the keyboard. Hit one the these keys...

F9 See all open windows
F10 See windows in current application

... and then use the mouse to pick from the miniaturized windows. Or if you're after a file or folder on the desktop:

F11 Hide all windows

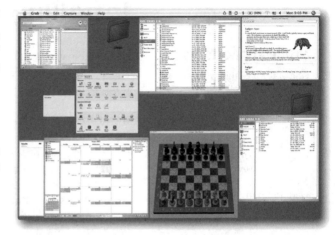

Hiding applications

Another useful way to cut through the clutter is to temporarily "hide" all the windows of a particular application (or all the other applications except the one you're working in). You'll find these options in the menu for an application, though its more convenient to hold down ⌥ or ⌘⌥ when clicking between applications via their icons on the Dock of via their windows.

Minimizing windows

To "hide" an individual window, minimize it to the Dock by pressing the yellow button in its top-right-hand corner. Or to minimize *all* the windows within an application (including Finder), hold ⌥ while clicking the minimize button. If you find the way windows "melt" down into their minimized state a bit too cute, change "Genie" to "Scale" in the **Dock** pane of **System Preferences**.

Tip: From the **Dashboard & Exposé** panel of **System Preferences** you can set up "Active Screen Corners" for the various Exposé commands. This way, simply moving your mouse pointer to one of the screen's corners does the same as pressing the shortcut.

Tip: While using Exposé or minimizing windows, hold down the ⇧ key and it all happens in slow motion – good when you have a hangover.

Installing & uninstalling

Though some applications take you through a step-by-step installer process (a bit like on a PC), in the majority of cases installing software on Mac OS X involves simply dropping a single file or folder into your Applications folder – or somewhere else if you prefer. Uninstalling is just as simple: drag the file or folder to the Trash.

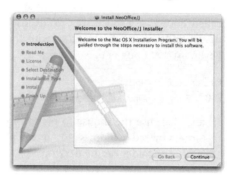

This ease of installing and uninstalling applications is one of the most user-friendly elements of OS X. It also makes it easy to share applications – copy a file or folder from someone else's **Applications** folder into yours, and in most cases it will work straight off. (Note, though, that in the case of commercial software, this might break the terms of the license agreement that your friend agreed to when he or she originally installed the software).

The only problem with all this is that when you drag an application to the Trash, you may be left with a few residual files (preferences and the like) in your Mac's Libraries. This is harmless, though if you're short of disk space, or you like to practise the Mac equivalent of Feng Shui, you may want to delete them. If the application came with a readme file, check that – it will often point you to all the relevant files. Otherwise, you could try using Spotlight (see p.90) to search for the name of the application to locate relevant files – but only delete the ones you feel sure aren't used by other applications.

If you find yourself becoming really obsessive about cleaning out residual files, consider downloading Allume's SpringCleaning tool.

SpringCleaning www.allume.com/mac/springcleaning ($50)

Downloading software

Though some data-heavy packages are only available on CD or DVD, most software these days can be downloaded from the Web. Simply go to a download site (see p.286) or the homepage of whoever produces the application you want, and look for a download link. Usually the download will start immediately, though in some cases you'll first be asked to choose a "mirror" site. These are simply various locations on the Internet where the file is stored. Software developers use mirrors because having too many people download large files from their websites can slow things down – and cost them money.

When the download is complete, you'll usually end up with a compressed file (see p.92) on your desktop. This might be a ZIP or a DMG file, or even a DMG file within a ZIP file. Also known as Disk Images, DMGs act like virtual disk drives: when double-clicked, the drive will be "mounted" on your desktop and Finder window Sidebars – just as if you'd plugged in an external hard drive.

Once opened up, the downloaded file will usually contain the application itself and possibly also a readme file. This is worth scanning as it not only provides general information about the software, but also typically gives some installation advice – such as which files will be installed where when you launch the application (useful if you later want to uninstall it).

Once the software is safely installed in your **Applications** folder, you can delete (or backup) the original downloaded file – and the uncompressed version of it, if there is one. If you installed from a DMG file, however, you'll need to "eject" the virtual drive – by dragging it to the trash or pressing the ⏏ icon next to its name in a Finder window Sidebar.

14 Dashboard

With the arrival of OS X Tiger came the much-hyped Dashboard feature, which provides a quick and easy way to do everything from check the weather forecast to find a phone number and search a favourite website... the list is almost endless. Though Dashboard appears in the Applications folder (and on the Dock), it's not so much an application as such – it's a "layer" of OS X that houses mini applications called widgets.

To quickly summon the widgets currently installed on your dashboard – which range from a calculator to an international weather tool – simply hit **F12**, or click the Dashboard icon in the Dock.

Tip: . If you always use the F12 key to access the Dashboard, there's no need to keep its icon in the Dock. Click and hold it and choose **Remove from Dock** from the menu. If you ever want to put it back, drag the Dashboard icon from **Applications** onto the Dock.

Tip: You can change the key that reveals your Dashboard in the **Dashboard & Exposé** pane of OS X's **System Preferences**.

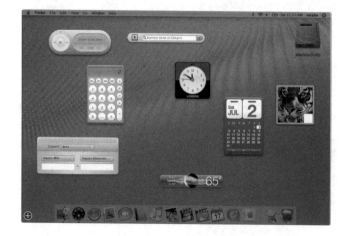

Have a play with what's available; you'll soon figure out what does what and which widgets are only going to do their thing if you are connected to the Internet. To close the Dashboard, hit **F12** again or click on some space between widgets.

When you first call upon Dashboard, the few widgets that are laid out before you are not the only ones in your OS X armory. Click the "+" icon in the bottom-left corner to show the Widget Bar along the bottom of the screen.

To add widgets to your Dashboard simply drag them out of the Widget Bar and watch as they ripple into life. To remove a widget from the Dashboard, click the "**x**" icon that is visible at its top-left corner when the Widget Bar is open.

Where widgets live

Each individual widget is a little application. But unlike "regular" applications, which tend to live in your **Applications** folder, widgets live in two special locations within your hard drive:

▶ **Macintosh HD/Library/Widgets** Widgets in here appear on the Widget Bar of all users on the Mac.

▶ **Your home folder/Library/Widgets** Widgets in here appear on your Widget Bar only – not those of other users.

Widgets don't have to live in these folders. As with other applications, you can keep them anywhere that's convenient and open them with a double-click. But if you want them in your Widget Bar, you have to use these folders.

Tip: To teasingly slow the Dashboard's animated blitz across the screen, hold down ⇧ while you click **F12**.

Tip: To close widgets without opening the Widget Bar, hold the ⌥ key as your mouse pointer hovers over the widget. This will reveal the widget-closing button.

Tip: If an individual widget becomes buggy or freezes, reload it with the shortcut ⌘R.

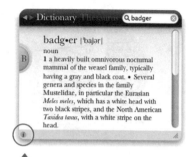

When your mouse pointer hovers over a widget, you may see a little "i". Click here to get access to the widget's settings.

Tip: Be warned. Though a Mac is unlikely to be affected by malware (see p.264), small, easily installed applications such as widgets offer an obvious way in for malicious software, so avoid any widgets that look remotely suspicious.

Widget preferences

If you want full control over your Dashboard environment, including the ability to turn it off and set widget security levels, try the Widgets Preferences Pane application from www.ego-systems.com

Get more widgets

The widgets that come with OS X are useful, but they're only the tip of the iceberg. There are thousands of widgets available online to download – and most of them are free. If you can think of a specific widget that you'd like, chances are that a developer somewhere has already thought the same and made it. As you might expect, your first port of call should be the Apple site, as their collection is vast and well organized:

Apple www.apple.com/downloads/dashboard

You can also go straight to this site from the **More Widgets...** option on the Dashboard bar. But it's not the only widget website:

DashboardWidgets.com www.dashboardwidgets.com/showcase
DashboardExchange www.dashboardexchange.com/widgets
DashboardExposed.com www.dashboardexposed.com
WidgetDeveloper www.widgetdeveloper.com

Always-on widgets

If you want to make a widget available all the time – not just when Dashboard is open, activate Dashboard Development Mode. To do this, open Terminal from **Applications/Utilities** and type this:

```
defaults write com.apple.dashboard devmode YES
```

Hit **Enter**, close Terminal and restart your Mac. When it's up and running again, hit **F12** to reveal Dashboard. While dragging the widget you want to keep active, hit F12 and hey presto – you have a floating widget. To put it back on the Dashboard, again press **F12** while dragging it.

To turn the Development Mode off, go back into Terminal and retype the same command with "NO" at the end in place of "YES". Hit **Enter** and restart.

Some widgets will automatically appear on your Widget Bar after you've downloaded them, but others may need to be dragged into one of the two widget folders already described.

Hidden features

Many widgets have fun extra features that aren't obvious from a first glance. Two examples, from the collection you already have:

▶ **The weather in Nowhere** Open the weather widget, hold down ⌘ ⌥ and click the widget a few times. You'll be taken to a mysterious city called Nowhere and shown all the weather systems the widget can describe.

▶ **Sort yourself out** If you've played with the Tile Game widget but got bored of the tiger image, try putting yourself in the picture. Pick an image and, while dragging the file, press **F12** – still holding down the mouse button. Keep dragging the image and drop it straight into the Tile Game.

Roll your own widgets

One of the reasons why widgets are so popular is the ease with which they can be created. Most comprise little more than HTML code, JavaScript and a couple of images. If you know what that means, you could probably have a crack at building a widget. To find out how it's done, read the tutorials at:

Apple developer.apple.com/macosx/dashboard.html
Dashboard Development For Newbies dashdev.djupet.se

For more developer resources, tips and Dashboard hacks, see:

DashboardWidgets.com www.dashboardwidgets.com/links

Tip: Some users have found that over time widgets can hog large amounts of RAM (see p.30), making both Dashboard and other applications slower. As a remedy, try closing widgets you're not using, and restarting your machine from time to time.

Konfabulator

Dashboard may have been introduced with Tiger, but the idea of widgets dates back to Konfabulator – a third-party product available for Macs and PCs. There are hundreds of free widgets available for Konfabulator, though you need to buy the main application ($20) to install them, since Konfabulator and Dashboard widgets aren't compatible. For more information, see: www.konfabulator.com

A few choice widgets

The following, all available via the Apple site, are some of our favourite widgets, and should give you an idea of the range on offer…

Asteroids widget

Play the classic arcade game. Your score is recorded online, and if you get into the top 100 chart of highest scorers everyone else who has this widget will know about it.

XwordLookup

Solve those impossible crossword clues by typing in any letters you have, along with the gaps. The widget reveals all the possible answers.

Wikipedia

One of many reference widgets, this provides instant access to the world's greatest wiki.

Air Traffic Control

Widgets are often quite geeky, so expect to see loads that delve into networking and the like. This one scans your area for available Wi-Fi networks.

TV Tracker

See what's currently playing on US TV channels. There are loads of similar widgets for everywhere from Australia to Sweden.

Panda Cam

See what's going down in the panda enclosure of the San Diego Zoo. For a completely customizable webcam widget, seek out SlothCam.

Ovulation Calculator

Find out the best time to make a baby during your monthly cycle.

Ceefax

The BBC's text-based information service, freed from the TV. News, listings and weather reports served up with a retro feel.

Customizing

15

We've already discussed various ways to customize how your Mac looks and works – by changing the Dock and Finder windows, for example. But there are many other tweaks that you can make, from picking a desktop image to installing techie tools for altering almost every aspect of the system. If you're happy to risk damaging your machine, and you don't care about details such as warranties, you could even try bypassing the software modifications and start hacking the hardware – see p.291.

Basic customizations

The desktop

The most obvious Mac customization is to substitute the rather corporate-looking abstract shape that, by default, occupies your desktop with something of your own choosing. This is easily done: either open **Desktop & Screen Saver** from **System Preferences**, or **Control-click** the desktop and select **Change Desktop Background...**

Here you'll find a bunch of Apple-supplied pics, plus direct access to your iPhoto Library and albums, and a **Choose Folder...** option to pick an image from anywhere on your Mac. You can even cycle through a folder of images at a frequency of your choosing.

Cool desktop tools

▶ **BackLight** (free) Put a live screensaver on the desktop background. freshsqueeze.com

▶ **Desktastic** ($13) Scribble and type onto the desktop. www.panic.com/desktastic

▶ **Stattoo** ($13) "Tattoo" the desktop with a clock, iCal and Mail info, battery meter, etc. www.panic.com/stattoo

Next, tinker with your desktop icons. Click on the desktop and hit ⌘J to open **View Options**, where you can pick the icon size and sorting options. Further changes to what appears on the desktop – hard drive icons, discs, etc – can be made by opening **Finder Preferences**, accessible via the **Finder** menu (or with the shortcut ⌘,).

Windows

Besides changing the View Options and Sidebar in Finder windows – as described on p.86 – it's possible to make various other modifications to how your windows look. **Control-click** the toolbar (the bit at the top with the buttons on) and you'll find a number of options, including **Customize Toolbar**, which will reveal a palette of buttons that you can drag onto the top of your windows. The same technique also works in many applications.

A few other modifications – including the colour of highlighted text labels, scroll button layout, etc – can be made under **Appearance** in **System Preferences**.

Menu bar

The menu bar can quickly fill up with notification icons and other symbols and menus, probably not all of which you need or use. Each one can be switched on and off in a preferences panel somewhere, but the easiest way to remove something is to hold down ⌘ and simply drag them off – or reorder them as you like.

Tip: You can quickly remove an item from your Finder windows toolbar by pressing ⌘ while dragging.

Customizing hotkeys

It's possible to customize many OS X keyboard shortcuts in various System Preference panels – most obviously in **Keyboard & Mouse**. Many applications also let you add or change shortcuts (look within **Preferences**, or in the **Tools** menu). But for total control over shortcuts in all applications, spend $10 on **Menu Master**, downloadable from www.unsanity.com.

Holding down the ⌘ key lets you drag items around on the menu bar. The same technique works on Finder window toolbars and elsewhere in OS X.

If there's something missing from your menu bar, look in the relevant pane of System Preferences, or the preferences panel of the application the item relates to, for a check box to reinstate it.

You can also enhance the menu bar with certain downloadable programs. iSeek (www.ambrosiasw.com/utilities/iseek, $15), for example, puts a customizable Google search box to the left of your menu bar icons. For more customization apps, see p.109.

Screensavers

Screensavers – animated displays that kick into action after your computer has sat unused for a set period – were first developed as a practical means of stopping static images "burning" into old-style screens. These days they're mainly for fun, though they also serve a security role, as you can set OS X to request a password when "awaking" after displaying a screensaver (see p.259).

To choose from the various screensavers that came with your Mac, open **System Preference** and hit **Desktop & Screen Saver**. There are a few good ones – including "RSS Visualizer", which displays headlines from any website newsfeeds you've subscribed to using Safari (see p.149). The design is over-clever, but the idea is great.

Obviously, you're not limited to the screensavers provided by Apple. There are hundreds more to be found online – some free, others pay-to-use, and ranging in style and concept from the sublime to the ridiculous. When you download and double-click a screensaver, you'll be offered the option of installing it only for yourself or for all user accounts on the machine. Depending which you

Tip: If you never see your screensaver because your Mac always goes to sleep before it appears, adjust the **Put the computer to sleep...** setting within the **Energy Saver** preferences pane.

Tip: At the bottom of the screensaver list, there are options for using pics from your iPhoto Library as slide-show-style screensavers.

Tip: Press the hot corners button within the **Screen Saver** preferences pane if you'd like to be able to instantly activate the screensaver by moving your mouse to a corner of the screen. This is useful with screensavers that serve some function beyond looking pretty.

customizing

Tip: Nearly every screensaver lets you make various tweaks to how it looks and works. Select one, and hit **Options...** in the **Screen Savers** System Preferences pane.

choose, OS X will drop the screensaver in either the **Library/Screen Savers** folder of your home folder, or the **Library/Screen Savers** folder of Macintosh HD. To uninstall a screensaver, find it in one of these two folders and drag it to the Trash.

Following are a few of our favourite OS X screensavers to get you in the mood. For more, look online, starting here:

Apple www.apple.com/downloads/macosx/icons_screensavers
OS X Screensavers macosxscreensaver.com

Marine Aquarium

Shame about the $20 tag, but could you ever put a price on the likes of butterflyfish and the yellow tangdo?

OOOkTunes

Turns your Mac into a "now-playing" display for your iTunes – in a colour and font of your choice.

ClockSaver

"A simple but elegant analog clock." Say no more.

SnowSaver

Snowflakes falling against a blue background. Surprisingly mesmerizing.

Holding Pattern

Become an international jet setter without lack of leg room or climate-change guilt trip.

Cavendish

Generates a random set of celestial bodies and then accurately models their gravitational effect on each other.

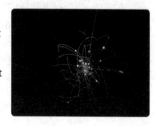

Serious customizations

If you want to tweak the way OS X looks and feels beyond the tweaks discussed so far, you'll need to download some extra tools. There are all kinds of customization utilities out there, so if there's something you'd like to change, there probably is a way. A word of warning, though: some customization programs let you make deep system changes that should be handled with care.

Among the most popular and useful customization tools are:

▶ **FruitMenu** www.unsanity.com/haxies/fruitmenu ($10)
Let's you do practically anything with the Apple menu and context menus: browse your hard drive, add and remove items, preview pictures and more. Great for quickly accessing files, apps and System Preferences panels.

▶ **Shapeshifter** www.unsanity.com/haxies/shapeshifter ($20)
Lets you install new OS X "themes", which affect the colours and designs of windows, the Dock, toolbars and more. You can download extra themes from www.interfacelift.com/themes-mac.

▶ **TinkerTool** www.bresink.de/osx/TinkerTool.html (free)
Display hidden files, disable sound effects, add Quit to the Finder menu, and make scores of other little changes.

▶ **Visage** keakaj.com/visage.htm ($10)
Tweak the log-in and boot-up screens and the system alerts ("Peter, are you sure you want to shut down?").

▶ **Mighty Mouse** www.unsanity.com/haxies/mightymouse ($10)
Change the style and size of your mouse pointers.

▶ **Cocktail** www.macosxcocktail.com ($15)
Unlocks all kinds of techie features and offers a few interface customizations: the way windows minimize, the position of the Dock, etc. Also lets you tamper with Exposé, Mail and Safari.

FruitMenu lets you access individual System Preferences panels and ferret through your hard drive, directly from the Apple menu.
▼

InterfaceLIFT

Mac OS X Icons

Customize the look of ap
icons. You can even chan
by following our detailed
our icon FAQ.

Please note that we also offer icons for W

Icon Set Preview

Download (mac) | More Info

Download (mac) | More Info

Download (mac) | More Info

Download (mac) | More Info

Download (mac) | More Info

Customizing icons

Scalable, high-res icons are one of the things that make OS X such a nice-looking system. And they're completely customizable, too – you can replace any icon with one that you prefer, or even one that you've made yourself. Thousands of icon sets are available for free download, making it easy to either subtly change the style of your set up or to fully convert it into a shrine to anything from retro design to, urm, sushi and powertools. Among the biggest and best icon collections are:

Apple www.apple.com/downloads/macosx/icons_screensavers
InterfaceLIFT www.interfacelift.com
Icon Factory www.iconfactory.com

For even more, try:

Icons.cx www.icons.cx/icons
IheartNY www.iheartny.com
Pixiland www.pixiland.de/osxicons
Pixelgirl Presents www.pixelgirlpresents.com

Changing icons

To replace an icon you don't like with one you've downloaded (or one that appears elsewhere on your system) first select the file or folder whose icon you want to use, and press ⌘I to bring up the Info panel. Click the icon at the top of the panel and then press ⌘C to copy it. Next, select the file or folder where you want to use the copied icon and, again, press ⌘I. Click the icon at the top of the Info panel, and press ⌘V to paste the copied icon into place.

This technique will work on all icons other than so-called System icons, such as the Trash and new folders. To edit those, you either need some in-depth technical know-how or the help of a tool such as Candybar, which lets you change not only icons but toolbar buttons in Finder, Mail and other apps. In case you change your mind, there's a one-click restore switch to put everything back.

Tip: For more icon software, see: interfacelift.com/icons-mac/software.php

Candybar www.panic.com/candybar ($15)

Icon managers

If you end up with a huge archive of downloaded icons, you might welcome the services of an icon manager such as Pixadex. Use it to browse your collection, create custom icon sets and save "iContainers" – packages of icons that can be installed with just a double-click.

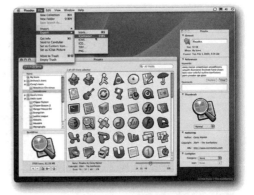

Pixadex www.iconfactory.com/px_home.asp ($19)

Making your own icons

Making a basic icon is easy. Using any decent graphics program, create a 128 x 128 pixel image, draw your icon and save it as a TIFF, JPEG or PNG file. The resulting file should automatically have an icon bearing the picture you drew, which you can then copy and paste to any other file in the normal way. (If no icon is displayed, grab the free Pic2Icon utility from www.download.com.)

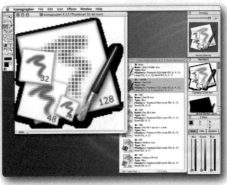

Creating a slick-looking icon with a transparent background is more fiddly. It's possible to do it by adding an alpha-channel mask to your icon in Photoshop and importing the result into **Icon Composer** (part of Xcode, which you can install from **Applications/Installers**). But it's far easier to use an icon-creation tool such as:

Iconographer mscape.com/products/iconographer.html ($15)

16 Automating

There's nothing more tedious than performing a repetitive task on a computer, be it a one-off pain (changing the names of a big stack of files, say) or a daily chore (such as downloading news headlines from the web, pasting them into a simple text doc and transferring them onto your iPod to read on the train). With a little effort up front, however, it's not difficult to get the computer to put in the legwork – leaving you free to do something more interesting.

Automating computers is nothing new. There are scores of programming languages designed expressly to create "scripts" for computers to follow – including Mac OS's own AppleScript (see p.114). But without learning a scripting language, we've traditionally been limited to the automation tools built into a few applications (such as "macros" in Word and "actions" in Photoshop). For Mac users, that changed with OS X Tiger – and the introduction of Automator.

▲
In case you were wondering, the Automator robot is called Otto.

Automator

Automator, which you'll find in **Applications**, lets you program your computer without a hint of technical know-how. The basic idea is that you assemble a time-saving "Workflow" by combining various off-the-shelf "Actions" (individual tasks such as finding unread emails, converting file formats, importing files into an application, and so on). Workflows have the power to do some pretty compli-cated things – publishing a Podcast, for instance, or harvesting full-size images behind an online gallery of thumbnails and adding them to your iPhoto Library.

Creating workflows

Automator comes installed with a large collection of Actions, arranged down the left according to the applica-tion they relate to. To start a Workflow, drag an action into the right-hand pane and, if necessary, tinker with its settings. Then add another action, but make sure it makes sense as a follow-up to the first. If it doesn't (if you try to follow **Find iTunes Items** with **Crop Image**, for example) you'll see red text where the two actions should link together.

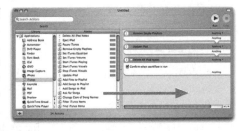

When you've strung a few actions together, hit the **Run** button to see if your Workflow functions as planned. Don't be put off if it fails at first; think logically through the Workflow from start to fin-ish, make some tweaks and try again. Once everything's working correctly, hit **Save** in the **File** menu and your Workflow will appear under **My Workflows** in the left-hand panel. Next, click **File/Save As...** and export your workflow as a standalone application. This way, you can run it without opening Automator – and you get to feel like a programming guru. You could even give your application its own icon (see p.110) and drag it onto the Dock.

Adding actions

You're not limited to the Action that came with Automator, as there are loads of extra ones available to download and import (see box). You could even have a shot a designing your own, though you'll first need to learn some AppleScript...

Automator online

For extra Actions, ready-made Workflows and Automator tips and tricks, drop in to:
www.apple.com/downloads/macosx/automator
www.automatoractions.com
www.automatorworld.com

AppleScript

To a certain extent, Automator is just a friendly interface for AppleScript, the long-standing Mac scripting language. Just like an Automator Workflow, an AppleScript is essentially a series of commands that can be opened and edited or exported as a mini application.

To see the sample scripts that came with OS X, open **AppleScript Utility** from **Applications/AppleScript** and check the box to activate the AppleScript menu. A new icon will appear up on your menu bar (near the clock), revealing scores of scripts when clicked. For thousands more, drop in to:

Apple www.apple.com/applescript
Doug's AppleScripts For iTunes www.dougscripts.com
MacScripter www.macscripter.net

Writing AppleScripts

If you fancy trying your hand at programming, and especially if you want to create your own Automator Actions, learning a bit of AppleScript is a good place to start. Compared with most programming languages it's very human-friendly, with code that even the uninitiated can make some sense of (eg `tell application "iTunes" to quit`). Yet AppleScript is also powerful, especially if you master AppleScript Studio, a development environment for building fancy graphical interfaces onto your scripts.

AppleScript Studio is part of XCode, an OS X programming toolkit that you can install via **Applications/Installers.** But don't try and run before you can walk. First download a basic tutorial (the starters' guide at www.applescriptsourcebook.com is excellent) and experiment with Script Editor, which you'll find in **Applications/AppleScript.**

Folder Actions

Folder Actions is an OS X feature that lets you associate a script with a particular folder. The script is triggered when that folder is opened, closed or moved, or when items are added to or removed from it. Try this as an example:

▶ Create a folder on the desktop.

▶ **Control-click** the folder and chose **Enable Folder Actions**.

▶ **Control-click** the folder again, choose **Attach a Folder Action** and then choose the **Image – Flip Vertical** script.

▶ Now drop any image file into the folder, look inside and you'll find a flipped copy of the image you dropped in.

To turn Folder Actions off , **Control-click** any folder and hit **Disable Folder Actions**.

Mac as office

Software for office & home

17

The Mac platform has long been the preserve of design and media professionals, so if you want to put something on paper – be it a simple letter, a glossy newsletter or a styled-up film script – there's plenty of software available to help you. And so it is with tools for presentations, number-crunching, note-taking, cataloguing and any other area of work and life management.

There isn't space here for in-depth articles on using word processors, DTP (desktop publishing) tools, spreadsheets and presentation packages. Instead, this chapter aims to give you an overview of which applications – and widgets – are best for which documents and which tasks.

Which office suite?

An "office suite" is a set of applications designed for work-related tasks. Most include a word processor for writing and editing text and a spreadsheet for manipulating numbers. Suites often add to this recipe a program for preparing and delivering presentations, a database app, and also email, calendar and organizing tools. The

software for office & home

Saving tips & tricks

⌘S is a standard shortcut for **Save**, while ⌘⇧S is often **Save As**. And when you're specifying where to save your work…

▶ Hit ⌘D to go to the desktop, or ⌘⌥H for your home folder.

▶ Use the ▼/▲ button to reveal or hide the file browser.

▶ If there's a search box, use it to find folders to save into. Or create a new folder using the button at the bottom-left.

▶ Just as in Finder, you can navigate back and forward, and change views, using the button on the top-right.

▶ You can drag the Sidebar pane on the left in and out.

various components of an office suite typically share the same look and feel, and a degree of functional integration.

Many Macs ship with Apple's own office suite – AppleWorks – which seems likely to be replaced soon by the newer iWork. Then there's the ubiquitous Microsoft Office as well as various freebies, such as OpenOffice. Each of these is described below.

Of course, you don't necessarily need an office suite. Even if your Mac didn't ship with AppleWorks, it will have come with **iCal** and **Address Book** for scheduling, **Mail** for email and **TextEdit** – a surprisingly decent word processor, capable of handling images and tables and offering detailed font control. TextEdit can even save – and in many cases open – documents in the Microsoft Word format.

AppleWorks

$79/£65; free with many Macs; www.apple.com/appleworks

Previously known as ClarisWorks, AppleWorks is a complete office suite – "word processing, page layout, painting, spreadsheet, database and presentations" – in a single application. It's very easy to use and more than powerful enough for most home users. The downsides are that it's not as fully featured as some suites, it looks set to be replaced by iWork (see below) and that, while it can save Word documents, it can't always open them.

Microsoft Office

$400/£349 standard; $150/£109 for students and teachers; $500/£449 for pro edition with Virtual PC: see p.11.

This is by far and away the world's most widely used office suite, to the extent that familiarity with its various components – **Word**, **Excel**, **PowerPoint** and **Outlook** (known as **Entourage** on the Mac)

– are prerequisites in many fields of employment. If you've used Microsoft Office before, you'll know what to expect: tools that are powerful but sometimes infuriating, especially the "helpful" features such as Word's determination to restyle your text as you type. If you want to be able to open every office document that you'll ever be sent, or to get good at using the applications found in practically every office, then this suite is essential. But if you only want to type the occasional letter or essay, don't go near it. You'll be paying for mail merge and pivot table tools that you'll almost certainly never use.

iWork

$79/£49; www.apple.com/iwork

iWork is Apple's attempt to reinvent the office suite according to its key design principles: ease of use and elegance. Currently, it consists of just two applications. **Pages** is a word-processing and layout tool, which is particularly good for nice-looking letters, newsletters and the like. It's a bit like a stripped-back, user-friendly version of Word, but comes with a wide range of highly usable templates to base your projects on. **Keynote**, meanwhile, is a similarly pared-back equivalent of PowerPoint. Again, what it lacks in features it makes up for in ease of use and elegant templates. It's rumoured at the time of going to press that a spreadsheet application (**Numbers**?) will complete the package in the not-too-distant future, at which point AppleWorks will be consigned to the vaults of history. But that remains to be seen.

OpenOffice & NeoOffice
Free; www.openoffice.org & www.neooffice.org

OpenOffice is a powerful and completely free office suite created by volunteer open-source programmers around the world. It's not yet quite as fully featured as Microsoft Office, but it's quickly catching up – and in many ways is easier to use. The project is partly funded by Sun Microsystems, who sell a version of the same software, but with various extra features, under the brand **StarOffice**. At the time of writing, OpenOffice is available in two versions for Mac, the easiest to use and install being **NeoOffice**. As well as word processing, spreadsheet, presentation and drawing programs, NeoOffice does a very good job of opening and saving all kinds of formats – including those of Microsoft Office. It's not as slick-looking as most Mac applications, but it's an astonishingly good freebie.

Publishing & design

Creating cards, newsletters, pamphlets – or even simple magazines – isn't too difficult on a Mac, as long as you have the right software. If all you want to do is print greetings cards bearing your own digital photographs, then select an image in iPhoto (see p.222), press **Print** and use the **Greeting Cards** presets in the **Style** dropdown. But for anything combining text and pictures, you'll need a word processor or desktop publishing (DTP) package.

OS X's built-in TextEdit application lets you paste in pics and style up text. Word (see p.118) provides much more flexibility, though it's far from ideal as a page-layout program – learning to use it properly, and to circumvent its annoying habits, can take quite a while. Instead, for foolproof professional-looking results, try Apple's Pages (see p.119), which comes with scores of template sets

The Pages approach to desktop publishing. Pick an Apple-designed template, such as this one, replace the text and images with your own and tweak the layout to fit.

– from "Personal Resume" to "Non-profit newsletter" – ready to adapt to your requirements.

If you're looking to create a specific kind of layout, however, look online to see whether there's a tool devoted to exactly what you have in mind. Comic Life, for example, let's you easily pull snaps out of iPhoto, apply filters, drag on some speech and caption buttons – maybe a Batman-style "ka-blam!" – and the job's done.

Comic Life plasq.com/comiclife ($25)

Likewise, if you want to produce business-style reports, with slick-looking tables and charts, RagTime beats any standard office suite – and it's free for personal use.

RagTime www.ragtime-online.com

No animals were harmed during the production of this page. Created with Comic Life.

Or maybe you're a wannabe screenwriter. Of course, you can type a script in a simple text editor, but if you're serious about getting noticed you'll want to lay things out properly. **FinalDraft**, makes it easy to align columns for instructions and dialogue, and will even export text to Keynote (see p.119) to create storyboard slides. Wannabe producers, meanwhile, may want to try **Gorilla** – for managing film budgets, schedules, crew and more.

FinalDraft www.finaldraft.com
Gorilla www.junglesoftware.com ($129)

For really serious magazine or book layouts, however, you'll need some professional tools. The industry standards are **InDesign** (used to create this book) and **QuarkXPress**, which provide more flexibility and features than anything else on the market. Combine either with a copy of Photoshop (see p.229) and Illustrator (see p.217), and you'll have the software kit used in most publishing houses. But put aside a few months to learn how to use it all properly.

InDesign www.adobe.com
QuarkXPress www.quark.com

Organizing life & work

If there's one thing that computers are good at, it's creating order out of chaos. So no surprise then, that there are scores of programs available to help manage the various parts of your life. We cover contacts and calendars separately (see p.130), but that only scratches the surface of what's available. Some pointers…

Notes & journals

OS X comes with a **Stickies** widget (see p.100) for scribbling notes and ideas. But you can't fit much text on each note and too many notes will quickly clutter your Dashboard. Instead, try **Notepad Widget** which lets you add multiple sheets on one "pad" – or **WikityWidget**, a wiki-based tool that automatically creates links between notes. Both are available from: www.apple.com/downloads/dashboard

Naturally, note-taking and journalling don't have to be confined to the Dashboard. You could also investigate some standalone applications such as:

▶ **MacJournal** www.marinersoftware.com ($30)
Purported to be the world's most popular journalling software for the Mac, this great program lets you easily create a daily (password protected) log of text and images.

▶ **ToDo X** www.nomicro.com ($15)
A great little notepad and "to-do" list organizer. Its very clean design makes it a dream to use.

▶ **myJournal** www.dereksoft.com ($10)
Another password-protected journal tool which this time supports multiple journals – so the whole family can have one. It also features blogging tools to help you publish your thoughts online.

Money & business

There are many personal finance tools available for Mac OS X, including **Quicken**, the powerful package popular in the US. But there are also many free alternatives, such as **SpendThrift**, which lets you keep accounts, import Quicken data, create graphs and much more.

Business widgets

There are loads of Dashboard widgets specifically aimed at business users – many are little more than corporate-looking notepads, but there are also real-time stock trackers, currency converters and more. Check out the listings at: www.apple.com/downloads/dashboard/business

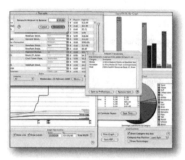

Quicken quicken.intuit.com
SpendThrift blackllamafaction.org/spendthrift

If you run a small business – or you're thinking of starting one – look online to see whether there's any software related to your specific field of activity. There are specialist tools for managing everything from dance schools (TanzProfi) to medical centres (Med-Center Office), as well as more general tasks such as time-billing and invoicing (iBiz) and project management (Merlin).

All of the aforementioned, and many more, can be found via the Business & Finance section of:

Apple Downloads www.apple.com/downloads/macosx

Catalogue madness

You probably already have a spreadsheet or database tool as part of AppleWorks or Microsoft Office. Though designed primarily for business use, these tools are also indispensable to the obsessive computer home user, as they can be used for cataloguing anything from recipes to film collections. But before you start creating any catalogue with Excel, AppleWorks or NeoOffice, search the Web to see whether there's a specialist option for whatever you're trying to achieve. For example:

▶ **About Wine XT** www.wine-software.net ($55)
This wine-lovers' software will help you manage the contents of your cellar and also provides tasting notes.

▶ **Readerware** www.readerware.com ($40)
A great cataloguing tool for book collectors. Enter an ISBN and it will grab the rest of the data from the Internet.

▶ **DVDpedia** www.bruji.com ($18)
Catalogue your DVDs using an intuitive and stylish interface. The same company also makes tools for cataloguing CDs and books, and offers a free widget to search all three simultaneously.

Fonts & special characters

18

If you want to create professional-looking documents or presentations, it's essential to choose appropriate typefaces – or fonts as they're known in computer-speak. OS X comes with a decent selection of fonts built-in, but you can also add your own, and switch your various fonts on and off to stop them slowing down your system. Equally important when dealing with text is to use all the suitable special characters, such as accents, umlauts and other diacritics.

Fonts

Though you might think of fonts as things that are hardwired into your computer, each font is actually just a file (or a set of files). When you open an application and look in the font menu, what you see is a list of all the font files residing in various special folders on your Mac. These folders are:

▶ **Your home/Library/Fonts** Fonts in this folder are available to you only – not other users on your Mac.

Apple typography

If you're into Macs and fonts, you might find yourself wondering which typefaces are uppermost in Apple's own font sack.

▶ **Myriad** On ads, product literature (and on the menus of photo-style iPods).

▶ **Lucida Grande** The system font in OS X, used in menus, windows, etc.

▶ **Garamond** The Mac branding font before Myriad.

▶ **Chicago & Charcoal** Widely used in pre-OS X Macs and many older iPods.

▶ **Macintosh HD/Library/Fonts** Fonts in this folder are available to every user on the Mac.

▶ **Macintosh HD/System Folder/Fonts** These are the fonts available for use in old-school "Classic" environment applications.

▶ **Macintosh HD/System/Fonts** The fonts used by OS X. Never meddle with these or your system might crash and refuse to boot up again.

Managing fonts

If you've downloaded, purchased or been sent new fonts, you can add them to your system by simply dropping them into any of the first three folders described above. Likewise, you can remove fonts you don't want by dragging them out of those folders. But, especially if you regularly deal with fonts, you'll find it much easier to use a font-management tool – such as **Font Book**, which is built in to OS X. Open it from **Applications**.

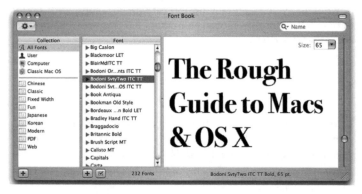

Font Book is a tool for browsing, previewing, adding and removing fonts, arranging them into sets, exporting them and more. Here's a quick breakdown of how it works…

▶ **Add fonts** Double-click any font file on your system and it will open into Font Book. If you like the look of it, click the **Install Font** button. It will be dropped into the User collection unless you change this in **Preferences**.

▶ **Preview** Font Book is great for browsing and choosing fonts. Choose **Custom** in the **Preview** menu, type some sample text in the right-hand pane and then click on different fonts to compare. Use the slider on the right to change the size.

▶ **User, Computer, Classic** These icons at the top of the Collection pane show you which fonts are available to you, to all user accounts, and to Classic mode. You can drag fonts from the main list to these icons.

▶ **Collections** Just like playlists in iTunes and albums in iPhoto, collections in Font Book are for grouping fonts together by project, by style or by any category you like. This makes them easier to browse, enable, disable and export. To create new collections, press the "+" button.

▶ **Enable/Disable** If you've got too many fonts "active" on your machine, font menus become impractically long and your computer will run more slowly. To get around this, select fonts or collections you're not currently using and choose the **Disable** option in the **Edit** menu. You can always enable them later.

▶ **Resolve duplicates** If you have more than one copy of a font installed on your system, the font in question will have a little dot next to it. Select the font and choose **Resolve Duplicates** from the **Edit** menu. Duplicate fonts can cause system instability.

▶ **Delete fonts** To send a font to the Trash, select it and press **Remove Font** in the **File** menu.

Tip: Click the arrow next to a font family name to reveal the individual styles, such as **bold**, *italic* and so on.

Tip: Automator (see p.112) includes all sorts of options for Font Book, allowing you to filter, find and otherwise speed up your type management.

Tip: If you get seriously into typography, you may want to replace Font Book with a third-party tool such as:

Suitcase www.extensis.com

Accents & special characters

Anyone who's worked on a PC will be used to the astonishingly bad Windows system for entering accents, diacritics and other special characters. Unless you're in Word, which features the **Insert Symbol** option, you have to hold down ⌥ and type the character's four-digit code on the number pad. Macs make it much easier, with a special-character input panel and a logical set of shortcut keys.

Character palette

Tip: To find a special character to match the font you're using, select **Glyph** from the Character Palette's **View** menu and then choose the font in question from under **Glyph Catalog**. Or to browse characters in all fonts, select **All Characters** from the **View** menu and browse by category.

OS X's built-in Character Palette lets you browse, find and insert all kinds of special characters (in your various fonts) into most applications. Simply put your cursor where you want the character and press **Insert**.

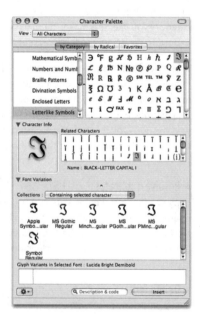

To open Character Palette, click the flag icon near the clock in the menu bar and choose **Show Character Palette**. If no flag is there, open **System Preferences** from the Apple menu, select **International**, then **Input Menu** and check the boxes next to **Character Palette** and **Show input menu in menu bar**.

Special character shortcut keys

Once you get used to the common special-character shortcuts, you'll never look back. First, you hit the keyboard combination relating to the type of accent you require. The common ones are:

´	⌥E
`	⌥`
¨	⌥U
^	⌥I
~	⌥N

Then simply press the key of the letter that you want to add it to. So, to create the accent ï, for example, you'd hit ⌥U followed by I. For é, you'd key ⌥E followed by E. Simple. And capitals work just as you'd expect. To create É, say, you'd hit ⌥E followed by ⇧E.

Note that these shortcuts will only work if the character in question exists in the font that you're using. So while you'll almost always be able to create common characters such as ñ, you might not be able to muster more unusual variations such as ū.

A few other useful special character shortcuts:

ç	⌥C
ø	⌥O
å	⌥a
•	⌥8
–	⌥-
#	⌥3
¢	⌥4
€	⌥2

Word

In Microsoft Word, if you're so inclined, you can use the in-built character palette. Simple select **Symbol** from the **Insert** menu.

Tip: If the font you're using doesn't feature the special character you need, you could try to combine two separate characters together if the application you're using lets you alter the spacing ("kerning") of the characters. For instance, you could create g̊ by typing ° and **g**, and then alternating the spacing between the two characters. Alternatively, use a different font. Try Lucida Grande for a particularly wide range of characters.

19 Contacts & calendars

Tip: To learn how to import your contacts and calendars from an old Mac or PC, turn to p.70.

Tip: If your Mac's date or time are wrong, correct them in **System Preferences** under **Date & Time**.

There are various Mac applications designed to help you keep your appointments and contacts organized. Some, such as Microsoft's Entourage (see p.153) are built into office suites and offer a wealth of tools useful in a big-office environment. But for home use, OS X's built-in organization programs – iCal and Address Book – are difficult to beat; they combine ease of use and plenty of features with the potential for syncing with other Macs and being expanded via downloadable plug-ins.

This chapter briefly explores what iCal and Address Book have to offer, and shows you how to use them in conjunction with iSync and iTunes to keep your contacts and calenders synchronized with PDAs, mobile phones and iPods.

Have you ever noticed that the iCal icon in the Dock always displays the correct date? ▶

iCal

iCal is essentially a computerized diary. You change the view in the main panel by clicking the **Day**, **Week** and **Month** buttons at the bottom (⌘1, ⌘2 and ⌘3 respectively), and add "events" by either double-clicking anywhere in the grid – or, in the Week and Day views, by dragging over a period of time.

You can also maintain a list of tasks in the To Do panel on the right (if it's not visible, hit the drawing-pin button). Again, a double-click will do the trick.

To make changes to an event or To Do item, select it and use the **Info** "drawer" that slides out of the side of the window. (If you can't see it, press the "i" button at the bottom-right). Here you can change the name, make events recur every day, week or year, and also assign an alarm and a calendar…

The buttons on the bottom-right and bottom-left let you display and hide the various iCal panes.

Calendars

The real beauty of iCal is the way it lets you organize events in separate colour-coded calendars – for holidays, work, school, sport or whatever you like. By default, your various calendars are all visible, but using the check boxes in the left-hand Calendars panel, you

---

Alarms

In the info panel, you can assign an alarm to any event (or a To Do item, though you'll first need to pick a "due date"). Besides a flash-up message and sound, you can have iCal send you an email reminder, run an AppleScript (see p.114) or open a file. The AppleScript option is full of potential – for example, you could have iCal fade out whatever you're listening to in iTunes and speak a reminder – though for this sort of thing it's probably easier to use the "open file" alarm option and choose an application your created in Automator (see p.112).

Tip: iCal's built-in **Birthday Calendar** automatically displays birthdays from your Address Book as iCal events. Turn it on or off from the **General** pane of iCal **Preferences**. You have absolutely no excuse for ever missing granny's birthday again.

Key iCal shortcuts

New event	⌘N
New calendar	⌘⌥N
New calendar group	⌘⇧N
New To Do	⌘K
To Do panel	⌘⌥T
Info panel	⌘I

can be selective about what you see. You could view just "Work" and "Travel" calendars in the office, say, and "Social", "Sport" and "Family" calendars at home. To add a new calendar, hit the "+" button at the bottom of the window. To delete one, select it and press backspace.

If you end up with lots of calendars, use the option in the **File** menu to create some calendar groups ("work" and "life", for example). Once you've dragged a few calendars into a group, you can turn all of them on or off with one click.

Subscribing to & importing calendars

iCal can import events in iCalendar, vCal and Entourage formats. To import a calendar you've downloaded or been sent double-click it or choose **File/Import…**

Tip: You can also drag a calendar into the main panel of iCal (to combine it with the currently selected calendar) or to the Calendar list (to be given a choice).

The best thing about this modular approach to time management is that you can import calendars that other people have created. Even better, people can publish calendars online in such a way that you can "subscribe" to them, with iCal regularly checking to make sure you have the latest version.

There are scores of freely available calendars covering everything from sports fixture lists and band tour dates via public holidays and meteorological events to political and academic timetables. If you know the address of a specific one, click **Calendar/Subscribe**. Otherwise, browse the thousands on offer at:

iCal Share www.icalshare.com
Apple www.apple.com/macosx/features/ical/library

Sharing your own calendars

If you'd like to send a calendar to friends or family, simply select it, press **File/Export…** and send them by email. The recipient will be able to import it as long as he or she uses a calendar program that supports the iCalendar format. That includes Outlook (not Outlook Express), Entourage, Mozilla Calendar and Lotus Notes.

To publish your calendars online so that other people can subscribe to them, you'll either need an account with .Mac (see p.32) or some other service, such as iCalx (www.icalx.com). If you're technically inclined, you could try publishing calendars on your own website, but you'll need webspace on a server that supports WebDAV. That's pretty rare, so your best bet may be to try setting up your own Mac to function as the server. For instructions, see:

Enabling WebDAv on OS X www.gregwestin.com/webdav_for_ical.php

Invitations

If you want to invite friends to take part in an event using iCal, select the event, type their email addresses in the **attendees** field of the **Info** panel, and hit the **Send** button at the bottom. The recipients will receive information about the event in an email and, if they use iCal and Apple Mail, the invitation will flash-up in their iCal Notifications pane.

You can also add attendees – and create new meeting events – by dragging names from iCal's **Address Panel**, opened from the **Window** menu or with the shortcut ⌘⌥A.

Tip: iCal features a superb printing palette that lets you print nicely presented calendars in any number of ways. Choose **File/Print...** (or hit ⌘P) to explore the options.

Tip: Exporting calendars is also useful for backing them up, but if you want to back up all your iCal events and information at once, use **File/Back up Database...**

Extra iCal tools

As with all Apple programs, there are plenty of downloadable tools to extend iCal's capabilities. For example:

▶ **iCal Events** (free) A widget that lets you view upcoming iCal events via the Dashboard. www.benkazez.com

▶ **MenuCalendarClock** (free, or $18 for full version) view iCal events via the menu bar. www.objectpark.net/mcc.html

Address Book

Address Book does what it says on the tin, though it also has a few fancy tricks up its sleeve. For example, you can wirelessly move names and numbers back and forth from a Bluetooth phone (see p.136).

The basics

To add a contact, press the "+" button below the **Names** panel. Edit the details as you like, clicking the ⬍ icons and the green and red circles to add and remove data fields. To add a little picture, double-click the small frame to the left of the contact's name and hit the **Choose...** button. Alternatively, drag an image directly into the square from Finder, iPhoto or even a webpage. (If you edit the picture on your own entry, it will apply to your user account pic, too.)

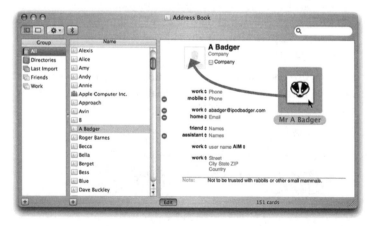

When you're done, click out of the **Edit** mode using the button at the bottom of the window.

Tip: You can edit the default card set-up settings in the **Template** pane of Address Book **Preferences** (⌘,).

Tip: Click a phone number's label and choose **Large Type** from the pop-up menu – guaranteed to stop you miss-keying phone numbers.

vCards

Each contact in Address Book is stored as a vCard – basically a virtual business card that contains your name, address, email, phone numbers, etc.

Groups & Smart Groups

You can organize your contacts into groups in the left-hand pane. This not only makes your address book easier to browse but also allows you to quickly send emails to a selection of people – and to export multiple contacts as a single vCard.

Press the "+" button to create a new group, and then drag contacts onto its icon. Note that (like iTunes playlists and iPhoto albums), you can add each contact to more than one group. Once the group is populated, **Control-click** it to either email everyone it contains, or export a group vCard.

Smart Groups, like other "Smart" items in OS X, populate themselves automatically according to conditions that you define. You might create one based on a dialling code to assemble everyone you know in a certain district, for instance, or one based on email addresses to group together people from a certain company. Select **File/New Smart Group…** to give it a go, or hold down the ⌥ key and hit the cog button at the bottom-left of the window.

Import & export

Address Book uses the common vCard format, and can also import various other formats, so even if your friends are using a different address-book application it's highly likely they'll be able to export contact cards (for themselves or for mutual friends) in a form that you can import. And vice versa.

To import contacts that you've been sent, simply double-click them or look under **File/Import**. Likewise, to get a contact out, choose **File/Export** or drag it straight onto the desktop or into a folder. You can even drag a contact directly onto your email program's Dock icon to quickly forward it to a friend.

Tip: Single-click a contact to view it in the main panel; double-click to view it in a new floating window.

Tip: Most labels – "work", "home", etc – will reveal relevant options when clicked: an online map for a US address, say, or a "send message" option for an email address.

Tip: With a .Mac account (see p.32), you can access your Address Book contacts via the Web. Set it up under **Sync** within **.Mac System Preferences** pane. You can even share your online address book with other .Mac users. In Address Book open **Preferences**, tick the **Share** box and use the "+" to add contacts.

Prefer it on paper?

Address Book's print options are nearly as good as iCal's. Select a contact, group or "All", choose **File/Print** and output labels, envelopes, lists or even a pocket address book.

Syncing

Modern life is a complicated beast, and it tends to get more complicated as you accrue extra gadgets. Say you bump into an old friend and they give you a new number: you add it to your mobile phone, but what about your Mac, your PC at work, your PDA or iPod? And it's not just phone numbers – addresses, calendars, bookmarks, passwords and files also end up strewn over multiple devices. You can get away with organizing things manually, but the ideal solution is to sync everything automatically – especially if you regularly use more than one Mac.

▶ **Multiple Macs** By far the easiest way to sync data across multiple Macs is to sign up for a .Mac account (see p.32). Once you've set things up under the **Sync** tab of the **.Mac System Preferences** pane, you can add contacts, bookmarks, appointments and passwords to any of your Macs – or via the Web at www.mac.com. As long as you choose to "merge data" whenever prompted, all locations will be kept up to date.

▶ **Phones & PDAs** If your phone/PDA and Mac both have Bluetooth, you can sync your contacts and calendars wirelessly; otherwise, it may be possible to connect them via a USB cable (ask in a phone shop if you don't have one already). With the device connected – or in discoverable mode if you're using Bluetooth – open **iSync** from **Applications** and choose **Add Device...** from the **Devices** menu. A picture of your phone or device should appear. Click the icon to view device settings and, when you're ready to sync, hit the big metallic button.

▶ **iPods** To add updated Address Book and iCal data to an iPod every time you attach it to your Mac, open iTunes and choose **iTunes/Preferences** with the Pod connected. Within the **iPod** pane set the options under **Contacts & Calendars**.

Tip: In **iSync/Preferences** choose to show syncing status in the menu bar. From the icon that will appear you can manage iSync and .Mac synchronizations and conflicts.

Tip: To get more than just calendars and contacts onto your iPod or PDA, download a third-party synchronization tool such as Pod2Go (www.kainjow.com/pod2go) or PocketMac (www.pocketmac.net). Also explore Automator (see p.112).

Print & fax

20

Whether you use your Mac for work or pleasure, at one time or another you're going to want to print your handiwork. OS X makes setting up printers a doddle, and offers useful tools for previewing your printouts and "printing" to PDFs. Furthermore, many Mac applications feature handy print presets, from greetings-card layouts in iPhoto (see p.222) to a pocket-sized contacts list in Address Book (see p.135). And with OS X's built-in fax feature you can say goodbye to that noisy, cumbersome old monster that lurks under your desk…

Setting up a printer

Most printers with a USB or Bluetooth connection will work fine with OS X (if you have an old model with only a long "teethed" parallel plug, it's probably time to upgrade). In most cases, there's no need to install the software that came with the printer, as your Mac has hundreds of printer drivers pre-loaded. Just plug it in, hit **File/Print** in nearly any application and the new printer should appear in the **Printer** dropdown.

If this fails, the **Printer** dropdown should at least contain an option to **Add Printer…**. This opens OS X's Printer Setup Utility, which can also be found in **Applications/ Utilities**. The utility scans for connected

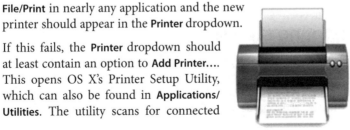

Buying a printer

There are hundreds of consumer printers on the market. The first choice is whether to go for an office-style laser model (fast and high quality), a special photo printer (the only way to get that glossy photo-lab look) or a cheap-and-cheerful ink-jet. Also consider resolution, speed, number of inks and refill costs. Visit these sites before opening your purse:

www.macreviewzone.com
printscan.about.com

You should encounter few setup issues with a machine from one of the big names (such as Epson, HP or Canon), but to find out exactly which models are supported natively by OS X, look here:

www.apple.com/macosx/up-grade/printers.html

*In the **Printing** pane of **Print & Fax**, in **System Preferences**, you can set the default printer and paper size and view the "print queue" – a list of not-yet-completed print jobs.*

Tip: From the **Printers** menu of the Printer Setup Utility, choose **Create desktop Printer...** (⌘⇧D) to place an icon on your desktop that you can then drag files onto to print them straight from Finder.

Tip: If your printer stops responding, visit the **Printing** pane of **Print & Fax** in **System Preferences** and try removing and re-adding the offending printer – this often does the trick.

devices; select the one you want and click **Add**. If it's a Bluetooth printer, or a printer that's connected to another computer on your network (see below), you may have to click the **More Printers...** button to browse for it. From the dropdown at the top you choose the type of connection you're trying to make – Bluetooth, Windows Printing, etc and see what appears.

Sharing printers on a network

If you have two or more computers, one of the best reasons for connecting them together into a network (see p.63) is that you can easily share one printer between them all. The ideal set-up is to connect your printer to the network's router. This is often impossible as most routers lack a USB port and most printers lack an Ethernet port. However, you can plug a USB printer to an AirPort or AirPort Express unit (see p.64); if it doesn't work straight off, launch the AirPort Setup Assistant from **Applications/Utilities**.

The more common setup is to attach the printer directly to one of the computers and to tell the computer to "share" it over the network. On a Mac, tick the box at the bottom of the **Sharing** pane of **Print & Fax**, in **System Preferences**. On a PC, run the Network Setup Wizard (within **Accessories/Communications** in your list of programs) and follow the prompts. Obviously, the computer the printer is connected to will need to be switched on in order for the others to print through it.

Printing & presets

In most applications you can print by choosing **Print** from the **File** menu or using the shortcut ⌘P. This will usually elicit a box where you can mess about with lots of customizable layout options and effects. If you create a configuration that you think you'll want to

Printing to PDF

PDF (Portable Document Format) is a file format, first developed by Adobe, that is widely used for everything from product manuals to press releases, as well as for sending publications (such as this book!) to a printer. The beauty of PDFs is that they combine text, fonts and images in a convenient bundle that can be viewed on practically any computer – regardless of which applications or fonts it has installed. Hence the "portable" tag.

Even better, the file size will be comparatively tiny compared with the original document, so PDFs are ideal for sending by email. The only downside (and this isn't always a downside) is that PDFs aren't editable – at least not to any useful degree.

Traditionally, to create PDFs you need a special application (such as Adobe Acrobat), but OS X lets you create PDFs from any application. Just hit **File/Print** and use the **PDF** button at the bottom of the box. The feature is placed here as the process of creating a PDF is akin to preparing a document to send to print. But rather than sending the information to a "real" printer, your Mac sends it to a "virtual" printer that renders your work as a PDF.

PDFs are a great way to send documents to other people, since you know they'll be able to open them, and that they will look on their machine exactly as they did on yours. When you press **Print**, you can even choose to create a PDF and attach it to an email in one fell swoop (look under the **PDF** dropdown). All the recipient will need – and they probably have this already – is either a Mac with OS X or a PC with a copy of the free Adobe Reader program:

Adobe Reader www.adobe.com/reader

PDFs can also be very useful for your own records. For example, when you register with a website, or book a holiday over the Internet, instead of copying out all the on-screen information and reference numbers, simply print a PDF of the webpage straight from Safari.

OS X opens PDFs with Preview, though there's also a version of Adobe Reader for Mac. It's worth having as just occasionally it will display a PDF that Preview is struggling with.

*One of OS X Tiger's most useful but unsung improvements is the updated PDF capabilities. You can now annotate PDFs with text labels and circles, as shown. Furthermore, it's possible to password protect a PDF: hit **File/Print** and choose **Encrypt PDF** from the **PDF** button's dropdown in the print dialog box.*

use again, choose **Save As…** from the **Presets** dropdown. Then you'll be able to quickly access that recipe of settings in the future, from almost any application. Finally, use the **Preview** button to get an accurate idea of how a printed page will look, and then hit **Print**.

Mac as fax machine

Faxing directly from a computer is *much* more convenient than using a fax machine. Instead of printing a document and then feeding the hard copy into another device, simply send the fax directly from your word processor, email or any other application – and have faxes you receive appear in your email inbox.

To send and receive faxes you need to connect your Mac's built-in dial-up modem to a phone socket using the supplied cable (if you can't find it, pick up another at any computer shop). A broadband connection won't get in the way, but neither will it handle faxing – you have to use the dial-up modem.

▶ **Sending faxes** Click **File/Print** in any application, and choose **Fax PDF** from the **PDF** dropdown. Enter the number of the recipient (or use the "silhouette" button to choose a contact from Address Book), add a cover page, if you want one, and hit **Fax**. The fax will be sent straightaway, unless you're already using your modem to connect to the Internet, in which case OS X holds the fax until the next time you disconnect.

▶ **Receiving faxes** If you'd also like to receive faxes on your Mac, open the **Print & Fax** panel of **System Preferences**. In the **Faxing** pane, check the **Receive faxes** box, enter your phone number and choose how you'd like your Mac to handle whatever arrives. You can have faxes automatically printed, or even forwarded to an email account so you can view new arrivals away from home.

Online

The Web

If you're coming to Macs from a PC background, you'll be used to surfing websites with Internet Explorer, the Web browser whose blue "e" icon is inseparable from the World Wide Web in many people's minds. OS X comes with a different browser: Safari RSS. In almost every way, this is an infinitely superior piece of software to Explorer, with lots of useful features that we'll highlight in this chapter. You'll find Safari's compass-style icon in Applications, and probably also on your Dock.

Other browsers

Safari is an excellent browser, but it's not the only player in town. There are scores of other Mac browsers available to download for free, and you may find one you prefer. For a start, it's worth having the Mac version of Explorer – not because it's any good (it isn't), but because, due to the laziness or incompetence of Web designers, a proportion of websites will display properly *only* on Explorer. So it's worth having this piece of junk in your toolbox; if a site does something weird on your main browser, try it in Explorer.

Internet Explorer www.mactopia.com

As for browsers that you may choose to use *instead* of Safari, the most tempting option is Firefox, a superb application created by

Set a default browser

If you do choose to use something other than Safari as your main browser, you'll want to let OS X know, so that when you click on a link in an email, say, the right browser opens up. To do this, open Safari, Click **Safari/Preferences** and you'll see the option in the **General** pane.

Save Page As...	⌘S
Send Link...	
Page Setup...	
Print...	⌘P
Import...	
Work Offline	

Firefox lets you browse and click between pages that you've recently visited without being connected to the Internet. Great for reading the news on the train, for example. You can increase the number of offline pages you have access to by upping the cache size in Firefox Preferences.

volunteer programmers from around the world. Firefox is better than Safari in some ways and worse in others – for example, there are more free plug-ins available for it, but it's generally a tad slower. In this chapter we'll discuss Safari and Firefox, so you get a sense of what each can offer.

Firefox www.getfirefox.com

There are many other browsers out there – Opera, Mozilla, Netscape, Camino and OmniWeb to name just a few. They all have something to offer, but few Mac users choose them over Safari. For the lowdown on just about every Mac browser ever released, see:

Mac Browsers darrel.knutson.com/mac

Browsing tips

There isn't room here for a step-by-step guide to surfing the Web – and you probably don't need that anyway. Instead, the next few pages focus on some of the cool features of Safari and Firefox that you may not be aware of.

Windows & tabs

One thing that marks out experienced Web users is that they very often have multiple webpages open simultaneously. It makes sense to work this way: you might have your webmail open in the background, for instance, while you read a blog in the foreground. Or you might fire open all the interesting-looking stories from the homepage of a news site; by the time you've read one, the others will have loaded, so you won't have to wait around. To open a link in a new window, **Control-click** it and choose **Open Link in New Window**.

Tip: In Safari, when you visit a webpage by typing its address or hitting a bookmark, the page is marked as a "SnapBack" point. If you then browse to other pages by clicking on links, you can return to the last snapback point by clicking the little orange button next to the current page's address.

An even better option is to open multiple pages within a single window, with "tabs" at the top to let you switch between them (see above). In Safari, you have to switch this feature on: open **Preferences** from the **Safari** menu and, under **Tabs**, check **Enable tabbed browsing**. Then, to open a link in a new tab, hold down ⌘ as you click it (or **Control-click** it and choose the relevant option). Even better, you can open tabs "in the background" by holding down ⇧ *and* ⌘ while you click – great for opening lots of links from one page.

Retracing your steps

Obviously, you can move back through the pages you've just been looking at using the **Back** button. But it's often quicker to click and hold on the **Back** (or **Forward**) button to choose the page you're looking for from a list…

Tip: If you visit a webpage all the time, drag its icon (to the left of its address in your browser) to the right-hand section of the Dock for 24/7 easy access.

Even with this technique, however, the menu will only show you a certain number of pages that you've viewed in the current window. To jump back to any page that you've viewed in the last week or so, use the **History** menu (or the **Go** menu in Firefox).

Bookmarks

When you find a page that's worth another visit, add a "bookmark" so you can quickly return to it later. You can do this via the **Bookmarks** menu – from where you can also access your bookmarked sites – or using the shortcut ⌘B (Safari) or ⌘D (Firefox). Get into the habit of using folders to group related bookmarks together or you'll end up with a huge menu in which it's hard to find anything. You can create folders, and delete unwanted bookmarks, by choosing the **Show All** or **Manage** option in the **Bookmarks** menu.

If you visit a page all the time, drop it onto the Bookmark Bar, located below the **Back** and **Forward** buttons. If it's not visible, you'll find an option for it within the **View** menu. Either drag page icons directly onto the bar (as shown) or save/move bookmarks into the Bookmark Bar folder, which lives with your regular bookmarks. You can even create sub-folders within your Bookmarks Bar folder to generate dropdown menus of your favourite sites.

Browser plug-ins

Whether you use Safari, Firefox or something else, there are bound to be various downloadable "extensions" available for adding extra functions and options to your browser – adblocking being one

example (see below). For Safari, you can find the best extensions (some free, others commercial) via the wonderfully named:

PimpMySafari pimpmysafari.com

Firefox has scores of extensions available, and they're nearly all free. Either choose **Extensions** from the **Tools** menu and click **Get More Extensions**, or simply pop in to:

Mozilla Update addons.mozilla.org

Kill the ads

There's nothing more annoying than pop-up ads and flashing banners offering you too-good-to-be-true deals. Fortunately, there are measures you can take to reduce the number of online ads you see.

▶ **Pop-ups** can be easily blocked: click **Block Pop Up Windows** in the **Safari** menu. The only problem is that Safari doesn't let you allow pop-ups on certain sites (such as webmail systems that use pop-ups for messages). Firefox offers a better pop-up blocker, with warnings when a window has been blocked and the option of adding sites to an "allow list" (open **Firefox/ Preferences** and look under **Web Features**).

▶ **Banners** If you download the right extension, it's possible to stop some banner ads appearing on webpages. For Safari, visit the "Adblocking" section of www.pimpmysafari.com; for Firefox grab the AdBlock extension from addons.mozilla. org. With Adblock you can simply **Control-click** an ad and choose **Block ads from….** Banners from that server should no longer appear in webpages you view.

Parental Controls

If you'd like to limit your child's browsing to certain approved websites, create a user account for him or her and enable Safari Parental Controls (see p.52). When logged in to their account, the child will only be able to access bookmarked sites. You can add and remove bookmarks using your administrator password.

Alternatively, try a special children's browser, such as KidBrowser, which makes browsing fun and easy as well as safe. KidBrowser, which costs €19, is available from:

www.app4mac.com

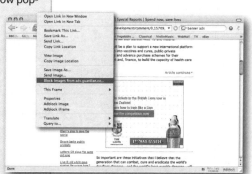

Keyword searching

One of the best things about Firefox is the way it lets you set up customizable searches. Let's say you regularly use MultiMap to view street maps, but its homepage is slow to load. Go to the site, **Control-click** the search box and choose **Add a Keyword for this Search**. When prompted, choose "map" as the keyword.

Next time you want to search for a map, you don't need to open the MultiMap homepage. Simply type the keyword, along with whatever you want to search for, straight into the bar where you usually type Web addresses. If you wanted a map of the London postcode W1D 6HR, for example, you'd type: map W1D 6HR.

You can do the same thing in Safari with the Safari SIA plug-in from horneddragon.com.

Searching

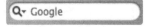

Safari (and Firefox) let you search Google directly from the toolbar, which saves you going to Google's homepage in order to search. When searching this way, all the regular Google tricks work, including:

Googling this:	Finds pages containing:
apple mac	the terms "apple" and "mac"
"apple mac"	the exact phrase "apple mac"
apple OR mac	either "apple", "mac" or both
apple -mac	"apple" but not "mac"
~mac	"mac" and related words ("Apple", etc)
"apple * macs"	"apple produce macs", etc
site:www.apple.com "safari"	"safari" within the Apple website

Being able to search Google directly from Safari or Firefox is great, (especially in Firefox, where you can search from the address bar to go straight to the top Google hit). But if you become a real search addict you might want to be able to search without even first opening your browser. You could use a search widget, so many of which are available that you'll find a whole category of them at:

Apple Downloads www.apple.com/downloads/dashboard

However, Dashboard can be slow to open, and you don't want to waste time clicking into the right widget. Better, then, is a tool for searching from anywhere with a shortcut key (Huevos) or even via a Google box on your menu bar (iSeek):

Huevos ranchero.com/huevos (free)
iSeek www.ambrosiasw.com/utilities/iSeek ($15)

Remember that you can also search Google for selected text in nearly any application using Services (see p.95).

RSS

RSS (Really Simple Syndication) is one of the best things to happen to the Web in recent years. In short, RSS allows blogs, news services and other websites to produce "feeds" or "newsfeeds" containing headlines and short descriptions of each new or updated article, complete with links to the full story. You can scan a feed at a glance and see if something's been added or changed without even having to visit and browse the website. Even better, you can "aggregate" the feeds from your favourite sites, in effect creating a totally personalized online magazine or newspaper.

Safari has RSS tools built right in. When you visit a site (or a section of a site) that offers a feed, an RSS button should appear to the right of its address; click this to view the feed. Occasionally, Safari fails to find a feed, in which case you'll need to find a link to the feed and click it (the link will often be an orange button labelled "XML").

Firefox doesn't currently feature full RSS support, but it does let you view feed headlines via the Bookmarks Bar. To create one of these "live bookmarks", go to any site with an RSS feed and click the orange button at the bottom-right corner of the Firefox window. For full RSS functions in Firefox, grab an extension (see p.146).

To combine RSS feeds from various sites, bookmark each feed and put the bookmarks into a folder, perhaps on your Bookmark Bar (see p.146). Then click the folder and select **View All RSS Articles**.

Another way to view RSS feeds is as a screensaver. Open **System Preferences**, hit **Desktop & Screen Saver** and, under **Screen Saver,** choose **RSS Visualizer**. Click **Options…** to pick from your Safari feeds.

Tip: If you'd like to be able to browse your newsfeed collection from any computer, sign up with an online aggregator such as:

www.bloglines.com
my.yahoo.com
www.waggr.com

*Anyone who can access your account can easily see all the sites you've recently visited. If that thought bothers you, clearing your history isn't enough, as your cookies, cache and auto-fill entries also show where you've been. Instead, click **Safari/Reset Safari…** to go back to a completely clean slate. Alternatively, choose **Safari/ Private Browsing** to prevent Safari from recording any traces of your surfing. In Firefox you'll find a **Clear All** button within the **Privacy** pane of **Firefox/Preferences**.*

Video & music online

Video and music can be made available over the Internet in two ways. They can be "streamed" (played straight off the Web in real time) or downloaded (saved to your hard drive and enjoyed at your leisure).

Streaming

Streaming is most commonly used for online radio stations, TV replays, concert broadcast, movie trailers and more. Usually, the quality isn't brilliant (especially with video), as the files are very compressed, and it's not possible to save the streams to your hard drive – at least not without special software (see www.bitcartel.com/radiolover).

Some streaming audio and video will play back using Apple's Quick-Time format, but you'll need a couple of software freebies to watch and listen to most of what's on offer. Download the free versions (not the free trials) of:

RealPlayer www.real.com
Windows Media Player www.windowsmedia.com/download

Downloads

At the time of writing, the vast majority of music and video downloading still takes place illegally via P2P file-sharing (see p.172). But, in the case of music at least, there's plenty of legal stuff available – freebies from labels and up-and-coming artists as well as pay-to-download services such as iTunes (see p.191). Aside from iTunes, few of the major online music services offer Mac-friendly files, though some specialists do. As a rule of thumb, any service that offers MP3 files should be fine; any that offers DRM-protected WMA files will be incompatible.

As for video downloads, there's not much available on the legal side, partly because the files would have to be huge to even vaguely compare to DVD or VHS quality. Instead, most movie downloading happens via P2P. Typically the files are highly compressed and arrive in MPEG or AVI formats. Depending on the "codec" (eg DivX) used to create the compressed video file, you may need a special program to play them back (see p.239). Of course, downloading copyrighted movies for free from P2P is illegal (see p.172).

Email

22

Email on a Mac works in much the same way as on any other computer. You get an account – most commonly from your Internet Service Provider, or an online company such as Yahoo! – and then send and read messages either through a special email program or via a webpage.

If you've already got an email account that you want to use, skip ahead to p.154.
Otherwise, have a think about what type of address you want; it pays to do this now, as it can be a real pain to switch accounts once you've given your address to everyone you know.

Pick an email account

When it comes to scoring an email address, there are three main options. You can get your address from…

▶ **An Internet Service Provider** Most ISPs provide at least one email address as part of any Internet access package. The advantage of these accounts is that they won't cost you anything extra, they're reliable and you don't have to view any ads along with your messages. The disadvantages is that if you ever switch ISP, you'll lose the address.

Andy Bouchard's wonderfully lo-fi reworking of the Mail icon (and others) can be downloaded from: www.andybouchard.com

POP3 & webmail

There used to be a clear distinction between "POP3" email accounts (with which you send and receive messages using an email program such as Mail or Outlook) and webmail accounts (such as Hotmail and Yahoo!, which you access via a website). These days, however, the boundaries are blurred: decent POP3 services offer web access and decent webmail services offer POP3 access. Only accept an account that offers both.

email

Hot or not mail?

Microsoft's webmail service, Hotmail, is hugely popular, but compared with Yahoo!, Gmail and other such services, it's a pretty crumby. The free version offers a comparatively tiny amount of storage space for messages, and if you don't use your account for just a few weeks it will be "frozen" – your messages will be deleted and you'll have to log in to "reactivate" the account.

.Mac email

There are various reasons why you might consider signing up for Apple's .Mac service (see p.32). But the email service alone isn't worth the money – unless you're absolutely desperate for an address ending in @mac.com. Although .Mac mail does have a few nice features, the online storage capacity is not exactly generous (at the time of writing, you get 250MB to share between email, iDisk and HomePage) and if you choose not to renew your subscription after a year, you'll loose your email address.

▶ **A webmail provider** The advantage of signing up with a web-based email provider is that they don't tie you to your ISP. Furthermore, the better services, such as Yahoo! or Gmail, provide so much online storage for your messages – up to 2.5 gigabytes at the time of writing – that you can leave all your emails permanently online (allowing you to access them from anywhere) as well as downloading them to an email program on your Mac ("POP3 access"). On the downside, when you're viewing your messages via the Web, you may have to view banner adverts on the page; there's no guarantee that the service will remain free forever; and, if you have a common name, you may end up with an address as catchy as johnsmith2972@yahoo.com.

Gmail www.gmail.com
Yahoo! www.yahoo.com

▶ **A domain registrar** One problem with both the above options is that you can't completely design your own address. Even if you can get the first half of the address you want – such as john.smith@my-isp.com or john@gmail.com – you're still stuck with the email provider's name after the @ sign. But if you register your own domain name (web address) you'll get control of all addresses ending in that domain. If you registered www.johnsmith.com, for example, you could use the email addresses mail@johnsmith.com, work@johnsmith.com, john@johnsmith.com, etc. Addresses such as these demand plenty of kudos and are also very practical (they don't lock you to any individual ISP or email provider). The only downside is cost: you'll have to pay an annual fee to control the domain and usually a hosting fee to get your mail up and running properly (you need POP3, not "email forwarding"). For more on registering a domain name, see p.169.

If your domain name of choice isn't available, you could try NetIdentity, which offers email accounts (and web addresses) based on the many domains that they own. For example, they might offer john@smith.net.

NetIdentity www.netidentity.com

Which mail program?

Though it's sometimes handy to access emails via the Web, there's no substitute for using a decent email application – or "client" – to compose, read, sort and organize your emails on your computer. There are many mail applications available, but none are better-suited to the majority of Mac users than Apple's own Mail. Though not always superbly fast, Mail is stable, user-friendly and has some very cool features – as we'll see over the next few pages. It also offers unmatched integration with Address Book (see p.134) and iCal (see p.130).

If you don't get on with Mail, or you require a specific feature that it doesn't offer, check out the alternatives. The best-known option is Microsoft's Entourage – essentially the Mac version of Outlook (not to be confused with Outlook Express). Entourage comes as part of Microsoft Office and is worth trying out if you've already paid for the Office suite or are familiar with Outlook on a PC. Otherwise, it's not worth the money, for while it does provide certain extra tools, most of these are designed for a big-office environment and are less useful than the features it lacks (such as Smart Mailboxes and iCal integration).

Entourage www.mactopia.com

Of the various other options, Thunderbird (see box) is probably top of the list, though small minorities of Mac users swear by alternatives ranging from Opera Mail (built into the Opera browser window, see p.144) to feature-packed clients such as Mailsmith and PowerMail.

Mailsmith www.barebones.com
PowerMail www.ctmdev.com

Tip: To get Entourage to sync your mail with a mobile device using iSync, grab PocketMac GoBetween from: www.isyncentourage.com

Thunderbird

The sister application of the Firefox Web browser (see p.144), Thunderbird is a powerful, completely free open-source mail application with some unique tools (such as a built-in RSS reader) and excellent spam filters. It doesn't integrate with other elements of OS X as seamlessly as Apple's own Mail, but it's worth test-driving nonetheless. Download it from:

www.mozilla.org/thunderbird

Using Mail

Apple's Mail application (also known as "Mail.app" to differentiate it from the generic term mail) should already be visible on your Dock. If not, you'll find it in **Applications**.

Setting up accounts

You may have entered your mail account details when you first turned on your Mac, or when you first launched Mail. If not, or if you want to set up Mail to send and receive extra email accounts, you'll need to head for the **Accounts** pane of Mail's Preferences panel (⌘,). Either hit the "+" button at the bottom to add an account or edit what's already in place within the **Account Information** pane. Here you'll see:

▶ **Description** Can be whatever you like (eg ISP Account)

▶ **Type** In most cases this will be POP3, though if you're using a .Mac, IMAP or Exchange account, specify accordingly.

▶ **Name and password** These are nothing to do with your OS X name and password; they're for your email account only.

▶ **Incoming mail server** The name of the computer (owned by your email account provider) where you messages live until you download them. It usually takes the form mail.yourprovider.com or pop.yourprovider.com.

▶ **Outgoing mail server** The name of the computer that routes your sent mail in the right direction. It usually takes the form SMTP.yourprovider.com.

Those are the only essential settings, but before closing the Preferences panel, have a look through **Mailbox Behaviors** and **Advanced** pane, where you'll find extra options to temporarily dis-

Server problems

Some ISPs only let you access their outgoing mail server when you're online using their connection. But you can use any functioning outgoing mail server for any email account, so if you're setting up multiple accounts, you may want to use your ISP's outgoing mail server for all of them.

Email on more than one computer

If you regularly use more than one computer – your Mac at home and your PC at work, say – you can easily set up your mail account on both. However, with the default settings in place, you'll usually find that if you download messages to one machine, they'll be deleted from the server and will no longer be available to download to the other. You'll end up with your mail archive spread across two computers.

One workaround is to set up Mail to leave a copy of the messages on the server after downloading: uncheck the **Remove copy from server...** box within the **Advanced** pane of the **Accounts** panel of Mail Preferences. On the other computer, choose to delete the server copy after, say, two weeks. That way, as long as you use both computers every fortnight, you'll always have a complete and up-to-date mail archive on both machines.

Other options are to choose an IMAP email account; to use the syncing features of a .Mac mail account (see p.32); or to grab a Gmail or Yahoo! account that provides enough server space to leave a copy of all messages permanently online.

able accounts, set "sent" and "junk" mail to be deleted, and choose whether you'd like to leave copies of your messages on the server after downloading them (see box above).

Now you're ready to start sending and receiving. All email programs are pretty much alike, so you shouldn't struggle with Mail if you're used to Outlook Express or any other tool. Even so, it's worth working through the following step-by-step guide to pick up a few tips.

Creating messages

To create a new message hit the **New** button (or press ⌘N) and enter one or more addresses in the **To:** and **Cc:** fields. You can either type

email

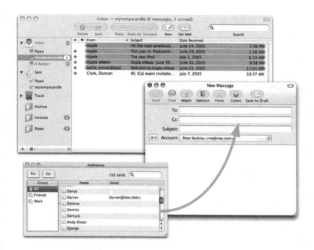

these manually or pull contacts in from Address Book (see p.134). Hit the **Address** button, select a contact and either hit the **To** or **Cc** button, or simply drag the contact into your message.

Add a subject, type your message and, if you like, click the **Fonts** and **Colors** buttons to change how things look. You might also want to add an attachment (see below) and a signature (see opposite). Finally, click **Send** or, if you'd like to come back to the message later, **Save as Draft**.

Responding

The other way to create a message is to respond to one that has been sent to you. You have various options, all of them accessible via the **Message** menu and in the menu that appears when you **Control-click** a message.

▶ Reply (⌘R) Responds to the sender alone.

▶ Reply All (⌘⇧R) Responds to all the recipients of the email.

Extra options

The **View** menu, and the button next to the Subject field, let you add two extra fields to your messages:

▶ Bcc Lets you copy in recipients without the other recipients of the email being able to see. Useful for sending group email when you don't want everyone's addresses to be visible to everyone else.

▶ Reply-To Add an address here (eg your work address) and any replies will go to that email account rather than the one you're sending from.

Attachments

You can include a photo, document or any other file along with your email. Just click the **Attach** button (or hit ⌘⇧A) and choose the file you want to send. Even simpler, drag and drop the files into the message window.

Note, however, that you shouldn't send attachments of more than a few megabytes – at least not unless you know the recipient has broadband and won't mind. Big attachments can take an age to download on a slow connection, and may even stop the recipient's email account working. One way to lessen the load is to compress your files before you attach them (see p.92 and p.168 for more information).

▶ **Forward** (⌘ ⇧ F) Sends the message on to someone else. Note that you can forward more than one message at once: simply highlight various emails (by clicking on them one while holding down the ⌘ key) and when you press **Forward** the text and attachments of them all will be combined in a single email.

▶ **Redirect** (⌘ ⇧ E) Forwards the message in such a way that it will appear to have come from the original sender (and at the original date and time). Useful when someone sends you an email in error.

▶ **Reply with iChat** (⌘ ⇧ I) If the person who sent you the message is in your iChat Buddy List (see p.162) *and* in your address book, you can use this option to start a text, voice or video conversation. When the sender of a message is available for an iChat reply, you'll see a green dot next to the message; if they're logged into iChat but "away", you'll see a yellow dot.

▶ **Bounce** (⌘ ⇧ B) The original email will be returned to the sender, to whom it will appear as if the message never got through. Useful for replying to unwelcome correspondents and for creating an excuse when you forgot to reply.

When you reply to or forward a message, the original text is quoted at the bottom of your email, coloured and styled to differentiate it from your reply. To change how quoted text looks, or to change how this feature works, look within the **Fonts & Colors** and **Composing** panels of Mail Preferences.

Sending & receiving

When you're connected to the Internet, mail will dispatch messages as you send them; otherwise, they'll sit in the **Outbox** until next time you connect. Likewise, when you're online, Mail will check for new emails at regular intervals. You can specify the frequency that this happens under the **General** panel of Mail Preferences, or check for messages at any time using the **Get Mail** button.

Signatures & vCards

You can add a personal touch at the end of your emails in the form of "signatures". Most people include their address, phone number and job title, sometimes rounding off with a recycled witticism.

To create or edit signatures, open **Preferences** from the **Mail** menu and look in the **Signatures** panel. You can create as many as you like and choose which to use case-by-case with the **Signature** menu (underneath the "Subject" in blank messages).

You can change the text style via the **Format** menu or even drag in a file such as your vCard from Address Book (which the recipient could then import into their own contacts list). If you do this, however, your recipients will end up with multiple version of your vCard in their inboxes, so you might consider putting your vCard online instead and then linking to it in your signature. Add some text, such as "Download vCard", then select the text, **Control-click** it, choose **Edit Link…** and enter the relevant URL (eg http://www.mysite.com/vcard.vcf).

When the lightening icon appears, it means Mail can't access the server for the account in question.

Smart Mailboxes

Smart Mailboxes are "virtual" mailboxes that display a list of emails that fulfil criteria of your choosing: unread messages, emails from a particular person... pretty much anything you like. This is a fantastic way to organize your mail, and it's low maintenance, too, as the mailboxes always stay up to date without any input from you. To create a Smart Mailbox, use the **Mailbox** menu or hold down ⌥ while clicking the "+" sign. If you set up many Smart Mailboxes, you might want to organize them into Smart Mailboxes Folders. Do this via the **Mailbox** menu.

When new messages arrive, you'll hear a sound (if the default tone annoys you, change the **New mail sound** under the **General** panel of Mail Preferences). You'll also find that Mail's icon in the Dock displays the number of unread messages in a little red star.

Within Mail, each mailbox also displays a number, referring to the number of unread messages it contains. And each unread message displays a blue dot; if you'd also like to have them display in bold type, look within the **Viewing** panel of **Preferences** (in the **Mail** menu).

Managing your mail

Incoming mail arrives in the inbox, which, if you have more than one account set up, breaks down into sub-inboxes. But to keep things organized, you may want to sort messages in "mailboxes" – essentially folders. To create a mailbox press the "+" button at the bottom-left or use the **Mailbox** menu, and then simply drag messages into it. If you want a message in more than one mailbox, hold down ⌥ as you drag.

Following are a few other useful techniques for viewing and organizing your mail:

▶ **Sorting** You can sort messages in any mailbox according to any column – "From", "Subject", "Date Received", etc. Simply click the text at the top of the relevant column. To add more columns, **Control-click** any column header and choose from the list.

▶ **Rules** You can set up "rules" so that when something happens (a message arrives from Uncle Jim, say) Mail does something (such as putting the message in your "Family" mailbox). To set up rules, open **Preferences** from the **Mail** menu and look under **Rules**.

Spam

Most email users receive a certain amount of "spam" – unsolicited messages – offering anything from free porn to get-rich quick schemes. Needless to say, such messages are invariably scams of some sort, so never reply to them and *never* follow links from them to websites to take up their "offers". To reduce your risk of landing lots of spam, avoid making your email address too public. Consider using a second account, or an alias (see right), for anything such as signing up to mailing lists, publishing online or giving out to customers or clients. If the new address gets too bogged down in junk, you can simply stop using it and set up another.

If the spam's already arriving thick and fast to your main address, however, you'll need to "train" your email application to filter out the junk as it arrives. In Mail, suspected spam messages are automatically marked in brown. If a legitimate message has been marked, select it and press **Not Junk**; likewise, if a spam message has been missed, select it and hit **Junk**. Do this for a month or two and you should find that Mail does an increasingly good job of spotting junk. Once you're happy with its success rate, open **Preferences** and, under, **Junk Mail**, choose to have junk messages automatically moved into a separate folder. This should cure the headache, though it's worth scanning through the junk folder occasionally for legitimate messages.

If Mail's junk-filtering doesn't do the trick, you may want to download some other anti-spam tools. You'll find plenty via:

Apple Downloads www.apple.com/downloads/macosx/email_chat

▶ **Threading** The **Organize by Thread** command in the **View** menu lets you view your emails as nested "conversations" – with a message at the top and all the replies to that message underneath. You can expand or collapse individual threads using the little triangles to their left; or deal with them all at once using the options in the **View** menu.

	Lockett, Andrew	Did you get that la...	17 Mar 2005	
	Lockett, And...	RE: Did you get th...	17 Mar 2005	
	Lockett, And...	RE: Did you get th...	17 Mar 2005	

*To set up aliases for a .Mac email account, click the **Create Alias** button in the **Account Information** pane of **Accounts** in Mail Preferences. You can colour-code each alias to see at a glance which address a message was sent to.*

Tip: For instructions on how to back up and restore your email, see p.270.

Tip: Messages that display a little curvy arrow are those which you've replied to.

Tip: Though most commonly used for shunting messages around as they arrive, rules can be run at any time on existing messages by clicking **Apply Rule** in the message window (or hitting ⌘⇧L).

Phone, video calls & chat

With a Mac and an Internet connection, it's free and it's easy to communicate in real time with other computer users around the world – in text, voice or even video. Even better, with the right software you can call "regular" telephones – both landlines and mobiles – for a fraction of the cost that your telco would charge. This chapter explains how.

Computer-to-computer messaging and calls

Instant messaging (IM) is like a cross between email and the phone, allowing you to communicate with one or more people by typing messages which pop up immediately on the screens of whoever's taking part in the conversation. Once you build up a list of contacts (or "buddies"), you'll be able to see at a glance which of them are at their computers and ready to receive messages. All this is done using a "messenger" application; and most messengers also let you make voice and video calls to other computer users.

iChat & other messengers

OS X comes with an excellent messenger built-in. It's called iChat, and it lets you communicate in text, voice and video with other iChat users, plus anyone who uses AIM (AOL's instant messenger) or Jabber (see below). The only problem is that millions of PC users who you might want to chat with use different messaging "networks" such as MSN, Yahoo! and ICQ.

It is possible to chat with all these people using iChat, but it requires a techie work-around using Jabber (see box). Instead, you might prefer to download the relevant messenger:

MSN Messenger www.microsoft.com/mac
Yahoo! Messenger messenger.yahoo.com
ICQ www.icq.com

If you get sick of switching between multiple messengers, try a multi-network tool such as:

Adium www.adiumx.com
Fire fire.sourceforge.net

Jabber

Jabber is an instant messaging system used in many universities, companies and elsewhere. iChat doesn't let you set up a Jabber account, but if you already have one, you can use iChat as a Jabber messenger. Enter your details in the Accounts pane of iChat Preferences, and then open the **Jabber List** from **Window** menu (⌘3) to see who's online and exchange messages.

One clever thing about Jabber is that it can utilize so-called "gateways" to log on to IM networks such as MSN and Yahoo!. And since Jabber is built in to iChat, it is possible via a slightly round-the-houses route to chat to MSN and Yahoo! buddies within iChat. To find out how, see: www2.hku.nl/~rogier9/jabberhowto

---

Tip: Account details can also be added, deleted and edited from the iChat Preferences panel, opened by the **File** menu (or the shortcut ⌘,).

*The Buddy List shows a screen name and picture for each of your "buddies". To change your own picture, go to the **Accounts** pane of System Preferences (see p.52).*

▼

Using iChat

Before you can use any instant messenger, you need to get yourself an account – basically just a "'screen name" (username) and password. You'll be prompted to do this the first time you launch iChat, which you'll find in the **Applications** folder, or perhaps already sitting in the Dock.

If you already have an .Mac or AIM account, you can log in to iChat with these details. Otherwise, choose **Get an iChat Account...** and you'll be taken to a page where you can sign up for a free .Mac trial (for more on .Mac, see p.32). At the end of the trial period, you'll get to keep your account name and password to use in iChat even if you don't sign up for .Mac. Alternatively, you can grab a username and password from:

AIM www.aim.com

Once you're logged in, you're ready to add some contacts and start messaging. If your friend already use iChat or AIM, email them and ask for their screen names. Next, open the **Buddy List** from the **Window** menu (or by pressing ⌘1) and hit the "+" button at the bottom of the panel to add a contact. If they're not already in your Address Book, click **New Person**.

From that point on, it's hard to go wrong. A glance at your Buddy List will show you which of your contacts are online and ready to exchange messages. To start a conversation, highlight a name and hit the "**A**" button at the bottom of list.

Audio & video calls with iChat

With a decent Internet connection and the right hardware (see box opposite) iChat enables you to make voice and video calls to other iChat and AIM users. You can "conference" with up to ten other

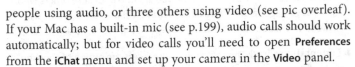

What you'll need for audio & video calls

To make computer-to-computer voice calls, both parties simply need some kind of microphone and speakers, either built-in or attached to their computer. However, a headset or USB handset (see p.166) will drastically improve the sound quality.

For video calls, you'll also need a webcam. Apple's own iSight (pictured) is extremely high quality, but has a price tag to reflect this fact. Alternatively, you could use a FireWire camcorder as a webcam, if you have one, or attempt to hook up an inexpensive PC webcam, though not all will work and you'll need to download, and maybe pay for, a third-party driver such as Webcam X.

Webcam X www.ioxperts.com/products/webcamx.html

Finally, for decent-quality voice or video calls, both parties will need to have broadband. Dial-up connections can be used, but the sound will be bad and the video will be more like an inch-wide slideshow, updating every second or so – worth it, perhaps, for a glimpse of a loved one on the other side of the world, but not a real means of communication.

people using audio, or three others using video (see pic overleaf). If your Mac has a built-in mic (see p.199), audio calls should work automatically; but for video calls you'll need to open **Preferences** from the **iChat** menu and set up your camera in the **Video** panel.

You can tell from your Buddy List which of your contacts is set up for voice and video calls – you'll see a phone icon when audio chat is pos-   sible, and a camera icon when video is possible. To start chatting or conferencing with someone, double-click the camera or telephone icon next to their name, or highlight them and use the buttons at the bottom of the list.

Why AV?

iChat's full name is iChat AV. In case you were wondering, the AV stands for "audio video", reflecting the introduction of voice and video chat features back in 2003.

iChat lets you video conference ▶ with up to three other people simultaneously.

> **Tip:** To enter full-screen mode when video conferencing, use the option in the **Audio** menu, hit the button at the bottom of the video window, or use the keyboard shortcut ⌘^F.

iChat tips & tricks

That's the basics covered, but there are various other functions and tricks that are worth knowing about:

▶ **Status menu** Below your name at the top of your Buddy List is a dropdown where you can choose how you want to appear to others whose Buddy List you appear on – "Available", "Away", "Offline", etc. You can also use this menu to type custom status messages ("At the shops, back in 5", etc).

▶ **Current iTunes Track** The same menu also offers the option of showing all your buddies what you are currently listening to in iTunes along with a link so that they can click through to the Apple Music Store and preview the track for themselves.

▶ **Groups** Select **Use Groups** from the **View** menu to divide your Buddy List into collapsible categories – Work, Family, etc. Groups can be added and edited using the "+" button at the bottom of the Buddy List, while individual buddies can be dragged from group to group within the list. To add a person to more than one group, hold down ⌥ while your drag.

*Under the **Messages** tab of iChat Preferences you can set the way text messages appear.*

▶ **Send files** Drag any file onto a name in your Buddy List – or into an open conversation – and, once the recipient has chosen to accept the file, it will make its way to their desktop. Unlike email attachments, this technique is great for sending large files.

▶ **Insert smilies** Using either the **Edit** menu option or the dropdown menu at the right-hand end of a chat box, you can add "emoticons" (emotion icons) or "smilies" to your messages. How much fun can you handle?

▶ **Blocking** To prevent a specific person from messaging you or seeing when you're online, open **Preferences** from the **iChat** menu and, under **Accounts**, click **Security**. Check **Block specific people**, click the **Edit List…** button and add your nemesis using the "+" button.

▶ **Parental controls** If you have children and you'd like to make sure they only chat to approved contacts, set them up with a "managed" OS X user account, and enable and configure iChat parental controls (see p.52 for more information).

Calling telephones

Not everyone is a broadband user who spends their life glued to their computer, ready to receive incoming calls. Good news, then, that it's also possible to use your Mac to call regular phones – landlines and mobiles – via your Internet connection. Doing so can save you money, especially if you regularly call long distance. It can also be very useful if your home phone is often in use, effectively providing a second line with no monthly charge.

The technology that allows computers to connect to normal phone lines is called VoIP (Voice over Internet Protocol), though various companies use an alternative term such as "Internet telephony" or "broadband phone". To get started, you first need to choose a VoIP service, such as…

Tip: To start a group chat, select multiple contacts in your Buddy List (by holding down ⌘ while you click), hit the "A" button and type a message. Each person who accepts will be able to chat with everyone else in the session.

Tip: To quickly add a person to your "blocked" list, click the **Block** button that appears in the window when you receive a message.

Bonjour

iChat usually works over the Internet, but it also lets you chat to other users on your office or home network – even when you're not connected to the Net. This is useful if, for instance, you want to quickly send files between laptops when you're out and about. Simply open the **Bonjour** panel from the **Window** menu (or hit ⌘2) to see all available buddies on your network with iChat running. For more information about setting up networks, see p.63.

Skype & Gizmo

If you want to improve the sound quality of your Skype calls, or to make VoIP feel a bit less like Star Trek, connect a USB handset, such as this TipTel 116, to your Mac.

The most popular VoIP service, partly thanks to its ease of use and reliability, is Skype. It's like a regular instant messaging program, with free computer-to-computer calls between users, but it also allows you to buy "SkypeOut" credit for calling regular and mobile phones around the world.

The prices are very low: roughly 2¢/1p per minute to landlines and mobiles in most of Europe, North America and Australasia, regardless of your location (note, though, that calls to UK mobiles cost more like 25¢/15p per minute). You can also receive calls to your Mac from regular phones, though you have to pay a monthly "SkypeIn" subscription.

Of the other pay-as-you-go services out there, the only one that looks set to give Skype a serious run for its money is Project Gizmo (name change due soon!).

Skype www.skype.com
Gizmo www.gizmoproject.com

Subscription plans

An alternative to a Skype-style system is a VoIP service that offers unlimited calls for a fixed monthly charge. These typically let you connect a regular telephone to your broadband router, missing out your Mac altogether. Services include:

BT Broadband Voice www.btbroadbandvoice.com (UK)
VoicePulse www.voicepulse.com (US)
Vonage www.vonage.com (US) • www.vonage.co.uk UK)

Tip: To keep abreast with what's new in the worlds of VoIP and Mac telephony, drop by Om Malik's Broadband Blog at: gigaom.com

Your own website or blog

Publishing a website with your Mac is as easy or as hard as you choose to make it. If your sole aim is to put a few pictures online to show your friends and family, then your best bet may be to avoid the nuts and bolts of site creation and employ some simple photo-sharing tools (see p.233). Likewise, if you just want to plot your daily thoughts – or even publish a Podcast – then sign up for a free, ready-to-roll blog (see p.170). If you're after more flexibility and kudos, however, you'll want to use your Mac to create a proper website…

Publish a website

The simplest way to build a website is to use an online service such as Apple's HomePage (see box). The result might look a bit prefabricated, but you can create a site through a step-by-step wizard, or by simply filling in a set of templates. However, there's no substitute for building your own site from scratch. The following pages outline roughly how this is done; for far more details, buy *The Rough Guide To The Internet*.

HomePage

If you have a .Mac account (see p.32) you can use the HomePage feature to create and publish a website in minutes – for no extra cost. The pages live within your iDisk, and are accessed via your .Mac web address. HomePage also integrates with several other Apple applications, allowing you to publish galleries of images to the Web direct from iPhoto (see p.222) and publish iMovie clips and films direct from iMovie (see p.248).

Tip: For a simple site, create and save all your images and pages in a single folder. This makes everything easier to manage and keeps the links between pages short and sweet.

Creating webpages

Though you wouldn't know it from browsing the Web, each webpage actually consists of a bunch of separate files: an HTML document plus a file for each image used in the page. Preparing your images is easy (see box), but putting them together with text in an HTML file is a bit more tricky. To get really good results, you should take the time to work your way through an online HTML tutorial (for example at www.w3schools.com), though if you're feeling impatient, you might want to go straight for the easier options:

▶ **Word** Using Word (see p.118) you can create a "standard" document with text and pictures then choose **Save As Webpage** from the **File** menu.

▶ **Web design applications** Dedicated Web design tools offer far more power and flexibility than Word and don't necessarily require you to know any HTML (though it certainly helps). There are some reasonably priced applications in this department which use templates and themes to make the whole process simple (such as Freeway, RapidWeaver and Site Studio). But if you're really serious, try an all-singing-and-dancing commercial alternative such as Adobe's GoLive:

Freeway Express www.softpress.com ($90)
RapidWeaver www.realmacsoftware.com ($35)
Site Studio www.dotsw.com ($30)
GoLive www.adobe.com/golive ($400)

When you've created your pages, save them with short lowercase names without any spaces or special characters (for example, pictures.html or contact_me.html). Most importantly, save your homepage as index.html. This way, when someone types www.yoursite.com into their browser, the homepage will automatically appear.

Park your pages

When your webpages and images are ready to go live, you'll need to make them available on the Internet, which means putting them on a server computer – a "host" – with an address where people can find them. There are three main options:

▶ **Free webspace** If your budget is tight, you could plant the files in some free space, perhaps thrown in by your ISP as part of your Internet connection package, or from a free webspace provider such as www. tripod.com or www.geocities.com. The problem is that you'll end up with an address such as http://webspace.myisp.com/peter. If you want something more like www.peter.com, you could register a domain name (see box) and use that as a front page to your free webspace. People will type, say, www.peter.com, which will redirect them to http://webspace.myisp. com/peter. Note, though, that some registrars will display – unless you pay a small surcharge – an ad banner at the top of your site to anyone who reached it via the new address.

▶ **A proper host** If you want to register a domain name and have it function properly, not just as a front door, you'll need to pay a few pounds or dollars per month to house your pages on a "proper" Web host. By far the easiest option is to buy a hosting package and domain name at the same time, and from the same company.

▶ **Host it yourself** If you have an always-on broadband connection with a static IP address (ask your ISP if you're not sure), you could consider setting up your Mac as a Web host. OS X makes this very easy, as it comes pre-installed with the world's most popular server software: Apache. All you need to do is open **Sharing** from **System Preferences** and turn on **Personal Web Sharing**. Then put your webpages and images in the **Sites** folder of your home folder; they can then be reached from anywhere by the address http://your-IP-address/~yourshortusername. If you'd rather have a non-numeric address, register a domain name and set it up to point all traffic to your Mac; visitors to your site will never know that you're hosting it yourself.

Get a domain name

If you'd like a personalized Web address, you'll need to register a "domain". You pay a fee and that gives you exclusive use of the address for a set period (usually a year or two at a minimum) after which you can renew it.

If someone else has already taken your ideal name – eg www.peter.com – you'll have to try changing the end (.net, .info, etc) or the name itself (eg www.peteronline. com). Any domain registry will instantly confirm what's available and let you bag your domain. Major registrars include:

123-reg.co.uk (UK)
www.domaindirect.com (US)
www.domainmonger.com (US)
www.uk2.net (UK)

When you register a domain name you'll usually be offered a hosting package for an extra fee. If you don't accept this offer, you'll need to either set up the domain to "forward" all traffic to some other address (your webspace or blog, say) or associate the address to a server – either a third-party Web host or your own Mac.

Upload your site

Tip: Many site-building tools also feature an FTP tool – so see what you already have before downloading a stand-alone tool.

Unless you're hosting your own site on your Mac, you'll need to upload your pages, images, etc, to wherever they're going to live on the Net. First, you'll need to get some log-in details from whoever is providing your online space. This will usually include a username, password and an FTP address for your space on the server.

You can access an FTP server using Finder (choose **Connect to Server...** from the **Go** menu) or even use an Automator (see p.112) Action (editkid.com/upload_to_ftp), but you'll find it easiest to install a dedicated FTP program, such as the free, open-source OneButton:

OneButton FTP www.onebutton.org

Publish a blog

A blog, or weblog, is a special kind of frequently updated webpage consisting of short "posts", arranged with the most recent at the top. Many major sites feature blogs, sometimes written by teams of people. But the archetypal blog is composed by an individual – a daily log of a person's life, thoughts and online discoveries.

Creating a blog can be extremely simple. Just sign up with a free host and choose a template to determine how your blog will look. Then log into the host's website from any computer and type a new post. People will access your blog via a sub-domain or your blog hosts's address – eg peter.blogger.com.

The best-known blog hosts include:

Blogger www.blogger.com
GreatestJournal www.greatestjournal.com
Sparkpod www.sparkpod.com

If you have your own website, choose a blog host that will let you display your new weblog at your own address – or download some tools that will allow you to manage your blog direct from your Mac. If you use .Mac (see p.32), try iBlog:

iBlog www.lifli.com ($20)Podcasting

Otherwise search for blogging applications and widgets at:

Apple Downloads www.apple.com/downloads/macosx

Creating a Podcast

Audio blogging – aka Podcasting – is the latest craze in the blogo-sphere. If you want to create a simple, voice-only Podcast, you can do it by telephone using a service such as www.audioblogger.com. But for something more professional – perhaps with a mixture of chat, music and interviews – you'll need to follow these steps:

▶ **Prepare your episodes** Use an audio editor such as GarageBand (see p.204) to record and mix your shows. Then export them to iTunes and convert them to MP3s (see p.188).

▶ **Create an enclosure** Publish your MP3 file as an enclosure (the weblog equivalent of an email attachment) on your blog. Check your blog host's site for details on how this is done.

▶ **Create an RSS feed** If you want people to be able to "subscribe" to your Podcasts, via iTunes or elsewhere, you need to create an RSS feed – the same technology used for online newsfeeds (see p.149). The easiest way to do this is to use an RSS feed provider, such as www.feedburner.com

▶ **Publish your Podcast** This basically means planting your RSS feed where people can find it to subscribe. You can do this via iTunes (head for the iTunes Music Store and follow the links), direct from your own site or blog, or via a website such as www.podshow.com.

> **Tip:** When recording your Podcast in GarageBand, add **Compression** to voice record-ings to give a smooth effect, and use **Gate** to prevent extra-neous noise from creeping in when you aren't talking.

> For more on Podcasting, see:
> www.ipodder.org
> www.podcast411.com
> audiofeeds.org

25 P2P file sharing

P2P ("peer-to-peer") file-sharing is a technology that allows computer users all over the world to "share" each other's files via the Internet. Even if you've never heard of P2P, you've probably heard of some of the programs that have made this kind of file sharing possible, such as KaZaA – and, historically speaking, Napster. And you've probably also heard people debating the legal and moral ins and outs of the free-for-all that file-sharing applications facilitate. If not, don't worry – the next few pages will bring you up to speed.

As we've already seen (see p.63), one of the reasons why people set up home and office networks is to allow each user some degree of access to the files stored on the other computers. P2P file-sharing applications apply this idea to the whole of the Internet – which is, of course, simply a giant network of computers. In short, anyone who installs a P2P program can access the "shared folder" of anyone else running a similar program.

With literally millions of sharers online at any one time, an unthinkably large quantity of files is available – from music and movies to images, software and documents. So, whether you're after a drum'n'bass track, a web-design application, a Chomsky speech or an episode of your favourite sitcom, you're almost certain to find it. But that *doesn't* mean that it's legal. If you download or make available any copyright-protected material, you are breaking the law and, while it's still unlikely, you could, in theory, be prosecuted.

In 2004, according to a study by Michael Goodman of The Yankee Group, five billion music tracks were downloaded via P2P, compared to only 330 million from online services selling legal, DRM-protected tracks.

The legal battle

Continuous legal action saw Napster – the first major P2P system – bludgeoned into submission (it has now resurfaced as a legitimate online music service, though it's not compatible with Macs). A similar fate befell Scour, this time because of movie rather than audio sharing. But these casualties just paved the way for others, such as KaZaA, which stands by some margin as the most downloaded program in the history of the Internet.

These new-generation P2P tools are genuinely decentralized: they don't rely on a central system to keep tabs on which files are where. Which means that, though the programs are mostly used for the illegal distribution of copyrighted material, the companies producing them can't easily be implicated in this breach of the law (just as a knife manufacturer couldn't easily be sued for a stabbing).

Current legal wranglings in the US look set to change this at some stage, but in the meantime the music, film and software industries have instead gone after the people who clearly *are* breaking the law: individual file sharers. Quite a few individuals have now been prosecuted – especially in the US – but with many millions of people using file sharing each day, it's pretty inconceivable that anyone could attempt to sue all of them.

Whether or not it's ethical to use P2P to download copyrighted material for free is another question. Some people justify it on the grounds that they only download music, software or video they're considering buying; others believe that intellectual property is akin to theft; others still that they only download non-controversial material, such as recordings of speeches, freeware software or music that they already own on CD or vinyl and can't be bothered to rip or record manually. It's a heated debate – as is the question of whether file sharing has damaged legal music sales, something the industry insists upon, but which many experts claim is questionable.

As this spoof poster (available from www.modernhumorist.com) shows, many on the "free distribution" side of the DRM debate see their adversaries – led by the Recording Industry Association of America – as draconian authoritarians committed only to profit, power and an outmoded and unsustainable business model. Unsurprisingly, many musicians disagree. For both sides of the argument, see:
www.riaa.com
www.eff.org
theregister.com/internet/rights

Mac P2P applications

There are various P2P "networks" – the main three being eDonkey2000, FastTrack and Gnutella – each of which can be accessed via various different applications ("clients"). Some of these clients are very sophisticated, with features such as the ability to download a single file from more than one source simultaneously or to import downloaded tracks directly into a playlist in iTunes. Among the most popular Mac P2P clients are these user-friendly tools for accessing Gnutella:

LimeWire www.limewire.com (Gnutella)
Acquisition www.acquisitionx.com (Gnutella)

But you might prefer to use something that won't badger you for a donation and which can tap into multiple networks, such as:

Poisoned www.gottsilla.net (Gnutella, FastTrack, OpenFT)
MLMac www.mlmac.org (eDonkey; BitTorrent; FastTrack; Gnutella; KaZaA)

There are many other programs and networks out there (as well as other ways of sharing files, such as via newsgroups and chat). For example, SoulSeek is popular for underground and alternative music and has an active "community", while BitTorrent – with which you start downloads via links on websites – provides superfast access to large, popular files, such as videos. Find out more at:

BitTorrent www.bittorrent.com (PC & Mac)
SoulSeek www.slsknet.org (PC & Mac)

For reviews of all the available programs, plus news and links to download sites, see:

Mac-P2P.com www.mac-p2p.com
Slyck www.slyck.com
ZeroPaid www.zeropaid.com

Sound

Sound basics

26

Macs handle sound in numerous ways. On the most basic level, they chirp on start-up, grunt when you hit a wrong key and offer congratulatory whistles when you save documents. More usefully, they allow you to play CDs and digital music files through programs such as iTunes (see p.183), produce your own compositions and record your own performances (see p.199) and speak to friends and family around the world (see p.161). You can even talk directly to your Mac (see p.182).

All this will most likely happen effortlessly, but it's still worth taking a few minutes to understand how to control sound on your Mac – especially if you intend to augment your setup with additional mics or a breakout box (aka an audio interface, see p.202).

Volume

You can change the overall volume on your Mac using the dropdown slider on the menu bar (by the clock). If it's not there, open **System Preferences** from the Apple menu, choose **Sound** and check the box at the bottom of the panel. Most Mac keyboards include keys for quickly changing the volume and muting the sound altogether – look for the three little speaker symbols along the top of your keyboard.

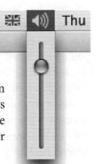

Tip: If you use a dial-up modem and you don't like the noises it makes when it connects to the Internet, turn off "modem sounds" within **System Preferences** – click **Network**, choose your modem from the **Show** menu, click into the **Modem** pane and turn **Sound** off.

Tip: When you're using your keyboard to change the volume, holding down ⇧ mutes the feedback sounds. Or, to avoid these sounds ever happening, uncheck the **Play feedback sounds...** box under the **Sound Effects** pane of the **Sound** section of **System Preferences**.

Inputs & outputs

Unless you have special additional hardware, your Mac will deal with one incoming sound source (eg a microphone) and one outgoing sound source (eg internal speakers) at a time. So if you have more than one input or output, you need to specify which you want to use. This is done within the **Output** and **Input** panes of the **Sound** section of **System Preferences**.

By default, you'll have one output set up – **Built-in Audio** – which covers your built-in speakers or headphone socket (the name will change depending on whether there's anything plugging into the latter). And, depending on your Mac model, you may have nothing – or just the in-built mic – in the **Input** pane.

If, however, you add external audio devices – such as a USB mic, an iSight or a full-on audio interface (see p.202) – you may need to open this preferences panel and select the device before you can get it to work.

Alerts & effects

The **Sound** preferences panel also contains the settings for **Sound Effects**. From the **alert sound** list, you can pick the noise you'll hear when you try to do something impossible. To toggle whether you hear sounds every time you copy or delete a file or folder, use the **Play user interface sound effects** check box.

Tip: Alerts can also be signalled visually instead of audibly. This is done using Universal Access (see p.49).

Tip: If you have more than one sound output set up, you can have your system alerts and sound effects play through one, and everything else (music, video, etc) through the other. You'll find this option under the **Sound Effects** tab in **System Preferences/Sound**.

Tip: If you intend to work on your Mac while listening to music through headphones, it's worth turning the volume of alerts down, as they can give you a bit of a shock, suddenly ricochetting across your ear drums at high volume.

Hi-fis & speakers

If you listen to music or watch DVDs on your Mac, you may find the internal speakers quiet and tinny, in which case consider hooking up your computer either to a hi-fi or a set of external speakers.

Connecting to a hi-fi with a cable

To get the sound from your Mac into your hi-fi, the latter will need an available line-in channel – look on the back for an unused pair of red and white RCA sockets. They may be labelled "Aux" or "Line-in", though any input other than "Phono" (which will have a built-in preamp) should be fine.

Next, pick up an RCA-to-minijack cable (pictured). When buying a cable, check all the plugs are "male" not "female" (they probably will be) and, if you want true high-fidelity, spend extra to get gold-plated jacks – they deliver a far cleaner sound.

Run the cable from the Mac's headphone socket to the hi-fi's Line-in. If you have a G5 Power Mac, or an audio interface, run the cable from a Line-out socket instead of the Mac's headphone socket.

Connecting to a hi-fi with AirTunes

If your hi-fi has a line-in socket, but you don't want to be limited by cables – perhaps you have an iBook or PowerBook, or your Mac is in a different room from your stereo – investigate Apple's AirPort Express wireless base station (see p.64), with its so-called AirTunes

(see p.64)

iPod to hi-fi

One problem with running your Mac through your hi-fi is that you need to have the computer on to hear anything and, unless you have an AirPort Express, you may have to run a cable across the room. An alternative, if you're mainly hooking up the stereo to listen to your iTunes Library, is to attach an iPod to the hi-fi. This doesn't give you quite the same ease of use and flexibility, but it's often more convenient. Simply run an RCA-to-minijack cable between your hi-fi's line-in and your Pod's headphone socket or, much better, the LINE OUT on the back of an iPod Dock. The Dock solution can be made all the more convenient when combined with a wireless iPod remote control.

feature. With this set up, your alert noises and other sounds will come through your Mac's speakers as usual, but you can stream music wirelessly from iTunes (see below) to the hi-fi.

The AirPort Express plugs into any convenient power socket and is attached to the hi-fi with a standard RCA-to-minijack cable; it communicates with your Mac using AirPort – so you'll need to buy an AirPort or AirPort Extreme card if your Mac doesn't have wireless built-in.

Once everything's in place, open iTunes Preferences and check **Look for remote speakers connected with AirTunes** in the **Audio** tab. Your hi-fi (which you will have given a name during the setup process) will automatically appear in a dropdown menu on the bottom of the iTunes window.

AirPort Express can also beam an Internet connection around your house, and allow you to connect to a printer wirelessly (for more information, see: www.apple.com/airportexpress). However, it doesn't allow you to stream music wirelessly from any application other than iTunes. Thankfully, this limitation can be easily circumvented with the help of a $25 application called Airfoil:

Airfoil www.rogueamoeba.com/airfoil

The solution isn't perfect however, as you manually have to select whichever program you want to send through the ether, and there is a significant delay between the time the sound is played by whichever program you are using and the time that it actually gets to your hi-fi speakers. This kind of time-delay is often referred to as "latency", and in the case of Airfoil, it means that the system is useless if you are trying to watch a DVD or play in sync with a backing track when using a multitrack recording application (see p.201).

Airfoil

Tip: If no signal seems to be getting to your stereo from iTunes, or whichever program you are using, and with whichever method you use to connect, make sure that your volume is turned up both in the program and on your selected output device's master volume.

HiFi-Link

If you are after a really clear sound through your hi-fi, consider Xitel's HiFi-Link. Essentially a pared-back audio interface designed specifically for connecting to a hi-fi, it connects to one of your Mac's USB ports (bypassing the built-in sound processors and sockets), converts the digital signal to analogue and pumps it through 30 feet of high-quality audio cable. Not bad for $50/£30. Find out more from:

HiFi-Link www.xitel.com/product_hfl.htm

Computer speakers

If all this talk of cables and sonic wirelessness smacks of overkill, but you're still unhappy with the sound that comes out of your Mac's internal speakers, the obvious solution is a pair of computer speakers. Most connect via a standard minijack plug, which will connect to the headphone/line-out port of your Mac, though a few models use a USB connection, in which case they take care of the digital-to-analogue conversion internally – which may be good or bad news depending on the quality of the speakers.

There are various speaker models designed specifically for Macs, with shapes and colours to complement Apple's computer aesthetic. Among the most striking examples are JBL's Creature II combo (pictured) and Harman Kardon's translucent SoundSticks – both of which feature a subwoofer for base and two "satellite" speakers for treble. Systems such as these provide a sound to rival medium-range home hi-fis, though you have to pay for the privilege. If you're on a budget, any pair of plain-old PC speakers should work fine.

Tip: If the Queen's English is your first language, you might find that speech recognition works better if you adopt a slight American twang.

Tip: Speech recognition also works with OS X's built-in chess program – found in the **Applications** folder.

Tip: Perhaps the most fun to be had with Macs and speech is with the "Tell me a joke" command. A simple "knock knock" gag becomes surprisingly entertaining when delivered by a white plastic box in a deadpan monotonal drawl.

Tip: For more speech access features look under Universal Access (see p.49).

Speech

Human to Mac

Though the technology is still in its infancy, computers are beginning to be able to interpret human speech with a degree of reliability. In OS X, you can use this technology to give commands in certain applications, hide the Dock, switch between programs, open an Address Book contact, and so on. First, open the **Speech** pane of **System Preferences** and click the **Calibrate...** button to teach your Mac to recognize your pronunciations.

Next, turn **Speakable Items** on to reveal a floating little speech tool, and decide how you'd like to tell your Mac that you're about to issue a command. Either define a "listening key" (by default **Escape**), or have your Mac permanently listen out for a spoken keyword (by default "computer"). Finally, look within the **Commands** panel to get a feel for the kind of commands that your Mac will recognize, and start speaking.

Mac to human

Beside speaking to your Mac, you can have the computer speak to you – reading out alerts, selected text and so on. Hit the **Text to Speech** tab of **Speech** in **System Preferences** and pick a voice (avoid Albert, who will give you nightmares). If you'd like to have the Mac read selected text – useful if you have difficulty reading small type on-screen – you'll need to set a key-combination to tell the computer when to start speaking. Pick something that's unlikely to clash with a key-combination in another program. ⇧+**Tab** is as good a choice as any.

iTunes & iPods

iTunes is OS X's built-in application for managing and playing the music stored on your Mac. It's also used for moving music from a computer to an iPod (see p.184), but you don't need an iPod to use iTunes. If you're mainly interested in creating a digital music collection to listen to at home – rather than carry around with you – you can do this using iTunes alone. After all, your Mac can do everything an iPod can do, including being hooked up to a hi-fi (see p.178).

Another function of iTunes is to provide access to Apple's iTunes Music Store, which is one of various Internet-based services from which you can legally buy and download music. Currently the only way to access the Store is via iTunes: you can't shop there by visiting the Apple website using a regular Web browser.

But you don't have to buy your music from the iTunes Music Store. You can use iTunes to play music copied from CD or other computers, or downloaded from elsewhere on the Internet (though music files from certain other online music stores may not be compatible).

The following provides plenty of information to get you up to speed with iTunes and iPods. But for the full picture, check out the bestselling *Rough Guide to iPods, iTunes & Music Online.*

Zeros & ones

Clever though computers and iPods are, they only deal with numbers: digital, rather than analogue, information. In fact, their vocabulary is limited to just zeros and ones: the "binary" number system.

So music on your Mac – regardless of whether it's a song or a symphony – is reduced to a series of millions of zeros or ones. Or, more accurately, to a series of millions of tiny magnetic or electronic charges, each representing a zero or a one.

A typical song stored in your iTunes collection would consist of around 30 million zeros and ones, while a 60GB hard drive in a Mac or iPod could hold around 450 billion zeros and ones – 75 for every person on the planet.

The idea of reducing music to zeros and ones is nothing new: CDs, MiniDiscs and every other digital format also store music as binary code. But none of these other formats combines the capacity, flexibility and editability of the hard drive found in a computer or iPod.

An iPod primer

What is an iPod?

An iPod is like a cross between a Walkman and the hard drive used to store files in a computer. Instead of playing from cassettes, CDs or other media, an iPod holds music internally as digital data, in just the same way as a computer stores word-processing documents and other files. iPods aren't unique in this respect: many devices do roughly the same. They're collectively known as digital music players or MP3 players. But Apple's iPod is currently by far the most popular on the market.

High-capacity digital music players – including most iPods – store their music on a hard drive, just like the one found in a computer (but a bit smaller). Less expensive, lower-capacity digital music players, however, including the iPod shuffle, store their music on tiny "flash memory" chips of the kind found in digital-camera memory cards.

The models

At the time of writing, there are three types of Pod available:

▶ **iPod** What was once the "iPod photo" is now the "standard" iPod, so as well as being the best choice for anyone who wants a high-capacity player, it features a colour screen that can display photos from your iPhoto Library (see p.222). It also has good battery life and scrolling menu text.

▶ **iPod mini** Small, sleek and available in four colours, the iPod mini combines a certain fashion appeal with a lower price than the bigger Pods and a hard drive big enough to satisfy most listeners.

▶ **iPod shuffle** The smallest and youngest member of the iPod family is very different from both the above. It's inexpensive and eminently portable, but lacks a screen and doesn't allow any browsing of the music stored on it. At any one time, it can store just one playlist – of up to around 125 or 250 songs, depending on the model – which you can work your way through either in order or randomly (hence the "shuffle" in its title). Rather like a "key drive", it plugs directly into a USB port as opposed to using a cable.

How much space?

Choosing between the various iPod models is above all a matter of choosing how much storage capacity to go for – as measured in gigabytes (GB). Bank on around 1GB for 20 albums. However, bear in mind that you don't need an iPod capable of storing your whole music collection. You can store your collection on your Mac and just copy across to your iPod the albums you want to listen to at any one time.

Note also that if you plan to use the iPod as a portable hard drive as well as a digital music player, you'll need enough extra space available for the kinds of files you're planning on storing. Word and Excel docs and the like are almost negligibly small, but backing up your whole system or storing image, video or program files quickly fills up space.

More than music...

iTunes and iPods aren't just for music. Here are some of things you can do with them – all of which are covered in this book's sister volume, *The Rough Guide to iPods, iTunes & Music Online*...

▶ Transfer or store any kind of file

▶ Record voice memos

▶ Read emails and news

▶ Create a universal remote control

▶ Download photos directly from a camera

▶ Navigate the road network

▶ Listen to a new poem each day

▶ Interrupt an FM radio signal with a DIY newsflash

▶ Deliver a PowerPoint presentation

▶ Backup key files

▶ Play games

▶ Run Linux

▶ Make a flipbook movie

▶ Shave off your beard

For more on using an iPod with iTunes, see p.198.

Left to Right:
iPod shuffle, iPod mini, iPod.

Import music from CD

The best way to get your head around iTunes is to plant some music in your Library and play. Let's start by copying some tracks from a CD to your computer's hard drive. This process is usually known as "ripping". iTunes, however, calls it "Importing".

You can't really go wrong. Load a CD into your computer and it will appear in iTunes as an icon in the Source List; click the icon and the CD's contents are displayed in the Song List.

Stage 1: Download the track names

If, when you first ran iTunes, you agreed to let it connect to the Internet whenever it likes, you'll probably find artist, track and album information for your CD automatically appear in the Song List. If not, make sure you're online and select **Get CD Track Names** from the **Advanced** menu.

This info is *not* pulled from the CD, which contains nothing but music, but downloaded from CDDB – a giant online CD database hosted by a company called Gracenote (www.gracenote.com). If you get no info from CDDB – or you get the wrong info – then you'll have to input the track info manually…

Stage 2: Edit the track info

You can enter information directly into any editable field of the Song List by clicking on its name twice (not too quickly). Any existing text will become highlighted and you're ready to type. Alternatively, to view, add or edit all kinds of information about one or more tracks simultaneously, select them in the Song List and hit ⌘I.

Selecting tracks…

To select multiple tracks in iTunes, either:

▶ Hold down ⌘ and click tracks selectively.

▶ Hold down ⇧ and click the first and last in a series of adjacent tracks. You can then unselect any individual tracks by clicking them with ⌘ held down.

▶ Open Browser mode (see p.192) and click on an Artist, Album and Genre to select all the tracks they contain.

Stage 3: Join tracks

Before importing the tracks from a CD, it's possible to "join" some of them together. Then, when they're played back on your computer or your iPod, they'll always stay together as one unit, and iTunes won't insert gaps between the tracks. This is useful if you have an album in which two or more tracks are segued together or if you just think certain tracks should never be separated – even in "Shuffle" mode. Select the tracks you want to join and then click **Join CD Tracks** from the **Advanced** menu. In the short term you can change your mind by clicking **Unjoin CD Tracks**, but once you've pressed **Import**, the songs will be imported as a single audio file that cannot be separated without the use of audio-editing software (see p.200).

> **TIP:** iTunes only allows you to join tracks before you import. If you want to join them after importing, seek out Track Splicer from Doug's AppleScripts For iTunes: www.dougscripts.com

Ripping services

It can take just a few minutes to rip a CD into iTunes – and you can listen to the music and/or do work in another application, while this is happening. But if you have more money than time, there are services that will take away your CDs and rip them into a well-organized collection for around $1/£1 per CD. See, for example:

PodServe www.podserve.co.uk (UK)
DMP3 www.dmp3music.com (US)
RipDigital www.ripdigital.com (US)

Lose the hard copy?

Unless you're a sound-quality connoisseur or a fan of sleeve notes, you might find that once your CDs have been copied onto your Mac, the discs start to seem like a waste of space. Some have advocated selling them: many will go for $10/£5 through online auctions such as eBay, so if you sell enough you can end up better off than before you bought your Mac. Strictly speaking, the moment you sell the CD you are no longer the owner of the music, so this is legally dodgy. But it's a tempting idea nonetheless.

Converting formats

It's easy to convert existing tracks in iTunes into a different file format. First, pick a format and bitrate within the **Import** pane of iTunes Preferences. Then select the relevant tracks and choose the **Convert** option in the **Advanced** menu. Converted versions will appear alongside the originals.

At that point you can delete the original versions, but be sure to first check the sound quality of the new versions. Converting between compressed formats (eg MP3 to AAC) can result in a noticeable deterioration in fidelity.

Which format?

iTunes allows you to import your CDs in the following formats:

MP3 [Moving Pictures Experts Group-1/2 Audio Layer 3] MP3 no longer provides the best sound-quality/disk-space balance. But its ubiquitousness means that, if you import your music as MP3, you can be safe in the knowledge that it will be transferable to any other player or software that you might use in the future, or which friends and family may already own.
File name ends: .mp3
Best for: importing music you want to be able to share with non-iTunes people and players, and for burning special MP3 CDs.

AAC [Advanced Audio Coding] iTunes' default import format, AAC is liked by Apple for two reasons. First, it sounds noticeably better than MP3 when recorded at the same bitrate. Second, it allows Apple to embed DRM protection into files downloaded from the iTunes Music Store, to stop people freely distributing them.
File name ends: .m4a (standard), **.m4p** (when DRM is included)
Best for: importing music you don't expect to share with non-iPod people and players.

Apple Lossless Encoder A recent Apple innovation, this format offers full CD quality, but only consumes around half the disk space – expect to fit between three and five albums per gigabyte. Currently the format only works on iTunes and iPods.
File name ends: .ale
Best for: importing music at the highest quality for computer or iPod use. Note, though, that it won't work with an iPod shuffle.

AIFF [Advanced Interchange File Format], **WAV** [Wave] These uncompressed formats offer the same quality as the newer Apple Lossless Encoder but take up twice as much disk space (and won't play back on an iPod shuffle). In their favour, they can be played on nearly any computer software and also imported into audio-editing programs. They also tend to rip more quickly than Apple Lossless.
File name ends: .aiff, .wav
Best for: importing music for burning onto CD and then deleting, or for editing with audio software, not for general iTunes/iPod playback.

Stage 4: Set the format & bitrate

Before importing your CD collection into iTunes, think about which file format and sound quality you want to use. iTunes offers various options, which you can access via the **Import** preferences, which you can open from **iTunes/Preferences** (or with the shortcut ⌘,).

The default setting (AAC format at 128Kbps) is fine for listening via headphone or computer speakers, but if you want to put your music on a non-Apple's MP3 player, then AAC won't do (see box opposite), and if you're bothered about sound quality you might want to up the bitrate.

This is the total amount of data (the number of "bits", or zeros and ones) used to encode each second of music. The relationship between file size and bitrate is basically proportional, but the same isn't true of sound quality – a 128Kbps track takes half as much space as the same track recorded at 256Kbps, but the sound will be only marginally different.

Most people will be satisfied with AAC 128Kbps (which is roughly equivalent to MP3 at 160Kbps), but if you listen to high-fidelity recordings of acoustic instruments, and if you connect your Mac to

Tip: It's sensible to mix different file formats and bitrates in your Library, as some kinds of music receive less benefit from high-bitrate encoding. Sludgy, stoner-type rock, for example, may not require the same fidelity as a carefully regulated Fazioli grand piano.

Tip: In the bitrate drop-down, click **Custom** for extra options. **Mono** (under channels) halves the file size when you're importing mono recordings. And if you're recording in MP3 format, **VBR** (which stands for Variable Bitrate) varies the bitrate in real time, according to the complexity of the sound, potentially saving lots of disk space.

The best way to determine the right sound quality for your own ear, headphones and hi-fi is to pick a particularly clear and detailed track and rip it at various bitrates and/or formats. Then do some comparative listening either on headphones or, ideally, connected through a decent hi-fi or speaker system (see p.179).

a decent hi-fi, you may find this setting leads to a distinct lack of presence and brightness in your favourite recordings. If so, either opt for the Apple Lossless Encoder (see p.188) or stick with AAC and up the bitrate.

Stage 5: Import…

Now you've sorted out the track details, it's time to import the songs into iTunes. To the left of each song title you'll see a checked tick box; if you don't wish to import a particular track from a CD, uncheck its box. Then hit the large, round **Import** button in the upper right-hand corner of the iTunes window and watch as each of your selections is copied to your hard drive.

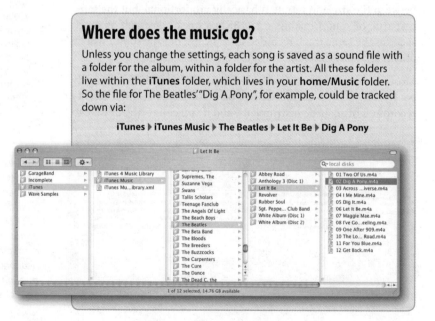

Where does the music go?

Unless you change the settings, each song is saved as a sound file with a folder for the album, within a folder for the artist. All these folders live within the **iTunes** folder, which lives in your **home/Music** folder. So the file for The Beatles'"Dig A Pony", for example, could be tracked down via:

iTunes ▶ iTunes Music ▶ The Beatles ▶ Let It Be ▶ Dig A Pony

Other ways to import

Apart from ripping music from CDs, you can expand your iTunes music collection by grabbing songs from…

▶ **iTunes Music Store** Apple's flagship music service offers more than two million tracks for ¢99/79p per shot. Simply hit the **Store** button, set up an account, and it's all quite self-explanatory from that point on.

▶ **Elsewhere online** You can download from other music services but only if they offer MP3 or WMA files *without* embedded DRM copy protection. For free downloads, try P2P (see p.172), though be aware that downloading anything copyrighted this way will put you on the wrong side of the law.

▶ **Sounds files** If you have music files on your computer, or an external hard drive, you can import these tracks into iTunes by simply dragging them into the main window – or directly into a specific playlist.

▶ **Vinyl or cassette** With sound recording and editing software, and the right cables, you can record music in from any source, including vinyl, cassette, MiniDisc and radio. For more information on how to do this, see p.199. You'll probably end up with a WAV file, which you can import into iTunes and convert to any format you like (see p.188).

▶ **Another computer** If you want to import iTunes music from another computer, you'll need to find the relevant files on the source computer and move them across to the destination folder. This can be done using file sharing (see p.66) or some external media such as a portable hard drive, CD or DVD. Once the files are on the destination computer, drag them into the main iTunes window or a specific playlist and they will be copied into the destination Mac's iTunes Music folder.

▶ **From GarageBand and iMovie** Most music and video packages will let you export WAV files of your compositions or soundtracks, which can be imported into iTunes and converted into something more space efficient. GarageBand and iMovie make it particularly easy – see p.208 and p.255.

Tip: iTunes will import standard WMA (Windows Media) files, though in doing so they'll be converted into AAC format, so the sound quality may be slightly degraded. If the WMA files have embedded DRM protection then iTunes won't import them – unless you burn them to audio CD and re-rip them in another format.

Tip: If there's more than one computer on your network running iTunes, you can share each others' Libraries. Open iTunes Preferences on each machine and under the **Sharing** tab check the relevant tick boxes; then look in the Source List for the links to the music on the other computers.

Play, browse & delete

Tip: When a song is playing but you've browsed elsewhere, use the SnapBack arrow in the right of the status window to reveal the track currently playing.

You can access a menu of the most useful iTunes controls by clicking and holding the mouse over the iTunes icon on the OS X Dock.

In its default state, iTunes will play whatever is in the Song List, in the order shown, and then stop. That might be your entire library, a CD, a playlist (see p.194) or whatever. But there are various other options. From the **Controls** menu, or using the buttons to the bottom-left of the window, you can choose from:

▶ **Repeat All** Plays whatever is in the Song List around and around forever.

▶ **Repeat One** Plays one track around and around forever.

▶ **Shuffle** Plays back whatever is on the Song List in random order.

Alternatively, choose **Party Shuffle** from the Source list. This generates a random mix of tracks drawn from either a playlist or your entire Library. When you hit the icon, a new panel appears where you can set parameters for how the list looks and where the tracks are drawn from, though you can also add selections from anywhere in your Library by dragging them onto the Party Shuffle icon in the Source List.

Browse & search

Though some people use iTunes for months without ever noticing it, the Browser option is a very important feature, allowing you to see tracks arranged by genre, artist and album. To open Browser, click the eye button on the toolbar – or hit ⌘B. The panel that appears automatically includes artist and album; if you also want a genre column, visit the **General** pane of **iTunes Preferences**.

The Search box, on the right-hand side at the top of the iTunes environment, lets you find a track by typing all or part of the name of the artist, album, track title, grouping or composer. Note you can search more than one field at once, so typing **Whi Elep**, for example, would quickly bring up The White Stripes' *Elephant*. If you want to limit your search to artists, albums or genres, use the triangle dropdown menu.

Note that iTunes will only search those tracks currently in the Song List. So if you want to search your whole collection, make sure that the Library icon is selected in the Source List, and "All" is selected in the Genre column before you start to type.

Delete music

To delete music in iTunes, first click the Library icon (as deleting tracks from a playlist does not really delete them). Then select one or more tracks, artists, genres or albums and…

▶ **Hit Backspace** on your keyboard.

▶ **Select Clear** from the iTunes Edit menu.

▶ **Control-click** and select **Clear** from the context menu.

▶ **Drag** the selections straight to the Trash.

Hit the green button to turn iTunes into a mini player.

Deleting from a Pod

Many new iPod users have spent hours trying to delete unwanted music from their Pod. The solution is simple: you do it via iTunes…

▶ Delete a track from iTunes and the next time you connect your iPod, it will disappear from there, too.

▶ If you want a track in iTunes but not on the Pod uncheck the box next to its name in iTunes and choose **Only update checked songs** in iPod Preferences (see p.198).

▶ If you don't want to uncheck the songs (since this will stop them playing in iTunes), use one of the manual update options to take more control over what gets transferred to your iPod (see p.198).

Playlists

A key feature of any computer jukebox software is the ability to create playlists: homemade combinations of tracks for playing on your computer or iPod; for burning to CD; for sending to friends; or even for publishing online. The first thing to understand about playlists is that they don't actually contain any music. All they contain is a list of pointers to tracks within your Library. This means you can delete playlists, and individual tracks within them, without deleting the actual music files; likewise, you can add the same track to as many playlists as you like without using up extra disk space.

Creating & editing playlists

To create a new playlist, hit the "+" button at the bottom of the iTunes window or press ⌘N. Give the new playlist a name, click on your Library, and drag tracks onto the playlist's icon. You can also create a new playlist by dragging songs, artists, albums or genres directly into some blank space at the end of the Source List – iTunes will even try to name it for you.

You can sort the contents of a playlist automatically by clicking the top of the columns in the Song List. Or, to arrange them manually, first sort by the number column (by clicking at the top of that column) and then drag the tracks around at will. To delete tracks from a playlist, simple select them and press backspace – this *won't* delete them from your Library.

Smart Playlists

Smart Playlists are just like normal playlists but, rather than being compiled manually by you, iTunes does the work on your behalf, collecting all tracks in your Library that fulfil a set of rules, or

To rename a playlist, click its name once and then again. To delete one, highlight it and press backspace – or drag the icon into the Trash.

Smart Playlist ideas

Smart Playlists give you the opportunity to be creative with the way you organize the songs in your Library; they can be both a lot of fun and very useful. So much so, in fact, that there are whole websites devoted to the subject (such as www.smartplaylists.com). Following are a few examples to give you an idea of the kind of things you can do:

Functional...

Tracks you haven't heard
> Play Count is 0
All the music you've ripped or downloaded but not yet played.

On the up
> Date Added is in the last 30 days
> My Rating is greater than 3 stars
> Play Count is less than 5
A playlist of new songs that you like, but which deserve more of a listen.

The old Johanna
> Grouping contains piano
If you use Grouping or Comment fields (see p.193) to tag tracks by instrument, mood or anything else, you can then create Smart Playlists based on this info.

...or inspirational

Compilation of questions
> Song Name contains "?"
For days with no answers.

Space songs
> Song Name contains "space"
> Song Name contains "stars"
> Song Name contains "moon"
> Song Name contains "rocket"
For those who love their sci-fi as much as their music.

Tip: iTunes probably came with a few Smart Playlists labelled "60's Music", "My Top Rated", etc. Don't be scared to delete them.

Tip: If you want more space in your Source List for playlists, consider hiding the icons for the Music Store, Party Shuffle, etc. You'll find these options under **General** and **Store** in iTunes Preferences.

Tip: If one song in a playlist is recorded more quietly than the next, select it, choose **File/Get Info** and use the **Volume Adjustment** tool in the **Options** pane.

"conditions", that you define. It might be songs that have a certain word in their title, or a set of genres, or the tracks you listen to the most – or a combination of any of these kind of things. A Smart playlist's contents will automatically change over time, as relevant tracks are added to your Library or existing tracks meet the criteria – by being, say, rated highly.

To create a new Smart Playlist, look in the **File** menu or hold down ⌥ and click the "cog" button at the bottom of the iTunes window. Next, select your parameters in the Smart Playlist box, clicking "+" and "–" to add and remove rules. It's a bit like a bizarre kind of musical algebra. To edit the rules of an existing Smart Playlist, select it and choose **Edit Smart Playlist** from the **File** menu.

And then…

So you've created a dream playlist, and it's just too good to keep all to yourself. What next? You could:

▶ **Burn it to CD** Insert a blank CD into your Mac, select the playlist and click the **Burn Disc** button.

▶ **Design the artwork** Highlight a playlist and select **File/Print** (⌘P). A box will pop up offering you options for printing the track details as either a regular document or an insert for a CD jewel case. This is all very handy, but rather artistically limiting. Another option is to hit **File/Export Playlist…** and export the track names as a text document, and then paste them into another program that will allow you more creativity over the cover.

▶ **Publish it as an iMix** on the iTunes Music Store for others to admire. Select the playlist and choose **File/Create an iMix**.

▶ **Send it to us**, using the address playlists@roughguides.com, and we might just publish it in *The Rough Guide Book of Playlists*.

Extra artwork tools

There are a number of third-party tools and scripts that can help you create CD covers. For example, the free **iTunes Publisher** (available from www.trancesoftware.com) lets you export playlists in various formats, including tabbed text and HTML. Or try the "Playlist to papercdcase.com" script from Doug's AppleScripts For iTunes:

www.dougscripts.com

Radio & Podcasts

iTunes offers access to a number of radio streams (hit the **Radio** icon in the Source List) but it's a pretty feeble selection compared with what you can access with RealPlayer and an online radio directory:

RealPlayer www.real.com
About Radio radio.about.com

Much more interesting is the Podcast option. Unlike most online radio, which is streamed across the Net in real time, Podcasts are audio "shows" made available as downloadable files, ready to listen to in iTunes or transfer to an iPod. Podcasts are usually free and often consist of spoken content (current affairs, poetry, etc). There are many musical Podcasts, too, though there's a grey area surrounding the distribution of copyrighted music in this way.

It's usually possible to download an individual Podcast "show" directly from the website of whoever produced it, but the idea is to use iTunes (or some other "aggregator") to subscribe to Podcasts that you're interested in. iTunes will then automatically download any new episodes at regular intervals, so you always have fresh news, debates, poems, music and more.

To start subscribing, click **Podcasts** in the Source List and hit the **Podcast Directory** link at the bottom. When you find one that looks like it might float your boat, hit **Subscribe**. Then return to the Podcasts icon in the Source List to find your downloaded shows. While you're there, click **Settings...** to choose how you'd like iTunes to deal with old episodes and how often it should check for new ones.

iPod tips

The iPod is uber-simple to use, but there are a few things worth pointing out here:

▶ **Resetting an iPod** If your Pod freezes up or does anything else that it shouldn't, reset it by holding **Menu & Select** (or ▶II **& Menu** on older Pods) for ten seconds.

▶ **Clicker** If you don't like the iPod's "clicking" noise, turn it off in the **Settings** submenu.

▶ **Customizing** Choose which categories appear on the top-level menu within **Settings/ Main Menu**. Classical buffs, for example, will want to add "Composer".

▶ **Rating tracks** Pressing the **Select** button twice allows you to rate a track. This info will be pulled back into iTunes next time you connect.

▶ **Making playlists** To create an "On-The-Go" playlist, browse through your music, pressing and holding the Select button each time you find a track you want to add. The resulting list will appear in the Playlists menu.

▶ **Deleting music** See p.193

Using an iPod

By default, an iPod will automatically synchronize itself with your iTunes Library, making an exact match of all your songs and playlists whenever you connect. However, if you connect the iPod and open **Preferences** from the **iTunes** menu, you'll find the following alternatives under the **iPod** tab…

▶ **Automatically update selected playlists only** This is useful if you have an iPod without the capacity to hold your whole collection; you want to save time when updating your iPod; or you're using multiple iPods with a single copy of iTunes (each user can simply organize their own material within a specific set of playlists).

▶ **Manually manage songs and playlists** This gives you complete control over the contents of your iPod. When selected, you update your Pod by dragging tracks, albums, playlists, genres or artists from the iTunes Library onto the iPod icon.

If you choose either of these modes, you'll have to "eject" your iPod each time you want to physically disconnect it. Either click the ▲ next to its icon, or drag it to the trash.

Copying iPod to iTunes

Regardless of which update option you use, updating an iPod is a one-way process. You can't add new songs to your iPod from someone else's computer and then transfer them on to your computer. If you want to move tunes from an iPod into iTunes, you need some special software, such as:

iPodRip www.thelittleappfactory.com ($15)

Record sound & make music

28

Though the two activities overlap, recording sound and making music on a Mac can be two very different things. One involves using audio recording software to get sound in from a hi-fi (for getting vinyl into iTunes, for example) or a microphone (for making Podcasts, recording voice memos, and so on). The other usually involves "multitracking" layers of recorded and synthesized sounds with the aim of creating professional-sounding songs and other compositions. This chapter provides a whistlestop introduction to both areas.

Recording from mic or hi-fi

With any luck, your Mac will have a line-in or mic socket, which will allow you to connect it to a microphone or hi-fi. However, some models, such as iBooks and Mac minis, lack this socket. iBooks at least have an in-built microphone, but for any serious recording – or if you have a Mac mini – you'll need to purchase a simple external audio interface (see p.202) before you can get started. Once that's taken care of, follow these steps…

Macs & mics

All recent Macs except the Mac Mini and the Power Mac have an internal microphone – fine for recording voice memos but not exactly hi-fidelity. An external mic will provide better quality; USB models are easily added to any Mac, while minijack mics can be plugged into Macs with audio line-in sockets or external audio adapters (see p.202). If you have an iSight, its built-in mic can also be set as the system-wide default audio input device from the **Sound** panel of **System Preferences**, though it won't work for recording directly into GarageBand.

199

record sound & make music

Apple's own **GarageBand** (see p.204) can be used for basic audio recording. You probably already have it, so you may want to give it a go first. However, GarageBand is primarily a multitracking tool, so you might prefer the clean look and feel, and the extra tools, of a dedicated recording and editing tool. The obvious choice is the free **Audacity**, a great little program with loads of built-in effects. Grab it from:

audacity.sourceforge.net

Another option is **CD Spin Doctor**, part of Roxio's CD-burning package Toast (roughly $80/£50), which is designed for recording and "cleaning up" audio from vinyl, cassette and other analogue media. Find out more here:

www.roxio.com/toast

For scores more audio editors, noise removers and other recording software, drop in to:

www.apple.com/downloads/macosx/audio

▶ **Stage 1: Hooking up** If you're recording from a microphone, attach it to your Mac or audio interface. If you're recording from a hi-fi, look on its back for a pair of RCA sockets labelled "Line Out" or "Tape Out" and run a cable from there to your Mac or audio interface (usually, the required cable will be an RCA-to-minijack, available inexpensively from any hi-fi shop). If your hi-fi doesn't feature a line-out or tape-out, you could connect it to your Mac via its headphone socket, though this isn't ideal. Finally, check that the correct device is selected as your Mac's sound input (see p.178).

▶ **Stage 2: Check your disk space** During the actual recording process, you'll need plenty of hard drive space: around 15MB per minute. (Once you've finished recording, you can convert the music that you've recorded into a space-efficient format such as MP3 or AAC, and delete the giant original.)

▶ **Stage 3: Choose some software** Recording from analogue sources requires an audio recording application. You may already have something suitable on your computer, but there are scores of excellent programs available to download off the Net (see box, left).

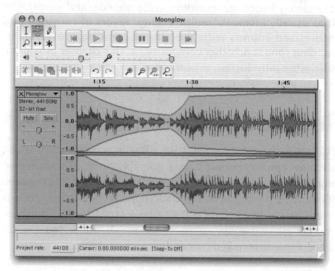

▶ **Stage 4: Recording** The details from here on in vary according to which program you're running and the source you're recording from, but roughly speaking the procedure is the same. When you create a new file and press "record", you'll be asked to specify a few parameters about the sound quality. The defaults – usually 44.1kHz, 16-bit stereo – should be fine. Hit the red button, start recording and use the "stop" button when you're done.

▶ **Stage 5: Tidy up the sound** A graphic wave form will appear on the screen. Use the "cut" tool to tidy up any extraneous noise or blank space from the beginning and end of the file, and the fade tool to hide the "cuts". If your audio editor offers hiss and crackle filters, try them. However, don't go clean-up mad: removing hiss and crackle is good, but over-processed sound can seem sterile and cold to the ear.

▶ **Stage 6: Normalize** If there's a "normalize" function you could also use this to maximize the level without distorting it. This will ensure that, if you record tracks from various old vinyl discs, for example, they will all end up sounding roughly the same volume.

▶ **Stage 7: Save the file** Save the audio in either WAV or AIFF format and drag the resulting file into iTunes. To add it to your iPod (or simply to save space on your Mac), convert the file into AAC or MP3 (see p.188) and consider backing up and deleting the original.

Multitracking

Multitracking means mixing and editing several separate audio recordings ("tracks") in one piece of music. The tracks might be the various members of a band, recorded simultaneously; they might be multiple takes of a single player or singer; or they might even be samples grabbed from CDs and vinyl, triggered from an electronic keyboard. But whatever they contain, each track can be individually chopped and changed, made louder and softer, and generally

Tip: You should aim to get as high a level as possible without causing the little metre to "peak" (go into the red). Try to get this right using the recording-level slider *before* you start to play or speak.

Tip: For a dedicated noise reduction application, try SoundSoap, available from www.bias-inc.com

Tip: If you find that your Mac struggles to play more than a few tracks at once, try setting **Processor Performance** to "Highest". In **System Preferences** look for the dropdown menu in the **Options** section of the **Energy Saver** pane.

played around with. Multitracking was pioneered back in the early 1950s by guitarist Les Paul and today almost every piece of popular music we hear is created in this manner – but on computers rather than reel-to-reel tape.

To start multitracking on your Mac, all you need is the right software. However, if you want to be able to record live sound from "real" instruments and singers, you'll also need a mic/line-in socket on your Mac. If you don't have one, or you want to be able to record

Tip: Some audio interfaces override the Mac's system volume control and recording level, instead providing a special mixer utility that allows you to make use of the multiple inputs and outputs.

Audio interfaces

You can add all kinds of sound connections to your Mac with an external audio interface. These plug in to your Mac via USB or FireWire, and carry a selection of input and output sockets; they take care of the conversion of analogue sound into digital data, and vice versa, in effect acting as an "external soundcard". This can not only result in improved sound quality, but it also relieves your Mac of some processing duties – which reduces the chances of glitches when recording and playing back lots of tracks simultaneously.

Audio interfaces range from simple devices such as Griffin's iMic ($35/£30), which provides basic line and mic sockets, to more professional units, such as M-Audio's FireWire 410 (pictured; $500/£300). These higher-end units typically feature studio-quality sockets, such as balanced phantom-powered XLR inputs for connecting professional microphones and MIDI ports (see opposite). Most also let you record multiple inputs simultaneously – essential for capturing a band session, for example – and come bundled with multitracking software.

iMic www.griffintechnology.com
FireWire 410 www.m-audio.com

For details and reviews of other models, visit:

PC Music Guru www.pc-music.com
SilentWay.com www.silentway.com/tips

multiple musicians or singers simultaneously, you'll need an appropriate audio interface (see opposite).

Finally, you might want to invest in a MIDI keyboard. You can get by without one and use your computer keyboard, or a clickable on-screen keyboard. But having a "real" keyboard is far preferable – especially if you already have a few basic piano skills.

Multitracking software

Among Mac owners, the most widely used multitracking application, or "sequencer", is Apple's own GarageBand. This is part of the iLife suite included with all new Macs, so you probably already have it; if not, iLife is available to buy for $79/£49. GarageBand is so fantastically easy to use that it makes an ideal choice for anyone just starting out with multitracking. Overleaf you'll find a brief tutorial on how to use it.

GarageBand isn't the only option, however. If you get seriously into music-making on your Mac, at some stage you'll want to check out a more serious sequencing package. Some of the industry standard applications – such as DigiDesign's Pro Tools – can only be purchased along with an expensive audio interface. However, others, such as Apple's Logic Pro and Steinberg's Cubase are available as standalone applications. The full versions are expensive, but both

are available in cut-down versions. Logic Express, for example, sells for roughly $300/£200, and Cubase SE costs around half that. To find out more, visit:

Logic www.apple.com/logic
Cubase www.steinberg.net
Pro Tools www.digidesign.com
PC Music Guru www.pc-music.com

MIDI instruments

MIDI (Musical Instrument Digital Interface) is a protocol that allows keyboards, drum machines and other electronic musical instruments to talk with one another – and with computers. Traditionally, MIDI instruments are connected to computers via MIDI cables (pictured below) but today some keyboards connect via USB. This is much more convenient, since you can't attach MIDI cables to your Mac without purchasing a suitable MIDI adapter (or an audio interface that features MIDI sockets).

For most home musicians, MIDI's primary use is to connect a keyboard, which you can then use to trigger (play) software instruments and samples stored on your Mac. However, MIDI works in both directions, and can also be used to give your Mac control over synths, drum machines or other MIDI instruments.

GarageBand

Like other competing packages, GarageBand allows you to record and edit layers of "real" sounds and "software instruments" (see box). What sets it apart is its foolproof user-friendly interface and its incorporation of "Apple Loops" – riffs, rhythms and sound effects that you can simply drag and drop into your songs. GarageBand takes care of the details such as making sure the loops you're using are all in the same key and playing at the same tempo, so absolutely no musical training is required to create something basic.

Following is a quick run through of how you might construct a song in GarageBand. It's certainly not comprehensive and neither is it prescriptive – if you're a musician, you may find Apple Loops appallingly limiting, and prefer to work from scratch.

Creating a backing track using loops

Launch GarageBand from **Applications** (or the Dock) and create a new song, or "project", when prompted. Pick a tempo, key and time signature if you like; otherwise go with the defaults. You can change them later if necessary using the master track settings (see Tip, left).

Your project will probably include a track for a grand piano. Ignore this for now and click on the eye button near the bottom-left (or hit ⌘L) to reveal the loop browser panel. Use the various category buttons and view options to browse what's

---

Recording Podcasts

Fancy trying your hand at broadcasting? If so, why not use GarageBand to create a Podcast? For more info, see p.171 or visit: www.apple.com/support/garageband/podcasts

Tip: To change the overall-tempo, key and time signature of an existing song, double-click the Master Track; if you can't see it, hit ⌘B or look in the **Track** menu.

on offer, clicking individual loops in the right-hand column to hear them. When you find something you like, drag it up into some empty grey space in the upper part of the window. A new track will appear, containing a coloured "region" of music. To extend it – for example to loop a rhythm throughout the duration of your song – hold your mouse pointer over its right-hand end and drag the region out to whatever length you need.

Keep adding more loops – drums, bass, guitar or whatever – until you've built-up a convincing backing track.

To quickly change the tempo of your song, click the tempo section of the digital display and drag the slider up or down.

Real & software instruments

A key concept in GarageBand is the disinction between "real" and "software" instruments. Every chunk of sound falls into one of these two categories – including non-instrumental lines such as vocals. You can distinguish real and "soft" sections at a glance: real ones bear soundwaves, while soft ones look more like pianola rolls (see right). Each track deals exclusively with either software or real instruments.

Real instruments include anything you record via a microphone or a hi-fi and Apple Loops based on recorded snippets (a wah-wah-style guitar riff, for instance).

Software instruments, by contrast, are virtual pianos, drumkits, violins, and so on. You can play them using a MIDI or on-screeen keyboard, or drag in loops based on software-instrument sounds. Either way, the "music" is essentially just a set of marks on a grid that instruct the computer to play particular notes at particular times. As such, you can change and delete individual notes, swap the instrument playing the passage, transpose the section between keys with no change in sound quality, and even view the passage in traditional musical notation.

When you're browsing for loops, the ones based on real instruments have a blue icon, and the ones based on software instruments have a green icon.

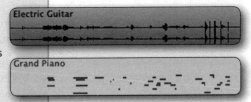

Real-instrument regions display the soundwave of the recording (top), while software-instrument regions display dots and dashes that represent the individual notes (bottom).

Recording software instruments

You should have an empty Grand Piano track at the top of the screen. If you'd rather pick a different instrument, either double-click the piano's name or add a separate track using the "+" button at the bottom-left of the window.

You can play your instrument of choice either with the on-screen keyboard (⌘K), your computer keyboard (⌘⇧K shows you which letter-keys are which notes), or a connected MIDI keyboard, which you can set up in the Audio/MIDI pane of GarageBand's Preferences (⌘,).

When you're ready to lay something down, make sure the relevant track is enabled for recording by pressing the little red button below its name. Then press the record button on the main GarageBand control strip and start playing. When you're done, hit the ▶ button – or your keyboard's spacebar – and a series of marks will appear on the track, each representing a note that you played.

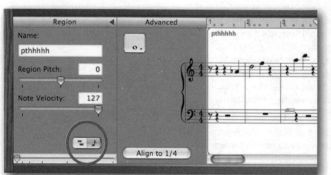

To edit the notes you just recorded, double-click the relevant segment of music – or select it and press the scissors button. Play around with the notes in the grid view and, if you like, hit the musical-note button to see what your playing looks like in traditional musical notation. Play around with the tools and buttons in both views to get a sense of what's possible.

Tip: The on-screen keyboard can be resized by dragging the bottom-right corner. To choose which range of keys is visible either scroll using the arrows to the left and right or click the top-right button to reveal a full-sized keyboard with a dragable range control.

Tip: To delete a track, select it and choose **Delete** from the **Track** menu (or press ⌘⌫).

Recording "real" vocals or instruments

To get some homemade sounds into GarageBand, attach a mic or instrument to your Mac's line-in socket or audio interface. If you're recording an electric guitar, don't connect it directly to the Mac: plug it into a normal guitar amp and take a line out from there (or simply mic-up the amp).

Next, click the big "+" button (or use the shortcut ⌘⌥N) to open the **New Track** box. Under the **Real Instrument** header, specify what you're recording in the left-hand column. If your instrument of choice isn't there, choose **Basic Track**. The right-hand column offers various "styles", which add effects

and EQs to the track. Note that the style isn't set it stone: you can switch off or change it at any time by double-clicking the track's title – or by selecting it and hitting the **Info** button (⌘I).

When you're ready to record, follow the same red-button procedure as before and hit the spacebar when you're done. A wave form will appear in the track to represent the sound you've recorded.

Double-click the newly recorded segment to open it in the wave editor. Here you can cut, copy and paste sections of wave (look in the **Edit** menu or use the standard shortcuts), tweak the tuning and tempo of a particular section, or change the overall pitch of the track. Have a tinker – if you make a mistake you can always go back a stage by pressing **Edit/Undo** (or hitting ⌘Z).

Tip: GarageBand's input/output settings work independently of OS X's. So set up devices and audio interfaces in the application's preferences, not System Preferences.

Tip: When recording with a microphone, use headphones to "monitor" what's going on. Otherwise you might end up recording feedback, and the sound from the speakers will "leak" into the microphone when you're recording.

Tip: GarageBand comes with a built-in instrument tuner. Look for the option in the **Control** menu, or use the shortcut ⌘F to start using it.

Tip: You can also import whole audio files (AIFF, WAV, AAC, Apple Lossless and MP3 formats) into your song by dragging them from Finder or iTunes directly into the GarageBand window.

Tip: You can temporarily silence a track, play it "solo" and lock it to avoid accidental changes using the row of buttons below its name.

iControl

If you get seriously into GarageBand, you may find that the humble mouse and keyboard are inadequate tools for music production. If so, check out M-Audio's iControl, which puts GarageBand controls – such as volume, pan, sends and effects – right under your fingers, and also features MIDI ports for connecting a keyboard or drum machine.

Mixing

Once you've assembled all the basic components of your track, it's time to get everything to work together. Obviously enough, you can cut, copy and paste segments of music, drag them around and delete them (by selecting them and pressing the backspace key). But mixing a song is not just about content – it's about fine-tuning volume levels and subtly "panning" tracks to the left or right side of the stereo spectrum – ie towards the left or right speakers.

You can change the overall level and pan for each track using its virtual knob and slider. But if you'd like to alter a track's volume over time, click the downward-facing arrow button to create a volume "envelope". Click points on the line and drag them about to plot the volume "shape" you'd like.

To create fade-ins and -outs for the whole song, open the master track (⌘B) and use the same technique.

Export your song

In the **File** menu you'll find options for saving your project and for exporting it to iTunes, from where you can burn it to CD, stick it on your iPod, use it behind an iPhoto slideshow, and much more. Before exporting your song, open **GarageBand/ Preferences** and, in the **Export** panel, choose an artist name that you'd like to use, which iTunes playlist you'd like the song added to, and so on. Then click **File/Export Songs to iTunes** and your track will be "bounced down" and dropped into your iTunes collection.

Getting more loops and instruments

GarageBand comes with a good selection of loops and instruments, but before long you may be hungering for more. Apple sells a selection of so-called Jam Packs, ranging from "Remix Tools" to "Symphony Orchestra". Each one costs $99/£65 and contains more than 2,000 royalty-free loops as well as numerous software instruments.

Jam Packs www.apple.com/jampacks

.Mac members (see p.32) can get hold of a bunch of free loops from the various Jam Packs. You'll find them in your iDisk under **Software/ Members Only**.

But you don't have to get your loops from Apple – the Net is swimming in them and some are available for free. Start here:

Samples4 www.samples4.com
Mac Idol www.macidol.com
Mac Audio Guy www.macaudioguy.com
PowerFX www.powerfx.com

To import purchased or downloaded loops and instruments into GarageBand, simply drag them into the Loops Browser. If you're given a choice, add them to your Apple Loops Library to keep things tidy. Once the loops are installed there, you can delete or archive the original source files.

Creating loops

It's easy to turn a track that you've played or recorded into a loop. Simply select a "region" and choose **Add To Loop Library…** from the **Edit** menu.

In iTunes, the song will appear in the high-quality AIFF format, which is ideal for burning to CD. But if you want to save space, stick the track on your iPod or email it to a friend, convert it to a more space-efficient format (see p.188). You could even share your creation with other Mac music-makers at:

Mac Idol www.macidol.com
iCompositions www.icompositions.com

Tip: If you're struggling to get GarageBand to do as you please, visit Apple's support site for tips and troubleshooting advice: www.apple.com/support/garageband

More music software

Besides the multitrack and recording applications already mentioned in this chapter, there are thousands of additional packages, plug-ins and software instruments out there. These range from analogue-modelling soft synths (Phoenix Analogue) and Moog emulators (Minimonsta) to drum machines (Doggiebox) and notation applications (Sibelius).

Phoenix Analogue www.rattlesnakehillsoftworks.com
Minimonsta www.arturia.com
Doggiebox www.doggiebox.com
Sibelius www.sibelius.com

And that's only the tip of the iceberg. For even more OS X audio software, drop in to:

HitSquad www.hitsquad.com/smm/mac
Pure-Mac www.pure-mac.com/music.html
OS X Downloads www.apple.com/downloads/macosx/audio

Confused by BPMs? Download the Audio Calculator widget from:
widgets.lensco.be

▼

Pictures

Image basics

Whether you want to accrue a weighty digital photo library, "draw" pictures from scratch, or prepare an image for online use, it pays to spend a bit of time getting your head around the basics of digital images: pixels, file formats, compression and the various software packages. This chapter takes a look at all these things, as well as providing a brief run-through of the various options for downloading, creating and importing pictures. To learn about managing your pictures in iPhoto, turn to p.222.

Load up with pics

There are many ways to create an image on your Mac, and many ways to import pics from external sources such as webcams, websites, scanners – even mobile phones. Here's a quick look at how to get images from…

▶ **Digital cameras** It's easy to import pics from a digital camera – you probably won't even need to install the software that came with the camera. For more on downloading images from your digital camera, turn to our iPhoto chapter (see p.222).

▶ **The Web** If you see an image online that you want, perhaps to use as your desktop background or to email to a friend, simply click the image and drag it from the browser window onto either the desktop or an open Finder

A pixel primer

Most of the images that you'll come across on your computer, including anything you import from a camera or scanner, or grab from a webpage, are so-called "raster" images, which means they're made up of thousands of individual dots known as pixels. From a computer's perspective, such an image is essentially just a database that specifies the hue and shade of each pixel.

The "size" of a raster image is most commonly expressed in terms of its dimensions: for example, an image might be 1500 x 1000 (1500 dots wide and 1000 dots tall). However, when you're shopping for a digital camera, its maximum-quality setting is described in terms of the total number of pixels in the image. Expressed this way, our 1500 x 1000 image would be said to be 1.5 megapixels (because 1500 x 1000 = 1,500,000 pixels, and "mega" means one million).

It probably goes without saying that the more pixels an image contains, the better it can look. However, images of any size can be poor quality. It might have been taken on a low-quality digital camera, for example, or been ruined by being heavily compressed (see p.168).

So how do pixels relate to "real" measurements such as inches and centimeters? On screen, when the image is viewed at 100% size, each of its pixels will take up one pixel on the screen, so the "real" size depends entirely on the resolution setting of your monitor. The higher the screen resolution, the smaller the image will appear. Of course, it's possible to zoom in and out on an image to make it take up more or less of the screen, but only at 100% will it look perfect.

When you're printing a picture, you're usually give the option of scaling the image up or down to make it fit as you want on the page. But the professional way to deal with print size it to specify the image resolution – the number of dots per inch (dpi) – using a program such as Photoshop. If we took our 1500 x 1000 pixel image and set the resolution to 100dpi, for example, the resulting print would be 15 x 10 inches. The higher the dpi, the better the quality, but the smaller the image. In the real world, images for Web and screen use are usually saved at 72dpi; images for printing are usually saved at 300dpi.

window. Easy. Alternatively, **Control-click** the image and choose **Save Image As…** from the context menu to save the pic to a particular location. Note, however, that online images are usually relatively low quality, because they've been scaled down and compressed so they will download faster (see p.168 for more on this).

▶ **Flatbed scanners** You can import a copy of a photograph, magazine page or drawing – just about anything two-dimensional – into your computer with a scanner. These are inexpensive, and work a bit like photocopiers, except that instead of printing, they send a digital image directly to your computer, usually via a USB cable. The software that comes with scanners is generally pretty easy to use, though scanning can also be handled, somewhat cumbersomely, from OS X's **Image Capture** program. Open it from the **Applications** folder, browse for your scanner from the **Device** menu – it should be under the **TWAIN device** submenu. Check the **Use TWAIN software** box, and then click **OK**. Return to the Device menu, select your scanner, have a play with the options, and start scanning.

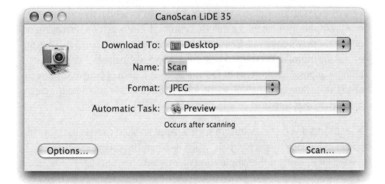

▶ **Bluetooth mobile phone** Most mobile phones these days take photographs, and they are easy enough to transfer wirelessly to your Mac – assuming both devices have Bluetooth capabilities (see p.31). First, pair your Mac and phone (as described on p.62), trigger your image transfers

> **Tip:** Google Image Search offers an easy way to fish for images online; use the size options to filter out pics that may be too small for your needs and be sure to grab the full size version of the image, not the thumbnail preview offered on the search page.
>
> **Google** images.google.com

> **Tip:** Image Capture can also be used to automate image imports from other devices, such as digital cameras and Bluetooth phones.

Up for grabs

As we've said, ⌘⇧3 deposits a snap of your entire screen onto the desktop. Also try:

▶ Use ⌘⇧4 to change your mouse pointer into a target icon and then drag across the area you want to grab.

▶ You can also hit ⌘⇧4 and then the **spacebar** to turn your target icon into a camera icon that will focus your grab on any individual window, palette or dialog box.

▶ Add ^ (**Control**) to any of the above to place your grab on the "clipboard", ready to be pasted (⌘V) into whichever application you want.

▶ In **Applications/Utilities** you will also find a handy little application called Grab, which lets you do timed grabs, TIFF format grabs, and also to include the mouse pointer in the snap.

▶ If you take a lot of screenshots, download the free Capture widget, that offers quick access to all of these screen grabbing options as well as a few extra file formats and a scale setting.

from the mobile and then wait for the **Incoming File Transfer** dialog box. If you are not sure where the image has been dumped, click the little magnifying glass icon to reveal the file in Finder.

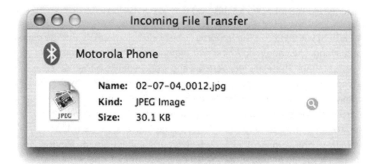

▶ **Screen grabs** A screen grab is a snapshot of whatever is on your screen, or in a particular window, at a specific moment. They can be useful for everything from capturing a weird error, in order to send it to someone for troubleshooting advice, or to quickly capture the information displaying on one or more windows in a format that anyone will be able to open. They are especially useful if you want to capture a whole webpage rather than just a single image. The shortcut ⌘⇧3 will deposit a snap of your Mac's screen onto the desktop in the PNG or PDF format, but there's a lot more to screen grabs than that (see box).

▶ **Webcams** If you use a webcam such as Apple's iSight (see p.163) you can copy a still image by pressing ⌘C when in iChat. This image can then be pasted (⌘V) into another application or location.

▶ **From scratch** Talent permitting, you could create images on your computer with drawing software (see opposite) or, at a push, using a photo editing program that features pencil and brush tools, such as **Gimp** or **Photoshop** (see p.229).

Drawing programs

Though it's possible to create pictures from scratch using an image-editing tool such as Photoshop (see p.229), it's certainly not ideal. Such programs are really designed for editing pixel-based images that already exist, so the tools they provide are essentially clever ways of tampering with one or more pixels simultaneously.

Instead, it's far easier to use a so-called "vector"-based drawing program that, instead of pixels, lets you work with editable lines and shapes. Once you're finished, you can export the image in a standard pixel-based format such as JPEG (see p.218) and treat it just like any other image – import it into iPhoto, email it, and so on. But you can also save the vector-based version so you can easily edit the shapes, lines, text and colours later.

The industry-standard drawing program is Adobe's **Illustrator**, which is part of the Creative Suite package. It's a great program, but costs big bucks and has more features than even professionals are likely to master in a lifetime. Just getting the basics right takes quite a while.

Illustrator www.adobe.com/illustrator ($500)

A more digestible and wallet-friendly alternative is **iDraw**, which features all the basic shape-drawing tools of Illustrator and lets you export your work in various different file formats (see p.218).

iDraw www.macpoweruser.com ($40)

For something far more basic, try **Tuxpaint**, one of the many drawing applications aimed at kids. It's not particularly pretty, and deals in pixels rather than vectors, but it's extremely easy to use and gets the job done. If you've ever used Windows Paint, this is a bit like a Mac equivalent.

Tuxpaint www.newbreedsoftware.com/tuxpaint (Free)

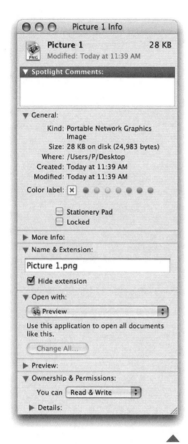

If you are unsure what format a file is, select its icon in Finder and hit ⌘I to call up the Info panel.

Formats & compression

In the same way that there are various types of music file (MP3, AAC) and document file (DOC, TXT, etc), there is a wide range of image file formats, each of which has its own advantages and disadvantages.

Most of the images you'll come across will be in compressed formats. These use some very clever, behind-the-scenes mathematics to considerably reduce the size of the file (in terms of bytes, not dimensions) while only marginally reducing the quality. That said, over-compressed images look terrible, so when saving one, you need to strike a balance between quality and file size. Compressed formats include:

▶ **JPEG (Joint Photographic Experts Group)** *File extension: .jpg*
The most common picture format of all, JPEG is the default file type for most digital cameras, and for photographs used on the Web. When you save a JPEG, you can choose from a sliding scale of compression.

▶ **GIF (Graphics Interchange Format)** *File extension: .gif*
Also widely used on webpages, the GIF is best-suited to images with large areas of flat colour (usually graphics rather than photographs). It also allows slide-show-style animations and transparent backgrounds – both widely used online.

▶ **PNG (Portable Network Graphics)** *File extension: .png*
PNG is a superior alternative to GIF, due to its fancy transparency abilities, and JPEG, though it's less widely used as less software supports it. Mac users are most likely to encounter PNGs when creating screenshots (see p.216).

You may also come across some non-compressed formats, especially if you get seriously into digital photography or image editing. The most common are:

A word about colour

Macs have long been favoured in the print and publishing industries, partly because of their excellent ability to manage colours. OS X features the most advanced colour-managment systems of any operating system, which means that, on a day-to-day basis, the colours your camera or scanner capture should be very close to the colours you see on screen and in turn the colours that are churned out by your printer.

A digital image can contain millions of colours, but each of those various hues and shades is made up of a mixture of three primary colours. In painting, that's red, yellow and blue, but on computer screens it's Red, Green and Blue (RGB) – the so-called "additive" primaries. If you want to know the exact RGB value of any colour on screen, perhaps to recreate a nice shade you've seen on a website, open the DigitalColor Meter from **Applications/Utilities** or play with the colour picking tool (the little magnifying glass) under the **Calculator** tab of ColorSync (also in **Applications/Utilities**).

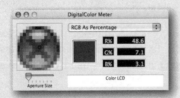

Occasionally, you might come across images saved in CMYK rather than RGB mode. CMYK images don't look any different, but they're processed differently by the computer. Here, each colour is defined as a combination of the so-called "subtractive" primaries: cyan, magenta and yellow (the opposites of RGB), with black (traditionally known as "key" in printing, hence the "K") added to provide extra clarity in darker colours. CMYK is used for professional printing, since cyan, magenta, yellow and black are the four inks used in a printing press.

Whichever colour mode is being used, OS X tries to ensure that all your devices and documents sing from the same songsheet: ie that they all have a common idea of the fundamental Red, Green and Blue ingredients. This is done using a system of so-called "colour profiles". It's too techie to go into in any depth here, but if you want to learn more, or if you have a colour-related problem in OS X, read:

ColorSync www.apple.com/macosx/features/colorsync

▶ **RAW (or Camera Raw)** *File extension: depends on camera*
Most digital cameras internally process their images into JPEGs to make them quicker to download and work with. This is convenient, but the resulting pictures are marginally less rich in terms of saturation, contrast, white balance and so on than the "raw" image data from the camera. So if you're serious about your photography, consider a camera that outputs RAW data instead of (or, ideally, as well as) JPEGs. Note, though, that different cameras have different RAW formats, so don't be surprised if iPhoto (see p.222) or any other image program fails to open them.

▶ **TIFF (Tagged Image File Format)** *File extension: .tif*
This flexible image format is most commonly used by publishing and graphics professionals, though many scanners and some cameras also generate TIFFs. It can be compressed, but very often it isn't.

There are numerous other image file formats, including BMPs, PICTs, TGAs, EPSs and more. Most are easily opened and resaved in an alternate format by OS X's **Preview** application…

Preview, convert & resize images

With the right tools, it's easy to change an image from one format to another, to add compression, and to change its size in pixels. This is extremely useful if you want to shrink the file size of an image in order to make it quicker to email or post on a website or blog (see p.167). It's also sometimes essential as not every program will recognize every file format, so you might need to convert the format simply to open a particular image in a particular application.

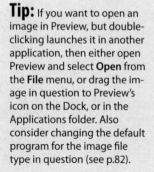

Tip: If you want to open an image in Preview, but double-clicking launches it in another application, then either open Preview and select **Open** from the **File** menu, or drag the image in question to Preview's icon on the Dock, or in the Applications folder. Also consider changing the default program for the image file type in question (see p.82).

Convert & compress

In OS X, double clicking most image formats will, by default, open them into the built-in Preview application, which is a handy tool for viewing and resaving images and PDF documents (see p.139). You can also open Preview from the Applications folder.

Though it doesn't give you as many compression and conversion options as a full-on image editor such as Photoshop (see p.229), Preview does let you resave most image formats via its **Export** option (which you'll find in the **File** menu). Clicking the **Options** button before saving will let you set compression and other preferences, depending on the format you've selected.

Resizing & batch processing

One thing Preview doesn't let you do easily is change the dimensions of an image: ie the number of pixels it consists of. Again, any serious image-editor (see p.229) will let you do this, but you can also resize an image using OS X Tiger's built-in Automator (see p.112). You'll find the "Scale Image" Action under Preview.

Using Automator to resize images is OK – especially if you want to process many images at once – but you might prefer to investigate some of the many free or inexpensive image processing tools and scripts that are available online. These are quicker and easier to use, and they also allow you to "crop" images – cut unwanted excess off the sides. For example, check out:

EasyBatchPhoto www.yellowmug.com/easybatchphoto ($25)
Graphic Converter www.graphicconverter.net ($30)
iZoom www.izoom.us (Free)

For more, browse: www.apple.com/downloads/macosx/imaging_3d

Preview tips

▶ **Opening images en masse**
If you want to open lots of images in one single Preview window, simply select the files and drag them to the Preview icon. The "Drawer" will appear, which provides an easy way to switch between the images; to toggle the draw in and out of view, use ⌘⇧D.

▶ **Opening a folder of images**
To open a whole folder of images into Finder, hold down ⌘⌥ and drag the folder's icon to the Preview icon.

▶ **Opening images from Preview**
The thumbnails displayed in the "Drawer" are live icons, meaning you can drag an individual image directly from there into a folder (to copy it) or onto the icon of another application (to open it into that application).

▶ See p.139 for more on PDFs and Preview.

Tip: Another way to batch convert images is using Folder Actions (see p.114).

iPhoto

iPhoto is Apple's flagship photo management application. It's a tool for importing pics from digital cameras and elsewhere, keeping them organized, removing red-eye and making other tweaks, and sending them on to friends, printers or print shops. You may have got a similar package on CD with your digital camera, though unless you believe that it's particularly good, you're far better off with iPhoto, perhaps supplemented by a more powerful image editor and some choice plug-ins.

If your Mac shipped with OS X Tiger, you should already have iPhoto 5, the most up-to-date version at the time of writing. You'll find it in the **Applications** folder or perhaps already on your Dock.

If you have an earlier edition of OS X or you purchased Tiger as an upgrade, you probably have an older version of iPhoto, since the new one is only available as part of the iLife suite, which ships with new Macs but otherwise has to be paid for ($79/£49). Earlier versions are OK, though the upgrade is worth considering, since iPhoto 5 boasts a number of new features, including support for RAW images (see p.220) and video clips. If you stick with the earlier version, you'll find some of the features described here are missing.

Import pics into iPhoto

From a camera...

The first time you connect a digital camera to your Mac, a dialog box should appear asking if you want to use iPhoto as the program for importing and organizing pics from that camera. If you say yes, from that point on, connecting the camera will cause iPhoto to launch automatically so that you can import your pics.

Importing with iPhoto is easy, but there is one annoyance: you can only import the entire contents of the camera, rather than browsing through your new photos before importing and deleting the duds. This isn't a serious problem, as you can always delete pics from iPhoto once they're imported (see p.227). But if you use a camera with a large memory, and you want a quick way to browse through hundreds of new photos to pick the few that you want to keep, iPhoto isn't the most efficient option.

At some stage iPhoto will doubtless be improved to get around this limitation, but in the meantime you may want to try a different program for separating the wheat from the chaff. You can continue to use iPhoto for managing the pics that are up to scratch. The obvious choice is PhotoReviewer, a neat $10 utility available from:

PhotoReviewer www.sticksoftware.com/software.html

...from elsewhere

You can also get images into iPhoto from other locations on your Mac or network. Simply drag them into the iPhoto window. Alternatively, choose **Add to Library...** from the **File** menu, or use the shortcut ⌘O, and browse for the files you want.

Tip: Most digital cameras need to be set to "Play" mode to be recognized by the Mac. If yours still isn't recognized, you may need to install the software that came with the camera. Or the camera may simply be incompatible with OS X, in which case investigate the possibility of getting a media card reader to download the pics from the memory card rather than the camera.

Tip: Check that the time and date on your digital camera are right, as this information is imported into iPhoto along with the images and becomes a useful means of searching for shots using the iPhoto Calendar.

Tip: Importing an image into iPhoto from anywhere creates a copy of the file in your iPhoto Library folder. So if space is at a premium on either your hard drive or camera, delete the original after you import.

Organizing photos

iPhoto works with pictures in just the same way as iTunes works with music tracks. Everything you import is added to your "Library", which is easily accessible at the top of the so-called Source List on the left. It's perfectly possible to browse through your entire picture collection in the Library, but most users prefer to organize their photos into albums and folders…

Albums & folders

Each image in iPhoto can be added to one or more albums, which are arranged down the left in the Source List – just like Playlists in iTunes. To create a new album, press the "+" button at the bottom-left of the window, or use the keyboard shortcut ⌘N. Then you can simply select one or more images in your Library and drag them into the album.

If you want to combine a number of related albums, create a folder to drop them into. This is easily done using the **New Folder** option in the File menu. Folders can also hold Smart Albums (see p.226) and Slideshows (see p.230).

Rolls

Even if you don't organize your pics into albums and folders, they're already organized into virtual rolls. Each time you add pics to your Library, those pics are grouped together as a roll. To browse by roll, click on Photo Library and choose **Rolls** from the **View** menu.

Tip: To select multiple images, hold down ⌘ while you click. Or, to highlight a range of adjacent images, select the first and last while holding ⇧. You can also click on one image, hold down ⇧ and use the **arrow** keys to quickly select the adjacent pics.

Tip: Remember that images in albums and Smart Albums are just aliases of the image in the Library, so a single image can be placed in multiple albums – and removing an image from an Album will not delete the original from the iPhoto Library.

Tip: If you have an iPod that can handle photos, limit the size of albums you create in iPhoto to 200 pictures or less to ensure smooth Slideshow playback from your Pod to a connected TV.

Add info & Keywords

It's worth taking a little time to "tag" images with comments, titles, ratings and Keywords. This makes it easier to search for images – either within iPhoto or via Spotlight – and also to stay organized using Smart Albums (more on these later). You can change and add comments, titles and Keywords at any time, but it's much easier to get into the habit of tagging new images as you add them.

To add or change titles and comments, click on the Info button ("i") at the bottom of the iPhoto window. Or, if you want to add the same information to more than one image, select the photos in question and call up the **Batch Change...** function from the **Photo** menu. Alternatively, hit the shortcut ⌘⇧B.

Using Keywords

Keywords provide an easy way to keep your photos arranged in categories. To define your own Keywords, open **Preferences**, from the **iPhoto** menu, and look in the **Keywords** panel.

Once you've set up the keywords you want, they can be added to images by simply dragging the selected images onto any of the labels in the **Keywords pane** – accessible via the "key" button at the bottom of the iPhoto window. Then, clicking on Keywords in the pane will reveal all the relevant images.

To remove all keywords from an image, drag it onto the **Reset** button. You can also apply and delete Keywords within an image's Info panel, called up by ⌘I.

If you use Keywords a lot, you might want to try viewing them under the images when browsing through your Library. You'll find an option for this in the **View** menu.

Smart Albums

A Smart Album is a special kind of iPhoto album that uses a set of parameters, determined by you, to decide which images it is to include. It's exactly the same principle as Smart Playlists in iTunes (see p.195), and just as much fun. However, Smart Albums only work well if the images in your Library are liberally tagged with comments, titles, ratings and Keywords.

To create a new Smart Album look in the **File** menu, or hold down ⌥ (**Alt**) and click the "cog" button that appears in the bottom-left. Experiment with the various options, pressing the "+" and "–" buttons to add or remove extra criteria. Once you're done, press **OK**. If you don't like the results, select the relevant icon in the Source List and click **Edit Smart Album** in the **File** menu.

Rotating images

Like babies, digital photographs don't always arrive the right way round, so it's worth taking a few minutes to make sure that each newly imported pic is orientated correctly. To do this, make selections in the main window and then hit the **Rotate** button at the bottom of the iPhoto frame; holding ⌥ as you click changes the direction of rotation. Rotations can also be handled from the keyboard:

▶ To rotate clockwise use ⌘R

▶ To rotate anti-clockwise use ⌘⌥R

Deleting images

Deleting images is simple: select one or more pics and then either hit the **Backspace** key on your keyboard; choose **Move to Trash** from the **Photo** menu; or simply drag them onto the Trash icon at the bottom of the Source List.

Note, however, that deleting an image from a playlist or slideshow won't actually remove the offending photo from your Library. To do this, first click **iPhoto Library**, and then delete the image, as described above.

Deleted images go to the iPhoto Trash, where they'll remain until you either drag them out or choose **Empty Trash** from the **iPhoto** menu (also achieved with the shortcut ⌘⇧⌫).

Editing photos

In the bad old days, photos came back from the lab as glossy testimony to our amateur photographer status. Though iPhoto isn't going to turn you into a world-class snapper, it does give you a second chance at getting things right, whether that means adjusting the frame of your shot, improving the colours and light or removing the scourge of red-eye. To start editing, select an image with a single click and hit the **Edit** button at the bottom of the window.

Tip: A quick way to rate images it to select one (or more) and then hit ⌘0 through to ⌘5.

Tip: You can also add Keywords to images using the Preview application. Choose **Get Info** from the **Tools** menu and make additions under the **Keywords** tab.

Tip: Deleted something by mistake? You can always undo your last action with the shortcut ⌘Z. Deleted it from your camera? Try the data recovery software listed on p.280.

Tip: In iPhoto **Preferences**, under **General**, you can choose to have an image open into a separate editing window when it is double-clicked. Here you could also choose to have the image open into another application for editing (see box overleaf).

iPhoto's editing tools are pretty straightforward, so they shouldn't take too long to get used to. And, in the event that everything goes pear-shaped, you can always choose **Revert to Original** from the **Photo** menu. Here are a few pointers to get you going:

▶ **Constrain** If you choose the **Custom** option, don't be scared off by the dialog box that asks for exact dimensions – just hit **OK** without entering any values and then drag out the shape you want by eye.

▶ **Enhance** This is little more than a heavy-handed preset; you'll get a much better understanding of how it all works if you mess about with the various settings revealed by **Adjust** (see below).

▶ **Red-Eye** This is that rare thing: a tool that does exactly what you want it to, nearly all the time. Simply click the button and then click on the affected eye to remove the red.

▶ **Retouch** Designed to remove blemishes from faces, clothes or elsewhere, the **Retouch** tool can be useful, but employ it sparingly, as the results are rarely perfect. And, when using it, always zoom right in to the image so you can see exactly what you're doing.

▶ **Adjust** Experiment with the Adjust palette settings, and also the order in which you make adjustments. For example, the **Sharpness** tool produces its best results when used last.

Image-editing software

iPhoto is essentially a photo management application. And though it offers a decent suite of tools for tweaking digital photos, they barely scratch the surface of what's possible with dedicated image-editing packages. These allow you to do everything from completely reworking colour and brightness levels, or filtering something flat to make it look three-dimensional, to merging images together to create an apparently realistic snap of some real-world impossibility (if you want a shot of yourself taking a keyboard lesson with J.S. Bach, say, this is the route you would need to take).

The professional's image editor of choice is Adobe Photoshop, which is fantastic, but has a price-tag that reflects its quality. Download the trial version from:

Photoshop www.adobe.com

The best of the free options is the open-source powerhouse known as GIMP. It's superb, though installing it can be a bit challenging as it only runs on OS X using the so-called X11 system. Read more at:

GIMP www.gimp.org/macintosh • www.macgimp.org

For help using these serious image editors, scour their respective websites, or try:

CreativeMac.com www.creativemac.com
Gimp Guru www.gimpguru.org

Or to find and download some smaller-scale freeware or shareware image editors, browse the "Imaging" section of:

OS X Software www.apple.com/downloads/macosx

Slideshows

Slideshows are a good way to view a set of images full-screen – either for a set number of seconds per pic, or forwarded at your leisure using the arrow buttons or mouse. They're also an entertaining way to show off a set of pics to family and friends, though bear in mind that not everyone will share your love of unusual Tuscan farming implements, or be delighted by dozens of near-identical shots of your sleeping toddler. So keep 'em brief.

Who's Ken Burns?

When setting up a slideshow, you might come across the Ken Burns effect. Born in 1953, Burns is the documentary filmmaker responsible for series such as *The Civil War* (1990) and *Jazz* (2001). One of Burns's favourite effects is to use still pictures, slowly zooming in on and panning them. This technique is now known as the Ken Burns Effect, and it shows up not just in many documentaries, but also in various image and video editing programs.

To create slideshows, click on an Album, or select a number of images in the main iPhoto panel, and then click the **Slideshow** button. Hit **Settings** and play around with the various options – these apply to the whole slideshow, though you can also change the transitions and effects for individual photos using the controls at the bottom.

Once played, the slideshow will appear in the Source List so that you can replay it and edit it as many times as you like.

When you are done with the main ▶ *settings, use the Music button to choose some accompanying tracks from your iTunes Library – worth doing (if you want music at all) as iPhoto's sample choices are likely to have you chewing your own leg off after the first couple of listens.*

Release your photos

Having a Library of edited, organized images is all very well, but before long you'll be itching to get your images out of iPhoto and into the wider world – on paper or online. Here's a brief run-down of your options…

▶ Print iPhoto provides a good set of printing options and presets for turning your snaps into greeting cards, cramming multiple images onto a single sheet, and so on. Select one or more images, hit **Print** in either the **File** or **Share** menus or toolbar (or press ⌘P) and explore the options listed under **Style**. Alternatively, if your printer's not up to the job, order a hard copy via the Web (see box overleaf).

▶ Email This toolbar option (also found in the **Share** menu) slots selected images into the body of an email ready for you to address and send. If you (or the recipient) have a slow Internet connection, select the smaller image size options. Another way to email one or more images is as a PDF document – press **Print**, and then choose **Mail PDF** from the **PDF** button at the bottom of the Print dialog box.

▶ Burn a CD This is useful for taking pics to be developed at a store or for sending snaps by snail mail. You could choose **Burn Disc** from iPhoto's **Share** menu but this will generate a CD with an array of folders, pic files and thumbnails guaranteed to confuse print shops and relatives alike. A better solution is to select the pics or albums you want to burn, drag them to an empty folder on your desktop, and burn the CD with Finder (see p.45).

The iDVD export option makes it easy to create DVD menu screens, but they're not very pretty in their raw state.

Tip: Before sending images to iDVD, crop them to a 4x3 aspect ratio (TV resolution) using the Constrain/Crop tool (see p.228). Many basic digital cameras use 4x3 anyway, but if you have a digital SLR you may well find that your snaps have a different aspect ratio.

▶ **As a movie** Click **Export** in the **File** menu, and you can save selected images or albums as a QuickTime movie (see p.256) – just like a Slideshow, complete with music and transitions. If your Mac has a SuperDrive, you could also send slideshows straight to DVD, complete with menu screen and effects, using the iDVD option. For more on iDVD, see p.241.

▶ **File Export** You can drag images out of iPhoto onto the desktop or any Finder window to export a copy, but for more options choose **Export** from the **File** menu (or use ⌘⇧E) and browse for a destination to save the new file to. This can be done for single and multiple files.

▶ **Sharing over a network** Just as you can share music across networks in iTunes, iPhoto lets you share your Library with other iPhoto users on a network; wirelessly or otherwise (see p.63). To enable this option, open **Preferences** from the **iPhoto** menu, and then check the **Look for Shared Photos** and **Share my Photos** options. If any other iPhoto users are on the same network, their Library will pop up on your Source List.

▶ **Desktop background** To set any Library image as your OS X desktop "wallpaper", select its thumbnail and hit the **Desktop** button on the toolbar. If you don't like the way your Mac crops the image, use the Constrain/Crop tool (see p.228), selecting the **Display** option from the dropdown menu, to crop and recentre the shot, and then try again.

Ordering prints, books & more

If your own printer isn't good at reproducing photos, you might consider getting someone else to commit them to paper. The obvious choice would be to use the service built into iPhoto, which Apple runs in conjunction with Kodak. Simply select some pics and hit the **Order Prints** button to kickstart the process. Note, though, that you may get a better price by either taking your images (on CD) to a "real" store, or by shopping around for alternative online services such as the following, both of which have international branches:

Bonusprint www.bonusprint.com
Winkflash www.winkflash.com

For something really fancy, and if you don't mind walking that line between stylish printing and full-on self-aggrandizement, you could have your pics turned into a bound hardback book. Use the iPhoto **Book** tool to lay out your images, add comments and so on, plug in your credit card details, and your personalized coffee-table tome will arrive within a week or so. Prices start at around £7/$10 and go up from there, depending on the number of pages and the type of binding.

Tip: From the **Share** menu you can choose which common export tasks appear in the toolbar below the main iPhoto frame.

Tip: As well as printing to paper, you can "print" to a PDF document. After you've pressed **Print**, explore the various options in the PDF menu.

Sharing your photos online

If you want to put your pictures on the Web, where everyone can see them, you have a few options:

▶ **Your own site** If you already have your own website, you could either manually create a page with your pictures on (see p.167) or select an album or group of images in iPhoto, click **Export** in the **File** menu (or hit ⌘⇧E) and choose the **Web page** tab.

▶ **HomePage** If you have a **.Mac** account (see p.32), you might be tempted by iPhoto's **HomePage** integration. Choose an album, press the HomePage button and the rest pretty-well happens automatically. The results can look a little cheesy, but it's certainly quick and easy.

▶ **A photoblog** If you fancy trying your hand at blogging (see p.170), the Flickr and Photon iPhoto plug-ins makes it easy to upload fresh images each day.

Flickr www.flickr.com
Photon www.daikini.com

▶ **Online Gallery** There are also many services that, for a small fee, will provide you with a ready-made photo gallery online. For example:

Fotki www.fotki.com
Phanfare www.phanfare.com

Again, there are alternatives to iPhoto's built-in service. The following let you upload your pics to be planted not only in books, but on everything from T-shirts and mouse mats to cushions and keyrings.

CafePress www.cafepress.com/cp/customize (US)
PhotoWorks www.photoworks.com (US)
PixDiscount www.pixdiscount.co.uk (UK)
PhotoBox www.photobox.co.uk (UK)

More tips

A few final hints for getting the best out of iPhoto:

▶ Learn from your mistakes Select an image thumbnail in iPhoto and hit ⌘I. The Info panel that pops up offers loads of information about not only the file, but also the camera settings when the shot was taken – very handy when trying to work out how to avoid problems with exposure, focus and so on.

▶ Search everywhere The iPhoto search window (bottom right) only searches the contents of the main iPhoto frame, so make sure **Library** is selected in the Source List before you start typing search terms.

▶ iPhoto Preferences Can be accessed via the **iPhoto** menu (and also with the keyboard shortcut ⌘,).

Video

DVDs & TV

31

All recently bought Macs have the capability to play back DVDs and, with the right software, it's also possible to "rip" the contents of a DVD onto your hard drive. If your Mac features a SuperDrive (see p.29), you'll also be able to burn DVDs – either to backup data files (see p.269) or create your own movie discs that can be played back on any DVD player. Less well known is the fact that, with the right hardware, it's possible to use your Mac as a TV. This chapter reveals all.

Watching DVDs

Bundled within OS X is a little application called DVD Player – slot a disc into your machine and the program will automatically launch. It's very easy to use and will either fill your screen instantly or present the DVD's menu screen in a smaller window. Explore the controls on the floating panel and you'll find buttons for slow motion, subtitles and special DVD features such as alternate viewing-angles. Here are a few more features and shortcuts worth mentioning before we move on:

▶ Open the **Audio Equalizer** and **Video Color** panels from the **Window** menu to make fine adjustments to sound

> **Tip:** To create a catalogue of your DVD collection on your Mac, use the DVD Database X program, downloadable from www.valencio.com

> **Tip:** If DVD Player doesn't open (or you want to use an alternate player as your default) alter the setting in the **CDs & DVDs** panel of OS X **System Preferences**.

and picture quality, respectively. Only one can be open at a time, the other then being available from the dropdown menu at the top of the panel.

▶ The same dropdown also offers the **Video Zoom** control, which lets you magnify and reframe the action in the viewer window. This option is also accessed from the **Window** menu.

▶ By selecting either **Bookmarks** or **Video Clips** from the **Window** menu you can open a panel that stores shortcuts to your favourite moments

DVD Player shortcuts

Play or pause	**Space bar**
Stop	⌘.
Skip to next chapter	→
Skip to previous chapter	←
Scan forward	⌘→
Scan backward	⌘←
Go to beginning of disc	⌘⇧D
Go to menu screen	⌘`
Turn closed captioning on or off	⌘⌥T
Add bookmark	⌘=
Volume up or down	⌘↑ or ⌘↓
Mute on or off	⌘⌥↓
Show or hide the Controller	**Escape**
Show or hide the Navigator	**⌥Escape**
Toggle full-screen mode on and off	**⌘0**
Switch to Finder	**⌘⌥F**

(Bookmarks) and segments (Video Clips) on a DVD, making them easy to find next time you play the DVD.

▶ Also within the **Window** menu can be found the **Navigator**, which offers information about the currently playing disc or clip.

Title: 1	Audio: English 1	Bookmark: *None*
Chapter: 5	Subtitle: Off	Video Clip:
Title Elapsed: 00:37:48	Angle: 1	Volume:

The "region" issue

Most purchased DVDs contain a region code (indicated by a number on the back of the packaging), which in theory determines where in the world the disc is to be distributed and viewed. In turn, most DVD players and drives contain a piece of software that locks them to the specific region of their owner (though "Region 0" players that can play any DVD are available, as are "Region 0" DVDs that should play in any machine).

In the case of the DVD drive in your Mac, you are given five opportunities to change the region setting before it becomes hardwired. If you only ever watch movies from your own region (in the US and Canada it's Region 1, and in Western Europe it's Region 2) then you don't have a problem – you will never see any dialog boxes asking you to choose. But if you are one of the growing number of film-lovers who buy obscure titles from around the globe, you certainly don't want to find yourself locked into playback of a single region code.

One way around this problem is to try using the free VLC Media Player (see overleaf), which you may find allows you to completely bypass the regions issue. Alternatively you could try an application such as Region X, which lets you reset your region code as many times as you like (assuming your drive is not locked already). But be aware that this kind of tinkering could void your Mac's warranty.

Region X xvi.rpc1.org/region

Still no joy? Try ripping the DVDs with Mac The Ripper (overleaf) and burning the files to a blank DVD using Roxio's Popcorn (see p.243).

Watching downloaded video

If you downloaded a movie file from the Internet, you may need a special application to play it back – even if it seems to be a "regular" file type such as AVI or MPEG. The reason is that both these formats can hold video encoded in various different ways (using different *codecs*).

The extra video players you're most likely to need are:

DivX
www.divx.com/divx/mac
Windows Media Player
www.windowsmedia.com

There are also now video equivalents of MP3 CD players – DVD players that can read DivX and the like. See:

Kiss-Technology
www.kiss-technology.com

VLC

XinePlayer

Other players

Apple's DVD Player is not the only player available for use in OS X. Of the alternatives, VLC Media Player is the best, largely because of its ability to handle DVDs with any region code. XinePlayer is also worth a try, though you might not notice that much difference between it and Apple's DVD Player.

VLC www.videolan.org/vlc
XinePlayer xineplayer.berlios.de

Ripping DVDs

In most countries, assuming you own the original discs, it's legal to "rip" movies from DVD to your hard drive, just as you would rip a CD's contents into iTunes. This is most easily done using a program such as the free Mac The Ripper. If you have the hard disk space available, this is a good way to back up your DVDs, or to get around the problem of region codes (see p.247).

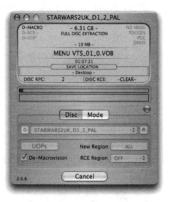

Tip: If you just want to "rip" individual still images from a DVD, the easiest option is to view the movie full screen and take a screen grab (see p.216). However, you'll find that OS X's screen-grab features are unavailable when OS X's DVD Player is running, so you'll need to either use VLC Player or use the screen-grab widget (see p.216).

The ripped files can be played back using OS X's DVD Player (clicking **VIDEO_TS Folder...** in the **File** menu) or an alternative such as the VLC Media Player. Mac The Ripper can also save your ripped footage into formats that can be imported into video editing programs such as iMovie, or be burned to DVD.

Mac The Ripper www.ripdifferent.com/~mtr

Creating your own DVDs

With a SuperDrive (see p.29), you can burn any type of files onto a recordable DVD either by using Burn Folders (see p.81) or by inserting a blank disc, dragging files onto it's icon and clicking **Burn Disc...** in the Finder **File** menu. But if you want to burn movie, music or photo DVDs for playback in standard household DVD players, you'll need to use a special application such as iDVD.

iDVD

If you have a Mac with a SuperDrive, you probably already have iDVD, Apple's own DVD authoring program (if it's not in the Dock, look in your **Applications** folder). For the home user, iDVD is an excellent program – especially the recent versions.

iDVD makes the whole process of creating a DVD – complete with fancy menu screens – extremely easy. Follow these steps:

▶ **Pick a theme** First, click **Customize** and pick from a selection of bundled "themes" for your menus. Some themes are picture plus text, others feature picture slideshows or audio tracks, and others still let you display pockets of active video. Some of the themes are a bit tasteless, but they can be reworked by clicking the **Settings** button. Once that's done, save your customization for later using the button at the bottom.

▶ **Add some content** First, click on the default header text and type a name for your menu. Then click the **Media** button to pull in audio and pics from your iTunes and iPhoto Libraries, and videos from the top level (ie not in subfolders) of your Movies folder. If you can't find what you want here, either drag content in from Finder, or use **Import...** in the **File** menu.

Tip: If you don't have a SuperDrive, but you know someone who does, you could create DVD projects on your own Mac using iDVD, save them as a disk image file when you're done, and move that file (see p.261) to your friend's Mac later for burning to DVD.

Tip: You can also buy more themes in the form of the third-party DVDPak (available from www.dvdthemepak.com) but expect "fun" not style.

Tip: If you're feeling really lazy, use the **OneStep DVD...** feature, found in the **File** menu: just plug in your camcorder, and iDVD captures all the footage, arranges the clips, and a few minutes later spits out a DVD.

▶ **Add extra menus** You can only have six items on your main menu. If you want more items than this, you'll have to create submenus. To do this, add "folders" to your main menu. Each folder, when clicked, will lead to another customizable menu, complete with a back arrow for returning to the main menu screen.

▶ **Map things out** Once all your menus and media are in place, click the **Map** button to see a tree diagram of the whole disc, and delete any unwanted bits (select the media in question and hit **Backspace**).

▶ **Add some files** You can add regular files to your DVD, which will be accessible if someone puts the disc in a computer. Choose **Edit DVD-ROM Contents...** from the **Advanced** menu, and drag the files you want to include into the panel from a Finder window.

▶ **Get burning...** Hit the **Burn** button and insert a blank disc when instructed. Or, to burn it later, or on another machine, choose **Save As Disc Image...** in the **File** menu. The result will be a file structured exactly like a DVD disc (it will even play back in your DVD Player application when **Double-Clicked**). This file can be burned to disc using use OS X's **Disk Utility** program, found in **Applications** under **Utilities**.

▶ **Save** Save your project so you can open and edit it later.

For much more information about iDVD, including in-depth technical information, see:

The Unofficial iDVD FAQ dvd.kentidwell.com

Tip: Only insert your blank disc when iDVD is ready for it. *Don't* insert it before running iDVD and give it a name in Finder.

Tip: If you burn to rewritable DVDs, they need to be blanked before each new use. This can be done using OS X's Disk Utility (in **Applications/ Utilities**) or with a program such as DiscBlaze, available from www.radicalbreeze.com

DVD Studio Pro

iDVD is great at doing what it does, but if you have real Hollywood ambitions, you might want to investigate something more powerful. The obvious choice for Mac users is DVD Studio Pro, part of Apple's Final Cut family (see p.248). It features an almost bottomless barrel of professional encoding variables and handles all the latest high-definition formats. Unfortunately, it has a price tag to match. For more information, see www.apple.com/dvdstudiopro

Copying DVDs

Duplicating a copyrighted DVD may be illegal, depending which country you live in and what you intend to do with the copy. In general, it's fine to make a back up for your own use, but not to distribute it to anyone else. Obviously, there's no limitations on duplicating homemade DVDs.

The procedure for duplicating a DVD depends on whether or not the disc includes any copy-protection. If not, you can create a disk image of the DVD using OS X's Disk Utility and then burn that to DVD using Finder (see p.45). If there is copy protection of some sort, however, you'll need to employ some extra software, such as Mac the Ripper (see p.240).

Of the commercially available DVD copying programs, the best-known is Popcorn, which allows you to do clever things such as compress a double-layer DVD so that it fits on a standard DVD-R, and also remove unnecessary baggage such as additional language tracks. However, you may have to combine it with other programs to get around copy protection (see p.239).

Popcorn www.roxio.com/popcorn

DVD discs

▶ **DVD-R** and **DVD+R** are formats that can be burned only once; these are each compatible with about 90 percent of household DVD players, but not necessarily the same 90 percent.

▶ **DVD-RW** and **DVD+RW** are compatible with fewer DVD players (around 80 percent) but let you record and rerecord many times. To use one of these discs in iPhoto, blank it first using Disk Utility.

As if that wasn't confusing enough, all the above can come in both single- and double-sided formats (stick to single), while DVD-R and DVD+R also come in double-layer versions. These can store twice as much information.

iDVD 5 supports the double-layer version of DVD+R (known as DVD+R DL) but this won't work unless you have a recent high-end SuperDrive that also supports the format. If you're prepared to invalidate your Mac's warranty, a Google search will take you to pages that explain how to hack other SuperDrives to add DVD+R DL capability.

Browsing through channels using the EyeTV software. Naturally, it's also possible to view in full-screen mode (as shown below).

Mac as TV

The distinction between computers and televisions has been slowly eroding for some time, and doubtless within a decade or two they'll be no line at all between the two. Though relatively few people yet know about it, it's already possible to use your Mac as a fully functional TV. Doing so may not only save you money and space (why have two screens in your house when you only need one?), but will also give you a whole raft of features such as the ability to pause and rewind "live" TV and record shows directly to your hard drive. The picture tends to look a tiny bit "digital", but is much clearer than you get from most regular televisions.

To use your Mac as a television, you need a TV receiver that will connect to your computer via a FireWire or USB cable. A handful of companies produce Mac TV receivers, but few are as good as Elgato's "EyeTV" series, which includes models for analogue and digital television on both sides of the Atlantic. Some models – such as the EyeTV for DTT (pictured) – are not much bigger than a matchbox.

Setting up an EyeTV system takes seconds: simply connect the device to your television antenna cable and your Mac (no need for a separate power plug), and drag the software off the included CD. The EyeTV automatically finds, saves and names channels, and you can flick between stations either using the on-screen controller or the included remote control. Some models even feature their own mini-ariel for use in areas with good signal strength, making it totally mobile – great for iBook or PowerBook owners.

Prices start at around $250/£200. For more information, see:

Elgato www.elgato.com

Making movies

32

If you want to make your own movies, then the Mac is the computer for you: Apple have created some of the most intuitive and friendly video-related tools available. Even many film students and professionals at times turn to iMovie (see p.248) and iDVD (see p.241), both members of the iLife suite, for their combination of powerful features and an unfussy interface.

But the iLife software is not the only option available, so the following pages point you towards some of the alternatives as well as showing you how to get the most from the Apple tools that you may well already have at your disposal. But before you start worrying about editing your masterpiece, you first need some footage. This could come from several sources…

DV cameras

Most camcorders on the market today fall into the DV (digital video) category. Compared with earlier analogue models, these mark a huge improvement both in picture quality and the ease with which you can transfer the footage to a computer – something typically done using a FireWire cable and a video-editing application such as iMovie (see p.248). Despite the availability of cameras that can record straight to DVD or hard drives, most consumers and semi-professional cameras store their footage on MiniDV tape.

> **Tip:** You can get video footage into a video-editing program in two distinct ways: either by **importing** files that already exist on the machine (or a connected drive) or by **capturing** footage from a connected camera.

Buying a camcorder

If you want to buy a camcorder to make movies in Apple's iMovie application (see p.248), the best place to start is the **Apple Store** – even if you don't get as far as opening your wallet. You can guarantee all the models that Apple stock will seamlessly integrate with Mac software and hardware, so it's a good place to do some research.

Apple Store store.apple.com

When choosing a specific model, consider what you actually want the camcorder for: indoor or outdoor use (cheaper cameras tend to perform poorly in weaker light); general holiday fun or serious amateur filmmaking (for the latter, you'll need a decent optical zoom and a good-quality mic). There's also the question of whether you want to make use of iMovie's "HD" function (see p.248) by buying a widescreen camcorder.

Also consider connectivity. FireWire – also known as IEEE1394 or i-Link – is a must. And, if possible, get a model with DV-in as well as DV-out, so you have the option of recording your edited work back onto the camera (see p.256). A regular video-in is also handy for copying footage from older video formats to stick into the Mac from your MiniDV camera.

You'll also have to choose which media to use for recording. At the time of writing, MiniDV camcorders offer better value than newer alternatives such as those that record to DVD-R or have an internal hard drive. But each has its own advantages. Furthermore, things change, so read recent reviews – and certainly don't be convinced by some Muppet in a chain store who claims to know his or her stuff. Visit:

CamcorderInfo.com www.camcorderinfo.com
SimplyDV www.simplydv.co.uk

Once you've decided on a model, head for a price-comparison agent (see p.17) to track down the best deal. As for actually using your new toy, don't expect to become the next Stanley Kubrick overnight. For a few pointers on composing shots, lighting and other such issues, see:

Exposure www.exposure.co.uk

TV

With a TV receiver such as an Elgato EyeTV (see p.244) you can record TV directly onto your Mac, ready to export as QuickTime and open into iMovie.

Ripped DVDs

Another way to get video footage onto your Mac is to rip it from a DVD. With a program such as Mac the Ripper (see p.240) you can save your ripped footage into a format such as MPEG-4 that can then be imported straight into iMovie (see p.248).

Video grabs

A video grab is a moving-image verison of a regular screenshot (see p.216), recording whatever is happening on your screen to a video file. Using a video-grab application such as Snapz Pro X or Display Eater, you can grab any video playing on your screen – even if it's streaming from the Web.

Display Eater www.reversecode.com
Snapz Pro X www.ambrosiasw.com

Photographs

iMovie lets you transform still images into video clips (see p.251), but there are other applications that do a better job. CameraMover is a good example – you drag and zoom a frame across an image in real time and end up with either a high-quality video clip or a bunch of individual JPGs if you want to edit frame by frame.

CameraMover www.info-services.net/cameramover

Tip: Many video-editing applications won't accept an iSight webcam as an input source, as they only recognize DV as a capturable format. iMovie HD, however, will import footage from an iSight.

Tip: If you have a mobile phone that can record video clips, you may well be able to move the results onto your Mac via Bluetooth, just as you would images (see p.215), and then import them into your video-editing program.

Choosing your software

There are many video-editing programs on the market. Apple's own professional alternatives to iMovie come under the umbrella of Final Cut. Avid is another industry standard – there are several versions available, including a free one, which may well be the best place to start if you are intending to go pro. Another free alternative is the feature-heavy HyperEngine-AV.

Final Cut www.apple.com/finalcutstudio
Free DV www.avid.com/freedv
HyperEngine-AV www.arboretum.com

The fundamental layout and process in all these packages is the same – you capture footage, organize clips in a timeline, add effects and transitions, and then export your movie. iMovie also adheres to these protocols, so even if you intend to go with one of the alternatives, it's a good place to get your bearings. You probably already have iMovie on your Mac, so read the rest of this chapter and have a play.

Hardware

If you do get serious with DV editing there are also several application-specific keyboards on the market, with scrubbing wheels and colour-coded shortcut keys. To find out more visit Bella:

Bella www.bella-usa.com

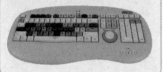

Tip: Video-editing programs such as iMovie and the others listed on this page are described as "non-linear editing systems" as they can access the footage on your hard drive in any order – as opposed to tape-based, linear editing system that emerged in the early days of video. Of course, old-style splicers-and-sticky-tape film editing is also non-linear.

Using iMovie

In a nutshell, iMovie (or iMovie HD, to give the current version its full title) is an application for importing and editing video footage. It allows you to capture raw footage from a digital video camera; import footage, audio and stills from pre-existing files; and to edit everything you have captured and imported into a professional looking film, complete with effects and transitions.

iMovie HD?

iMovie's HD tag refers to HDV (high definition video), the newest standard of digital video to have filtered through to the domestic camcorder market. HDV can be recorded onto the most common existing media – MiniDV cassettes.

As is so often the case with such technology, we are talking about bigger being better, and in this case widescreen. Cameras that support HDV can capture an image with an aspect ratio of 16:9 (compared with standard 4:3) and at a frame size of 1280 x 720 pixels.

This format looks set to become the norm over the coming years, especially considering the popularity of widescreen TVs.

As an interesting footnote to all this, the widescreen aspect ratio was originally developed in the movie industry in reaction to the popularity of television, which had pinched the 4:3 ratio from the traditional cinema "Academy format". To get bums on seats, the cinema movers and shakers reinvented the cinema experience to differentiate it from TV, and simultaneously to ensure that movies shot in 16:9 would have to be either cropped or "letterboxed" on a standard 4:3 TV.

Capturing footage from your camera

When you connect your camera to your Mac using a FireWire cable to capture footage from MiniDV tapes, make sure that, first,
your camera is in its "Player" mode (sometimes labelled "VTR"), and, second, that the mode switch in iMovie HD is in the capture position: move the slider from the scissors icon to the camera icon. With any luck you will have established communication with the camera, the iMovie HD preview screen will now be displaying the

Tip: If you don't get on with the video capture software built into iMovie or whichever video editing package you use, you might consider using the Pro version of Apple's QuickTime player as a video capture tool. It'll cost you a few bucks, but's easy to use. Download it from:
www.quicktime.com

making movies

Tip: If you have a DV camera and an iSight connected, **Control-click** the mode button to choose which device you wish to capture from.

Tip: With one of those brand spanking new cameras that capture video in the MPEG-4 format on an SD flash card, you can get the footage into iMovie by browsing from the **Import** command.

Tip: Make sure the time and date are set on your camera, as this can sometimes be the cause of camera-to-Mac communication problems.

Tip: Within the **Import** panel of iMovie Preferences (⌘,) you can specify whether you want newly captured clips to appear in the **Clips** pane or the timeline.

contents of the DV tape, and the on-screen controls can be used to play, pause, rewind and fast-forward the tape in the camera. If the connection doesn't work, it may be because your camera has gone to sleep; turn the camera off and then on again (this is known as "cycling the power") before toggling the iMovie mode switch (to scissors and then back to camera). Before you know it, you should have a bunch of clips in iMovie ready to go.

It's worth bearing in mind, however, that digital video is a disk-hungry beast and it will rapidly consume the free space on your hard drive. For this reason, it's worth:

▶ **Logging your MiniDV cassettes** Go through your footage before you start capturing and make a note on the time-codes where you want to start and stop capturing; this will save you both time and disk space.

▶ **Monitor your available space** While capturing footage keep half an eye on the indicator in the bottom-right corner of iMovie. If you do find yourself running low on space, empty both the iMovie Trash (using the command in the **File** menu) and the general Trash (see p.45).

Magic iMovie

If you're working to a deadline, trying to knock together something rough, or are just feeling lazy, the Magic iMovie feature is for you. You'll find it as a new project option and also on the splash screen when you open the application.

Basically, you just hook up your camera and iMovie captures all your footage, places each clip on the timeline, adds transitions and effects, and even chooses a soundtrack from iTunes before sending the whole thing to iDVD to be burned.

Of course, you don't have to use the feature in this way. You could just let Magic iMovie do all the preliminary work and then step in to fine-tune the transitions and adjust clips where necessary.

Importing footage from a file

As we've said, when editing using iMovie you're not limited to footage captured from a camcorder. From the **File** menu choose **Import** to browse for video, image or audio files. And by using the **Photos** and **Audio** buttons (to the right of the main window), you can access the contents of your iTunes and iPhoto Libraries.

Finally – if your Mac has an internal mic or a sound input port (see p.199) – you can use iMovie's **Audio** pane to record sound or speech directly into your movie.

Edits & effects

Once you've assembled all your footage, its time to arrange your clips in the timeline, adding audio, effects and transitions from their respective panes, as and when you need them. Switch

Tip: Use the **Spacebar** to stop and start video capture; also to play and stop when editing and previewing.

Tip: From the **Photos** pane you can add Ken Burns effects (see p.230) to a still image as you import it, thus creating a moving clip ready to drop into your movie.

Tip: You can also copy (⌘C) clips from a timeline in one project and then paste (⌘V) them into another project's timeline.

making movies

Tip: If you make a mistake in iMovie you can always undo it using the **Undo…** command in the **Edit** menu or the short-cut ⌘Z. And even if you made your mistake twenty clicks earlier, you can keep undoing as many times as necessary. Alternatively, choose **Revert to Saved** (again in the **File** menu) to discard all changes made since you last pressed save.

Tip: It's often helpful to pull a musical soundtrack in at the start, as the rhythms and shape of the sound will influence your edits almost as much as the video footage. Listen through the track and add Bookmarks (⌘B, or from the **Markers** menu) to use as guides as you edit.

Tip: Anything you cut or delete is sent to the iMovie Trash and is easily retrieved – double-click the trash icon and then drag whatever you need straight back into the timeline.

the mode slider to its "scissors" position and start experimenting. That's really the best way to learn. Here are a few pointers to get you going:

▶ You can drag clips from one position to another in the timeline, but they need to be dragged upwards slightly before they will go either left or right.

▶ To shorten the length of a clip, hold your mouse pointer over its end and drag in the direction of the little arrow.

▶ When editing, get used to **Control-Clicking** the clips to reveal their context menus. This offers the quickest route to many useful functions. The timeline's triangular "playhead" also yields a context menu, its most useful feature being the **Split…** command, which splices the clip into two.

▶ Set Chapter Markers from the **Markers** menu (or hit ⌘⌥M) as you edit – these are then translated into scenes on the DVD menu screen if you burn the movie to a disc in iDVD.

▶ To make adjustments and fades to audio levels, choose **Show Clip Volume Levels** from a clip's context menu. The volume level then appears on the clip – you can then drag it up and down and add anchor points for more precise adjustments.

iMovie shortcuts

As well as all the standard shortcuts (see inside cover), iMovie features loads of hotkeys that should drastically speed up your editing and generally turn you into a cutting-room guru:

Undo	⌘Z
Redo	⌘⇧Z
Scroll to playhead	⌘⌥P
Scroll to Selection	⌘⌥S
Zoom to Selection	⌘⌥Z
Switch viewer mode	⌘E
Show volume levels	⌘⇧L
Show audio waveforms	⌘⇧W
Move playhead to end of movie	End
Move playhead forward one frame	→
Move playhead forward ten frames	⇧→
Move playhead back one frame	←
Move playhead back ten frames	⇧←
Move playhead at speed	Hold down ← or →
Move clip to create black frames	^← or ^→
Cancel rendering	⌘.
Split clip at playhead	⌘T
Add Bookmark	⌘B
Delete Bookmark	⌘⇧B
Move to previous Bookmark	⌘[
Move to next Bookmark	⌘]
Extract audio	⌘J
Paste over at playhead	⌘⇧V
Save frame as JPG or PICT	⌘F
Lock audio clip at playhead	⌘L
Share movie	⌘⇧E

Tip: By selecting more than one clip at a time (hold ⌘ as you highlight them) you can add effects and transitions to many clips in one go.

Tip: For complicated visual effects, try adding multiple effects to a single clip.

Tip: At any time you can create a still frame from the current location of the time-line playhead by choosing **Create Still Frame** from the **Edit** menu, or hitting ⌘⇧S. The newly created image is dropped into the clip pane.

Tip: The timeline viewer gives you loads of control of individual clips, but you can also edit using the slightly less busy clip viewer. Use the two buttons just above the viewer to select these view modes, or toggle by pressing: ⌘E.

▶ Use the **Preview** buttons to check that transitions and effects are doing what you want them to – when you are happy, hit **Apply**.

▶ To add special audio effects choose **iMovie Sound Effects** from the dropdown at the top of the Audio pane, preview the ones you fancy and then either drag them straight onto the timeline or click the **Place at Playhead** button.

▶ To separate the audio from a video clip, select the clip and choose **Extract Audio** from the **Advanced** menu (or hit ⌘J).

▶ If you'd like to add titles and credits to your movie, hit the **Titles** button and play with the options.

More effects

There are hundreds of third-party iMovie plug-ins and standalone applications available online – for everything from cleaning grainy footage (Discreet's Cleaner) to removing unwanted wobble (iStabilize). Some cost a few dollars or pounds (depending on where the developer is based), but others are free. Start here:

PluginsWorld imovie.pluginsworld.com
Stupendous Software www.stupendous-software.com
OS X Video Software www.apple.com/downloads/macosx/video

Many plug-ins are installed by a downloaded installer (see p.99), while a few may need to be dragged to the **iMovie/Plug-ins** folder, found within the **Library** folder in your home folder.

There are even more plug-ins available for some of the other video-editing packages, one of our favourites being the Russian Lomo Kompakt Automat for Final Cut Pro, which allows you to achieve that retro Soviet look in order to "exceed the limits of that which was formerly known as maximum hipness":

RussianKamera
riverrockstudios.com/riverrock/pages/russianKamera.html

Find an audience

There are various options for getting your new flick out of iMovie and into the wider world, many of which are to be found via the **Share...** command of the **File** menu. From here you can export to:

▶ **Email** Click here to whisk your movie into a blank email as a compressed QuickTime file, ready to send. Note that, despite the compression, the file may still be 10MB or so, which may crash some email accounts – and is guaranteed to annoy recipients with slow dial-up connections. So try to use this function only for sending short movies to friends and family with broadband connections. Conversely, if you want to email a very short clip at a higher quality, export the movie via the QuickTime pane (see overleaf) and then attach it to an email yourself (see p.156).

▶ **HomePage** If you're signed up with .Mac (see p.32), click here to export your movie directly onto your Apple-created webpage. If you don't have .Mac, you could always publish the movie to a self-built website (see p.167) if you export it through the QuickTime pane (see overleaf) using either the **Web** or **Web Streaming** presets.

Tip: If you only want to export certain parts of your movie, select the clips in the timeline viewer, choose **Share...** from the **File** menu, and make sure the box at the bottom of the dialog box is checked.

Tip: To export any frame as an image file (JPEG or PICT), position the triangular "playhead" on the frame and choose **Save Frame...** from the **File** menu (the shortcut is ⌘F).

Tip: If you only want friends to see your HomePage movies, you can protect the page with a password.

making movies

Tip: Check how much available space you have on your iDisk before sharing your movies via your .Mac HomePage – and remember that nobody is going to bother viewing anything online if it takes more than a couple of minutes to stream – so keep 'em short.

Tip: As well as burning a playable DVD of your movie through the **Share...** option, you can simply burn a dupli-cate of the project file to a CD or DVD by choosing **Burn Project to Disc...** from the **File** menu.

▶ **Videocamera** If you have a camcorder with DV-in (analogue-in won't work), you could use this pane to export your edited film back to the camera – useful if you're out of blank DVDs and need the space on your hard drive, if you don't have a SuperDrive, or if you want to play the movie on a TV without a DVD player. Be sure that your camera is in "player" mode (sometimes labelled VTR) and a tape is inserted.

▶ **iDVD** If you want to transform your edited footage into a proper DVD, complete with menus and extra, click here to prepare the hard copy using Apple's iDVD program. For more on using iDVD, see p.241.

▶ **QuickTime** Of all the options, this one gives you the most flexibility, especially if you choose **Expert Settings** from the dropdown menu (see box). Even if you don't go for the advanced stuff, you at least get to choose a level of compression and where the file is to be saved.

▶ **Bluetooth** OK, the quality won't be great, but being able to send your movie to your mobile is great fun. You'll first need to "pair" your Mac and your phone – see p.62.

Advanced exports

If you have specific video-export needs, know what you are doing with video file formats, and understand PAL and NTSC modes, choose **Expert Settings** from the dropdown menu in the QuickTime pane of the iMovie **Share...** dialog box. Here you'll find all kinds of options, including loads of file formats to export your creations into – either the whole package (AVI, MPEG-4, etc) or perhaps just the audio (AIFF or WAV).

Security & maintenance

Privacy & passwords

33

From emails and Web histories to saved passwords and work documents, computers store all sorts of data about their owners and the people they know. Choosing a Mac, as opposed to a PC, makes you significantly less vulnerable to Internet-based privacy invasions (for more on online security, see p.264). But anyone with a little bit of know-how and physical access to your computer – a thief, an unpleasant flatmate, or whoever – could probably access all your data. The following pages explain what you can do about it, and also takes a look at Keychains, which OS X uses to store all your passwords.

First, the obvious stuff. If you're worried by the prospect of someone else being able to access your data, make sure you have a password set up for your account (see p.51), and make sure you've turned off **Automatic Login** so that no one can access your account just by switching on the Mac. To do this, open **Accounts** from **System Preferences** and click **Login Options**. You may first have to click the lock icon at the bottom.

Next, get your Mac to request your password when it is awoken from sleep (standby) or from a screensaver. You'll find this option in the **Security** panel of **System Preferences**.

Forgotten password?
If you're locked out of your account, see p.51 for instruction on getting back in.

Tip: Unless you're in the habit of saving or moving files to random places on the hard drive, all your private data lives in your home folder. That includes not just your documents, movies, etc, but all your emails, Web cache, saved passwords (all of which live in your **Library**) and everything on your desktop.

Tip: If you share your Mac with friends or family members, but you find it more convenient to have only one user account set up, consider locking the various **System Preferences** panels by opening them and clicking the padlock icon. That way, if anyone accidentally (or deliberately) tries to change any settings, they'll need to enter your password.

Tip: If you have problems with FileVault, but you want to encrypt your data, look into PGP desktop, a third-party application that offers a similar level of protection.

PGP desktop www.pgp.com

These tricks will make sure that no random outsider can get immediate access to your files. But that doesn't means they're safe. As we've seen (see p.50), anyone set up as an administrator on the computer can easily reset your password and log in as you. And even if you're the only administrator, someone with a Mac OS X install CD can reset your password; it's also possible to pilfer data by booting a Mac as a hard drive (see p.278). For more security, investigate the following.

#1. FileVault

FileVault, introduced with Mac OS X v10.3, brings military-grade file encryption to your home folder. It scrambles the folder, so that even if someone can access your system by booting from CD – or even removes the hard drive – they won't be able to access your files without your password.

One problem with FileVault is that, since it encrypts and decyrpts your data in real time, it can marginally slow down your computer. The effect shouldn't be all that noticeable (unlike with the first version of FileVault that was released) but it bothers some users. Others have also reported strange problems that have been solved simply by turning off FileVault.

To switch on FileVault, look in the **Security** panel of **System Preferences**. Before doing so, though, consider setting up a master password for the computer – if you haven't done so already. This is basically just a backup in case you ever forget your account login password. Make a note of this one somewhere – if you forget both, you can kiss goodbye to all your files forever.

#2. Encrypting files & folders

If you don't want to use FileVault for any reason – perhaps because you're not the only person who knows the master password, or because you only have a small selection of private documents – you could make one or more specific files or folders safe by putting them in an encrypted disk image file (see p.99 for more on what that means). It's a bit like making a password-protected folder.

First, assemble the files you want to protect in a folder. Then open **Disk Utility** from **Applications/Utilities**. In the **File** menu click **New Image/Disk Image from Folder...**, pick a name and location, choose **AES-128** from the **Encryption** menu and hit **Create**. When prompted, enter a password and deselect **Remember password** for extra security.

Alternatively, click the **New Image** button to create a disk image of any particular size, which leaves room to drag in extra files later.

Your new disk image file will appear and be "mounted" (see p.45) as if it were a hard drive. Once all your private files are in the DMG file, you can delete (maybe "secure" delete: see p.45) the originals. Next time you want to access the files, or add extra files to your protected area, double-click on the disk image file and enter your password. Don't forget the password or, as with FileVault, your files will be lost forever.

DES & AES

FileVault and encrypted disk images are based on the Advanced Encryption Standard (AES), a very sophisticated system that marks a vast improvement over the earlier, but still widely used, Digital Encryption Standard (DES). AES is, at the moment, essentially impossible to crack. According to Apple's calculations, a computer capable of "cracking" DES in a single second, would take nearly 150 trillion years (longer than the life of the Universe) to work out your FileVault or disk image password.

Top Secret Folder.dmg

Top Secret Folder

Double-click the DMG file to reveal the password-protected virtual drive. Don't forget to "eject" the drive when you've finished.

#3. Open Firmware Password

If you don't want to use FileVault but you want to protect your files – or if you're keen to protect the entire computer rather that just your home folder – then employ the Open Firmware Password utility (found on your OS X software installation CD under **Applications/Utilities**). Once installed, the system won't allow any of the special start-up routines that can compromise security – such as booting from CD or starting up as a target drive.

If for some reason you *do* need to boot from CD, or use any other special start-up routine, hold down ⌘⌥**OF** and power up your Mac. When the Open Firmware prompt appears, type reset-nvram and hit **Enter**. Key in the password you created when installing the application, and hit **OK**. When the **Open Firmware** prompt appears, type reset-all and hit **Enter**.

Password Keychains

Computer users quickly accumulate lots of pass-words: for Internet connections, email accounts, websites, routers, network folders, online banks, disk images… the list goes on. When you enter a password on your Mac, OS X will usually offer to remember it. If you accept, you shouldn't need to enter that password again, as it will be stored in your virtual "Keychain", and OS X will insert it when required.

Keychains are very handy, but if you're worried about someone being able to access all your passwords when you leave the room for a few minutes, you could ramp up the security by asking OS X to "lock" the Keychain, either permanently or after a period of

Tip: If you ever forget a pass-word that has been stored on your Keychain, open Keychain Access (see opposite) and locate the relevant item in the list. Double-click it and select **Show Password**. You'll need to enter your Keychain password (the same as your account password unless you've changed it) and then the missing password will be revealed.

inactivity. When locked, the Keychain will request your overall Keychain password before dishing out any information.

By default, this Keychain password is the same as your account password – which is handy, but it means that if someone can access your account, they can also access your passwords. For even more security, you could change your Keychain password, or even add a second Keychain with a separate password.

All these changes can be made within the Keychain Access utility, accessible from the **Utilities** folder within **Applications**. Click the padlock icon to toggle the lock on or off; or select **Change settings** or **Change password** for "Keychain Login" (your default Keychain) from the **Edit** menu.

Tip: If you just want to password protect some text information – numbers and the like – create a Secure Note using Keychain Access.

Other privacy issues

▶ **Deleting files** When you delete a file, it goes to your Trash (see p.45), so anyone with access to the account can recover it. Emptying the trash stops this happening, though in theory the deleted files could still be resuscitated using special recovery software. To avoid this possibility, select **Secure Empty Trash** from the **Finder** menu, and the files will not only be deleted but completely blanked from the hard drive.

Tip: Also consider privacy threats on the Internet (these are covered overleaf) and over your wireless network (see p.63).

▶ **Private browsing** Your browser records all the websites you've been to in your History, cookies, searches and more. To stop this happening, enable **Private Browsing** from the **File** menu in Safari. Or choose **Reset Safari** to delete all the saved info (see p.150).

▶ **Recent Items** If you don't want all your recently accessed files and programs – as well as any servers you've connected to – listed for all to see, go to **Recent Items** in the Apple menu and click **Clear Menu**. Individual applications usually have a similar list in the **File** menu.

34 Hackers, viruses & scams

As we've already mentioned, one of the best things about Macs, when compared with PCs, is that they're so much less prone to online security threats. It's not that OS X is the computer equivalent of Fort Knox – though undoubtedly the solid UNIX foundation helps. Much more important is that "hackers" and the mischievous programmers who dream up viruses and "malware" tend to focus exclusively on Windows, since that's what most of the computing world is stuck with.

This is all cause for celebration for Mac users, but it shouldn't be cause for complacency – not least because Mac users are just as prone to scams as anyone else. Here's a quick breakdown of what you need to know about hackers, viruses and scammers.

Hackers

The term "hacker" is somewhat fuzzy, as its original meaning – still in use among the computerati – is a legitimate computer programmer (see en.wikipedia.org/wiki/Hacker). But it's the popular definition that concerns us here: someone who wants to break into, or meddle with, your computer. They may be a professional out to steal your secrets or a "script kiddy" playing with a prefab Trojan. They might be a vandal, a spy, a thief or simply just exploring. As far as you're concerned, it doesn't matter. You don't want them, or their handiwork, inside your computer. The best way to avoid hackers is to activate a firewall.

Firewalls

A firewall, which can be either a hardware device or a piece of software, prevents people from being able to detect and invade your computer via the Internet. Mac OS X comes with a pretty decent firewall installed, but you'll need to switch it on. To do this, open **Sharing** from **System Preferences**, click the **Firewall** tab and press **Start**. For most users, that's all you need to know. But if any Internet-related applications stop working after you switch on the Firewall, it probably isn't a coincidence. Try turning the Firewall off again and, if that solves the problem, look online for help about tweaking the settings to open the relevant "ports" for the application in question.

The firewall built in to OS X is perfectly good enough for most home users, but if you're really worried about intrusions, or you want to be able to monitor all the "network traffic" coming in and out of your machine, grab a third-party application such as:

Little Snitch www.obdev.at/products/littlesnitch ($25)
Norton Firewall www.symantec.com/firewall ($70)

> **Tip:** You're much less prone to all kinds of online privacy threats if you regularly install the latest patches and updates. Run Software Update (see p.45) every week or so and always accept any security fixes or OS X upgrades that you are offered.

◀ *When you activate any of the sharing options under the Services tab, the relevant type of network traffic is automatically added to the Firewall's "allow" list.*

Viruses

Worms to wabbits

A virus is actually a very specific type of computer "malware" (malicious software). But it's widely used as an umbrella term for the full range of malware, including worms, wabbits, Trojans, backdoors and spyware. In this book virus is used in this broad sense.

Are Mac users at risk from viruses? Any company with scanning software to sell says "yes", and it's true there's no reason why a killer OS X virus shouldn't emerge next week. But that doesn't mean that virus protection software is necessarily worth the money. After all, there are nearly 150,000 PC viruses in circulation, and the majority of PC users have suffered only a certain amount of inconvenience at the hand of viruses. For OS X, by comparison, there has never been a single virus circulated. If, despite this, you still want the extra protection of virus software, the most popular choices are:

Norton AntiVirus www.systemtec.com/nav/nav_mac
McAfee Virex www.mcafee.com

One point to note. Most of the viruses that have affected pre-OS X Macs were macro viruses, spread via Microsoft Word and Excel docs. If you ever receive a doc with embedded macros, choose the **Disable Macros** option when asked.

What about spyware?

Spyware is software designed to snoop on your computing activity. Most commonly it's planted by some kind of marketer, who wants to find out about your online surfing and spending habits. But it might be more sinister: a keystroke-logger that records whatever you type when, say, logging in to an Internet banking site.

Recent reports suggest that the majority of PCs are infected with some kind of spyware (mostly the non-dangerous types), but, once again, Macs users are relatively safe. No widely employed Mac spyware applications are known. So unless you have a particular reason to believe there's a snitch in your system, you shouldn't need this Spyware scanning package:

MacScan macscan.securemac.com

Scams

Mac users, understandably, get a little bit smug over their lack of virus woes, but they're no less susceptible to online scams, and these are often more threatening than any kind of malware.

▶ **Beware the phishermen** "Phishing" is a cunning form of online scam in which someone pretends to be from your bank, ISP, online payment system or any other such body, and asks you to hand over your personal information either directly or via a webpage. The classic example is a scammer sending out a mass email claiming to be from a bank, with a link pointing to a webpage purportedly on a real bank's website. In fact, all the details are slightly incorrect (for example, the page might be at www.hsbc-banking.com instead of www.hsbc.com) but the recipient doesn't notice, assumes the email is legitimate and follows the instructions to "confirm" their online banking details on the fake site – in the process giving them to

◀ *A classic phishing attack, received on a Mac by one of this book's authors a few months before publication. The payment never took place, but the sender was hoping to scare recipients into logging in to a fake site to find out more, in doing so handing over their user names and passwords.*

hackers, viruses & scams

TIP: If you get one of the notorious messages inviting you to make millions from taking part in African money-laundering, beat the scammers at their own game using this site: www.flooble.com/fun/reply.php

a criminal, who can then empty their account. The moral of the story: never respond to emails – or instant messages – requesting private information, however legitimate they seem.

▶ **Don't respond to spam** Those "get paid to surf", "stock tips", "work from home", "recruit new members", "clear your credit rating" and various network-marketing schemes *are* too good to be true. It should go without saying that ringing a number to claim a prize will only cost you money.

▶ **Paying by credit cards** online is actually usually safer than sending a cheque in the post, since most cards offer some degree of protection against fraud, businesses going bankrupt before you receive your goods, and so on. Read the fine print on your agreement for specifics, but normally you're only liable for a set amount. You also might be able to pay a yearly surcharge to fully protect your card against fraud, though this is usually bad value unless you think you're more at risk than others. If you suspect you've been wrongly charged, ask your bank what to do, but also contact the site in question – even some auction sites will pick up the bill if you've been conned.

▶ **Only enter card details on secure webpages** When a webpage is secure, the beginning of the address is https:// and a little lock symbol appears on your browser window. If you're concerned about a site's security, shop elsewhere or phone through your order, but never send your credit card details by email.

▶ **Don't give extra information** To make an online purchase you should only need to provide your name, billing address, delivery address, credit card number, account name, expiry date and, sometimes, the three-digit security code on the signature strip. You should never need any other form of identification such as your social security number, health insurance details, driving licence or passport number.

Backing up

Any computer file, whether it resides in a scruffy old grey PC or an elegant iMac G5, can be deleted or become corrupted. Though it's often possible to "recover" files that seem to have been erased or overwritten, this is of no use if your computer gets stolen or destroyed. So if your Mac contains valuable documents, a library of music or a collection of irreplaceable digital photographs, it's unquestionably worth regularly backing up your files to some kind of external media. Let's take a look at which files you should consider backing up, where you can store them, and the special tools available to speed up the process.

What to back up

When backing up your Mac, you ideally want to cover everything that could be a pain to lose – including emails, photos, music, movie footage, documents, bookmarks, preferences, contacts and calendars. The obvious way to make sure you don't forget anything is to back up the entire contents of your hard drive.

A slightly more efficient alternative is to back up just your home folder. This way you should get all your personal files and data but you won't waste time backing up applications or OS X system files that could be easily reinstated from the original discs or downloads (see box overleaf).

> **Tip:** If you're only backing up your home folder, have a think about whether you've ever saved anything elsewhere – such as shared widgets, screensavers or fonts in **Macintosh HD/Library**.

If there's more than one user account set up on your Mac, there will obviously be more than one home folder. If you have administrative powers, you could deal with them all at once by backing up the entire **Users** folder, found in the top-level of **Macintosh HD**.

Backing up selectively

You may find that backing up your entire system or home folder is impossible, since they contain too much data. If so, you'll need to be selective about which files you back up. A few pointers:

▶ **Music** The music files that make up your iTunes Library live within your home folder under **Music/iTunes/iTunes Music**. You can back up individual artists or albums from there, but if you want to retain playlists and other such extras, you'll need to back up the entire **iTunes** folder.

▶ **Photos** Again, you can back up individual pics, but if you want to safeguard your albums, Smart Albums and other such data, you'll need to back up the whole **iPhoto Library** folder, found within **Pictures**.

▶ **Library** If possible, back up the entire **Library** folder within your home folder, as this contains things such as emails, contacts and calendars. If you don't have space for it all, at least grab the following…

▶ **Email** If you use Mail, you'll find your email files within **Library/Mail**. For other email clients, look for a folder named after the application in either your home folder's **Documents** or **Library** folders.

▶ **Bookmarks** For Safari bookmarks, back up the **Bookmarks.plist** file (found within **Library/Safari**). If you use Firefox, back up the **Library/ Application Support/Firefox** folder.

Applications

There's little point backing up applications that came with your Mac or that you purchased "boxed" – you can easily reinstall them from the original discs. Likewise, downloaded software can usually be downloaded and installed again. However, do consider backing up any downloaded applications that may no longer be available (or only available in new versions that you'll have to pay for) or are so big that they're a hassle to re-download. One strategy is to keep a copy of the original compressed files that you downloaded in a folder (named "Installers" perhaps) within your home folder and back up these.

▶ **Contacts & Calendars** Address Book contacts and iCal calendars are found under **Library/Application Support/AddressBook** and **Library/ Calendars** respectively.

▶ **Fonts** Don't worry about fonts that came with OS X, but any that you've added can be backed up via the various **Fonts** folders (see p.125).

Tip: The items on your desktop are covered if you back up your whole home folder, but if you are backing up selectively, don't forget anything important that you keep there.

How to back up

Backing up files into a folder on your Mac's hard drive offers some basic protection, but if your computer gets stolen or the drive dies, you'll lose both your original and the backup copy. Hence the only satisfactory solution is to back up your files to some kind of external media such as hard drives, iPods, CDs and DVDs, all of which are discussed below. Wherever you back up your files, you can do it either manually or with special backup software (see p.273).

Tip: If you're struggling to squeeze your essential files onto any kind of backup media, consider compressing them first (see p.92).

External hard drives just a few inches across can store hundreds of gigabytes of information. This model by LaCie features fingerprint recognition security to stop prying eyes accessing your backed-up data. ▼

External drives

The most convenient way to back up your files is to drag a copy of them onto an external hard drive. Such drives are fast, capacious enough to back up your entire system and very easy to use: simply connect one to your Mac (via a FireWire or USB2 cable) and the drive's icon will appear on your desktop and Finder Sidebars, ready for you to drag and drop files onto.

External drives start at around $75/£50, with prices varying according to capacity, quality and any special features. If you want something less expensive, or to be able to carry your backed-up documents with you at all times, consider a USB flash drive – also known as "pen", "key" or "thumb" drives. With a capacity of up to a few gigabytes, these are small

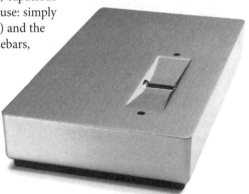

Tip: Some backup applications let you create an exact copy ("image") of your Mac's hard drive on an external drive. However, you can also do this manually with OS X's built-in Disk Utility tool, which you'll find in **Applications/ Utilities**. Simply select your Mac's hard drive in the list on the left, click the **New Image** button and specify the attached drive where you want to save the disk image.

iPod as back-up drive

iPods are basically just external hard drives in pretty white cases, and you can use one to back up and transfer all kinds of files – without even affecting its ability to play music. First, attach your iPod to your Mac, open iTunes and click **iTunes/Preferences**. Under **iPod**, check **Enable disk use**. From now on, the Pod will function exactly like any other hard drive: when you attach it, its icon will appear on the desktop and Finder Sidebars, ready to receive files. Note that, like any other drive, you'll now have to eject the Pod (see p.45) before physically disconnecting it – even if you're just using iTunes.

If there's room on the iPod, you could back up your entire home folder. But if you're short of space you may want to drag files on selectively – perhaps avoiding music and/or photos that are already stored on the Pod. That said, bear in mind that you'll need to use special software if you ever want to move your iPod's music archive back onto your Mac (see p.198). And if you're relying on your iPod's picture archive as a back up of your photos, make sure you have it set up to grab the full-resolution versions each time you connect the Pod to the Mac: open **iTunes Preferences** and click the **Photos** header; in the **iPod** panel, check the **Include full-resolution photos** box.

▲

USB flash drives such as this one from Samsung, are inexpensive and eminently portable – great for backing up essential documents.

enough to reside on a keyring (see pic left). They plug directly into any USB socket.

Before backing up to any external drive, create an empty folder on the drive and name it with a date (eg backup 04.02.06). Each time you overwrite its contents, rename the folder with the new date. This way you can always see at a glance when you last backed up.

CDs & DVDs

If you don't want to buy an external drive, you could back up files onto writeable CDs – or DVDs if your Mac has a SuperDrive. CDs are not ideal because of their relatively small capacity (around

Backup software

There are scores of applications on the market for streamlining the backup process. These let you save time by only copying files that have changed since you last backed up, and offer features such as scheduled backups and checkbox-style lists of important files.

Hard drives often come with backup software, but you might be better off with a downloadable application such as:

ChronoSync www.econtechnologies.com ($30)
Deja Vu propagandaprod.com ($25)
iBackup www.grapefruit.ch/iBackup (Free)

These all work with drives, including iPods – but not CDs or DVDs. If you're using an iPod, also consider Pod2Go.

Pod2Go www.pod2go.com ($12)

Apple's own application – Backup – is intuitive, offers loads of options, and makes restoring files very easy; it also works well with an iDisk. However, you can only use it as a .Mac member (see p.32). Similarly, rival-service Spymac comes with a tool called WheelGuard.

700MB per disc); DVDs are better, but the whole process is still slower and more cumbersome than using an external drive.

CDs and DVDs come in "R" and "RW" formats. The latter are more expensive and slower to use, but they can be blanked and reburned many times over. "R" discs, by contrast, can't be changed once they're burned (although it is possible to gradually fill up a CDR disc in discrete sessions using Disk Utility, which you'll find in **Applications/Utilities**). For more on DVD discs, see p.243.

Some backup software can handle CDs and DVDs, but it's also easy to manually back up files to either type of disc. By far the best technique is to drag the files into a Burn Folder (see p.81), press **Burn** and slide in a blank disc.

Rewriting CDs & DVDs

Before you can reuse a CDRW or DVDRW disc, you first need to blank it. To do this, insert the disc and launch Disk Utility from **Applications/Utilities**. Select the relevant disc in the left-hand panel, and click **Erase**.

Online backups

In a sense, backing up data online is ideal, insofar as your precious files are duplicated to a remote location. However, online storage space costs money, and uploading lots of data can take an age, so in reality this is only an option if you have broadband and you want to back up certain key files rather than your whole system.

Services such as .Mac and Spymac (see p.32) feature tools for backing up online, though you'll get more webspace for your money with a dedicated online storage service such as:

Xdrive www.xdrive.com
IBackup www.ibackup.com

Another option is to set up an email account with an online provider such as Yahoo! or Gmail (see p.152) and back up key files by emailing them to that account. However, with most accounts you'll be limited to sending around 10MB per email.

Restoring from a backup

In the event that you do lose data, in most cases you should simply have to copy the relevant files or folders from the external media to where you originally backed them up from. Obviously, you should only restore what you've actually lost. If you've accidentally binned a song or photograph, for instance, dig that individual file out of your backup and drag it into the iTunes or iPhoto window – don't overwrite the entire iTunes or iPhoto folders.

Of course, if you lose everything, you will first have to reinstall OS X from the disc that came with your Mac.

Help!

In terms of reliability and ease of use, Macs have come a long way since the dark days of OS 9. Still, no personal computer functions flawlessly, and your Mac may occasionally refuse to co-operate. There are whole books dedicated to OS X troubleshooting and it's obviously beyond the scope of a guide such as this to tackle every problem that you may encounter. Still, this chapter covers all the most common headaches.

My Mac has frozen

When your Mac is busy processing something, or it's frozen up ("crashed"), your mouse cursor will turn into a colourful spinning disc. Affectionately known as the spinning beachball of death, the colourful disc will sometimes disrupt only one application, but at other times everything will grind to a standstill. Either way, give the Mac a few minutes to sort itself out (see Tip), and then try to quit the application, either from its application menu or with the shortcut ⌘Q.

If that doesn't work, roll out the three-fingered salute: hold down the ⌘ and ⌥ keys and press **Escape (Esc)**. A box will appear listing the applications that you currently have running. If one of them says "Not Responding", select it and then press the **Force Quit** button; if "Not Responding"

> **Tip:** When you Force Quit an application you'll lose any unsaved work in that application. So if you're working on something important and you haven't saved for a while, give the machine five minutes or so to find its feet before trying to Force Quit.

Startup modes

When troubleshooting your Mac, there are various key combinations that do useful things during startup – some of which are referred to in this chapter. In each case, you have to make sure the Mac is switched off (hold down the power button for five seconds if you're not sure). Then switch on and as soon as you hear the startup "chime" hold down one of the following until something appears on the screen.

⇧	Safe Mode
⌘S	Single User Mode
C	Boot from CD

doesn't appear, pick the application you suspect has caused the problem and Force Quit that. If the application isn't in the list, see whether it shows up in the Activity Monitor list (see opposite) – if it does, select it there and press **Quit Process**.

If this doesn't work, try selecting Finder in the Force Quit box and pressing the **Relaunch** button. Still no joy? You may have to force your Mac to shut down: hold down the power button for around five second. After that, wait for ten seconds or so and then restart. Hopefully, everything will now be fine. If not, try repairing permissions (p.278). Or if the machine won't start up again…

My Mac won't switch on

If your Mac won't even begin to start up, check the obvious stuff. Is it definitely plugged in? Is the wall-socket working and switched on? All fine? Could it be that the Mac is already turned on and has frozen up with a dark screen? If so, hold down the power button for five seconds. After ten seconds or so, try again.

Still no joy? Try unplugging any external devices (scanners, printers etc; but not your mouse and keyboard). If you recently installed any internal parts, such as extra RAM, remove those too. Finally, if you have an Mac mini, an iBook or a PowerBook, try pressing ⌃⌘ (**Control** and **Command**) at the same time as the power button.

My Mac freezes-up during startup

First, force your Mac to shut down by holding the power button for five seconds. After ten second or so, start up again. Still freezing? Force shut-down again and, if you have an Ethernet cable attached to your Mac, disconnect it. Switch back on. No joy? Try Emptying your PRAM. Don't worry about what this means, just restart your Mac and as soon as you hear the "chime", hold down these four

Activity Monitor

Activity Monitor, which you'll find in **Applications/Utilities** is a useful tool for seeing what your Mac is up to behind the scenes. One thing it lets you do is select and Force Quit individual "tasks" – such as utilities and Finder plug-ins that have frozen. But Activity Monitor also allows you to keep an eye on your system's CPU, RAM and disk activity – which can often be useful when troubleshooting. If a small inactive application is consistently using up 50 percent of your processing power, say, that's a good signal that all is not well with that application.

To keep an eye on CPU, RAM or disk activity while you work, click and explore the options at the top of the menu. If you like, it will even display a real-time graph of your CPU usage on the utility's Dock icon.

keys: ⌘⌥PR. Keep them held down until you hear the chime again. Then release the keys to let the Mac start up.

If the problem persists, reboot in Safe Mode (see box opposite) and delete any non-Apple items found within these two folders: **Macintosh HD/Library/StartupItems** and **Macintosh HD/System/Library/StartupItems**. It that doesn't fix it, boot in Safe Mode again, open **Accounts** from **System Preferences** and, under **Login Items**, select each entry in turn and remove it by clicking the "-" button. Restart.

Still won't work? Try booting in Single User Mode (see box opposite). When the scary-looking white text appears, carefully type the following lines, hitting the **Enter** key after each line…

Startup beeps

If your Mac makes one or more beeps when you switch on, there may be something wrong with its memory (RAM). Assuming you can get to the internal slots, make sure the chips are firmly pushed into place. If you recently upgraded the RAM, remove the new chips and try using only the originals.

```
mount -uw /
mv /Library/Preferences/com.apple.loginwindow.plist preferences2.old
mv /Library/Preferences/com.apple.windowserver.plist preferences3.old
reboot
```

Mac as hard drive

Mac OS X's Target Mode allows you to boot your Mac as an external hard drive to another Mac. Turn off the Mac you want to use as a hard drive and connect it to the other Mac with a standard FireWire cable. Then hold down the **T** key on the first Mac and restart. Its hard drive should appear on the desktop of the other Mac. This can be a lifesaver if you can't start up your Mac and you want to access its files; or if you've forgotten your password and don't have your OS X startup disc to hand.

Repair permissions

OS X's permissions settings (see p.56) sometimes go pear-shaped, leading to all manner of problems. To repair permissions, open Disk Utility from **Applications/Utilities**. Select your Mac's hard disk in the list and click **First Aid** then **Repair Disk Permissions**.

If you can't access Disk Utility, insert the Software Install disc that came with your Mac and reboot while holding down **C**. You'll find Disk Utility in the **Installer** menu.

Finally, if you can't even access either of these modes, try running repairing permissions via Disk Utility from the Software Install CD that came with your Mac (see box).

Other Mac misbehaviour

When your Mac does anything strange – such as messing up your icons, continually freezing up or running slowly – and you don't know what the problem is, follow these three steps, in this order, before trying anything else:

▶ **Restart the Mac** This will fix the majority of problems.

▶ **Check your hard drive space** A full hard drive can cause slowness and other problems. Select your hard drive's icon on the desktop and click **Get Info** in the **File Menu**. If the figure next to **Available** is in megabytes (MB) rather than gigabytes (GB), then delete or back up some unwanted files and empty the trash.

▶ **Repair permissions** (see box).

OS X won't let me access a file or folder

If you can't open, delete or move a file or folder, make sure it isn't locked (see p.84) and that you have "Read & Write" selected under **Permissions** (see p.56). Still no access? Repair permissions.

The Trash won't empty

If you get an error message when you try to empty the Trash, quit all applications and try again. Still no luck? Open the Trash from the Dock and check through each of the files to see if any of them are locked (see p.84).

iBook & PowerBook batteries

Mac laptops are powered by Lithium-ion batteries that can keep going much longer than the batteries found in most PC laptops. However, over the years, all Lithium-based batteries gradually lose their ability to hold a decent charge, and in the end they give up the ghost completely. If you run your iBook or PowerBook from the battery every day, you may find that it needs to be replaced after a year or two. This is, unfortunately, quite normal, and is true of PC laptops – and iPods – as well as Macs. New batteries can be purchased from the Apple Store for $129/£89.

To increase the overall life of your battery:

▶ **Stay up to date** Among the various good reasons for accepting all updates to OS X (see p.46) is the fact that they sometimes relate to battery management. Also accept updates for your various applications, when offered.

▶ **Temperature** Your battery will last much longer if you use and store your laptop at room temperature or thereabouts. Avoid any extremes of temperature – hot or cold – especially for extended periods of time.

▶ **Plug it in** Plug in your laptop whenever possible, including when the battery is half charged. However, if you leave it plugged in nearly all the time, let the battery run down completely around once a month.

▶ **Storage** If your laptop is likely to remain unused for six months or more, switch it off when the battery is around 50% charged. To view your battery's charge status in the menu bar, check the box within the **Options** pane of the **Energy Saver/Battery** panel illustrated below.

To increase the time you get from a single charge:

▶ **Contrast** Turn down your screen contrast to the lowest acceptable level using the **F1** and **F2** keys.

▶ **Quit applications** Quit all programs that you're not using.

▶ **Switch off AirPort** If you're not using it, switch off AirPort via the fan-shaped icon in the menu bar. Also switch off Bluetooth, if you have it on.

▶ **Explore the settings** Open the **Energy Saver** panel of **System Preferences** and select **Battery** from the **Settings For** menu. Then choose **Better Battery Life** from the **Optimization** menu. Your Mac will be slightly slower, but slightly more energy efficient. To tweak the settings further, click **Show Details**.

help!

CD/DVD problems

▶ If a CD or DVD makes a rattling noise in your Mac, it's probably a fault with the disc – this is quite common. If it happens on all discs, the drive may need to be repaired.

▶ If a disc won't eject, even after restarting, then reboot the machine again and, the moment you hear the "chime", hold down these four keys: ⌘⌥OF until the text appears. Type these lines, hitting **Enter** after each:

```
eject cd
mac-boot
```

Tip: If you're worried about the possibility that your hard drive might crash, download SMARTReporter, a free application that will try to warn you in advance – by email or with an on-screen alert – if disaster is about to strike. Grab it from: homepage.mac.com/julianmayer

My Mac won't sleep

First, make sure DVD Player (see p.237) isn't running. Next ensure that Sleep isn't turned off in the **Energy Saver** panel of **System Preferences**. Finally, if you have a Mac laptop, make sure the keyboard hasn't come loose; if it has, push it back into position.

My Mac kicked the bucket

If your Apple's truly crumbled, resist the temptation to throw it in the kitchen bin. Find out how to dispose of it properly here:

Mac Recycling www.apple.com/environment/recycling

I deleted the wrong file!

If you've accidentally deleted – or overwritten – an important file or folder, and it's no longer in the Trash, you can probably still dig it up from the dark depths of your hard drive using data recovery software. Do this ASAP, as the longer you leave it, the smaller your chances of getting your data back. The best Mac recovery applications are:

Data Rescue www.prosofteng.com ($89)
Tech Tools Pro www.micromat.com ($100)

You can download a free trial of Data Rescue and use it to see which files you'll be able to recover (and salvage one file of 500k or less) before having to cough up for the full version.

Macology

Mac websites

There are thousands of sites on the Web that focus on all things Mac, from simple blogs to vast portals with discussion forums, troubleshooting tips, news and reviews. We've gathered together many of the best over the following pages, though you'll find hundreds more links scattered throughout this book. We've dedicated a separate section to online Mac weirdness (see p.289).

Apple

Apple's own site is a very useful resource, though if you can't resist a hard sell, it can be an expensive place to visit. It features stacks of downloads, patches, articles, info and tips.

Apple www.apple.com
Apple Store www.apple.com/store

If you're having problems with your hardware or software, drop into the Software Updates and Support sections:

Software Updates www.apple.com/support/downloads
Service & Support www.apple.com/support

But don't forget the discussion forums. Post a question or quandary and you may get a reply from a Mac know-it-all within minutes.

Apple Discussions discussions.info.apple.com

> **Tip:** Peeved with your Pod, PowerBook or Power Mac? Send feedback to Apple via:
>
> www.apple.com/feedback

Mac websites

Mac newsfeeds

The best way to stay up to date with Mac news is to subscribe to some RSS feeds (see p.149 for instructions). Many of the sites and blogs listed here offer feeds. But possibly the best technology news on the Net comes from *The Register*, whose Mac feed can be found at:

www.theregister.co.uk/ personal/mac/excerpts.rss

Mac gaming

Despite what those big bullies with overclocked PCs might tell you, there's plenty of gaming to be done with your Mac. Head to:

www.macworld.com/games
www.apple.com/games
www.macgamesandmore.com
www.macgamer.com
www.gamedb.com
www.insidemacgames.com

And if you like miniaturized, lo-tech games, don't forget the scores of widgets in the "Games" section of:

www.apple.com/downloads/ dashboard

Supersites, magazines & forums

For news, reviews, opinions and discussions, drop into any of the following:

About This Particular Macintosh www.atpm.com
EveryMac www.everymac.com
MacAddict www.macaddict.com
Macworld www.macworld.com
Insanely Great www.insanely-great.com
LowEndMac www.lowendmac.com
Mac Observer www.macobserver.com
MacMinute www.macminute.com
MacNN www.macnn.com

Rumour sites

Wondering what's in the Mac pipeline? Don't expect to find out from Apple, who usually only make advance announcements about their software. Instead, drop into one of these rumour sites. Expect around half of what you read to be true:

AppleInsider www.appleinsider.com
Mac Opinion www.macopinion.com
Think Secret www.thinksecret.com
Mac Rumors www.macrumors.com

Mac blogs

There are blogs covering everything these days, and Macs are no exception. A few of the best are:

AppleWatch apple.blognewschannel.com
Daring Fireball daringfireball.net

Tao of Mac the.taoofmac.com
The Unofficial Apple Weblog www.tuaw.com
The Apple Blog www.theappleblog.com
The Cult of Mac Blog blog.wired.com/cultofmac

Mac & accessories retailers

Reading the advice offered on p.22 – and scanning the reviews on the supersites listed opposite – should stand you in good stead when buying or selecting a Mac or accessory. Aside from the Apple store (see p.18), major stockists include:

Amazon www.amazon.com (US) · www.amazon.co.uk (UK)
Cancom www.cancomuk.com (UK)
MacConnection www.macconnection.com (US)
Mac Zone www.maczone.com (US)

Mac minis

From the day of its release, the Mac mini has been a source of fascination and wonder to many people. No surprise, then, that there are a number of sites and blogs devoted to using, upgrading, discussing and generally worshipping the crab apple of the Mac family.

123Macmini www.123macmini.com
Mac Mini Blog macmini.blogspot.com
Mac HTPC machtpc.com

Mac laptops

Despite their names, the following sites cover iBooks as well as their more expensive cousins.

PowerBookCentral www.powerbookcentral.com
PowerBookZone www.pbzone.com

Software downloads

Have you ever wished there was a bit of software devoted to carrying out some very specific task? Well, in all probability it already exists and is available for download via one of the following sites, all of which are overflowing with free or inexpensive apps for Macs.

Mac Update www.macupdate.com
Pure Mac www.pure-mac.com
Version Tracker www.versiontracker.com
Download.com www.download.com
TuCows www.tucows.com/downloads/Macintosh

Mac creative

These sites should help you get the best out of the iLife suite and, in the case of design, industry-standard "creative" packages such as Photoshop and Illustrator:

Apple www.apple.com/ilife
Mac Design www.macdesignonline.com
MacJams www.macjams.com
Jim Heid's Macintosh Digital Hub Site
www.macilife.com

Macs & PCs

If you want to make Apple and Wintel work together, see:

Emaculation www.emaculation.com
MacWindows www.macwindows.com

And for in-depth facts regarding the Mac vs PC debate, visit:

OS X Tiger vs Windows XP www.xvsxp.com
PC versus Mac pcversusmac.com

Mac programming & AppleScript

OS X software tends to have a friendly face, but behind the shiny icons lies a sprawling sub-culture of pale-skinned scripters and programmers, beavering away on everything from Actions (see p.113) and AppleScript (see p.114) to full-on applications. If you fancy joining their ranks, the *de facto* introduction to hacking – which among the computerati simply means programming, and doesn't imply anything illegal – can be found here:

How To Be A Hacker www.catb.org/~esr/faqs/hacker-howto.html

Once you're prepared, visit the following websites for links and inspiration – or simply to grab a sack-full of readymade scripts to automate your Mac.

AppleScript www.apple.com/macosx/features/applescript
Apple Developer Connection developer.apple.com
Doug's AppleScripts for iTunes www.dougscripts.com
MacScripter www.scriptbuilders.net
MacTech www.mactech.com
ScriptWeb www.scriptweb.org

MACTECH.

Linux on a Mac

Want to score maximum geek points? Then why not use your Mac to run the open-source operating system Linux, either instead of, or as well as, OS X. Find out more here:

www.lowendmac.com/linux
www.mklinux.org
www.terrasoftsolutions.com

Mac websites

iPods online

Gone are the days when the iPod was simply a cool Mac accessory. The music player has spawned its own vast online culture of sites…

www.ipodlounge.com
www.everythingipod.com
www.ipoding.com
www.ipodhacks.com
ipodstudio.com

…and blogs:

ipod.blogfreaks.com
www.ipod-news.blogspot.com
myipodblog.blospot.com
www.theipodblog.com

Help, hints & hacks

Whatever your Mac-related problem or question, the answer is bound to be online. A good place to start looking for help and advice is the Apple Discussions site (see p.283), but there are loads more sites out there. Try one of these:

About macs.about.com
Apple www.applefritter.com
MacFixit www.macfixit.com
MacZealots maczealots.com
MacOSX.com www.macosx.com
Mac OS X Hints www.macosxhints.com
XLR8yourmac www.xlr8yourmac.com

Troubleshooting Solutions for the Macintosh

Old Macs

Wondering what to do with, or need a driver for, your old Mac Quadra or Performa? Drop in to:

Classic Mac Addict thor.prohosting.com/classicm
MacDriverMuseum www.macdrivermuseum.com
LowEndMac www.lowendmac.com

Apple history

Want to know how it all started? These links offer the story of Apple – the highs, the lows, the beige boxes…

Apple History www.apple-history.com
Wikipedia en.wikipedia.org/wiki/Apple_Macintosh

Mac madness

Endemic among the Mac-using minority is a condition known as Apple Obsession Syndrome. While some AOS symptoms are serious (casual first-name references to Steve Jobs, for example) others can be entertaining, from gratuitous Mac modifications to ridiculous software. So grab your iHymn sheet and join us to pay homage at the high alter of Macdom.

iBook picture frames

Bored of using your iBook or PowerBook as a laptop computer? Why not turn it into an all-singing, all-dancing wall-mountable digital picture frame? A surprising number of people have done just this, and posted instructions online. Grab your glue gun and screwdriver, and head for:

DuoDigital www.applefritter.com/hacks/duodigitalframe
PowerBook Picture Frame barr104.spymac.com

The HollowScreen project

A "project" in the loosest sense. Take a digital photograph of something and set it as your desktop background on your iBook or PowerBook (see p.105). Then cunningly position your laptop in such a way that the screen appears to be transparent. Disarmingly funny.

HollowScreen www.hollowscreen.com

SlashNOT

SlashNOT is a pasquinade of the computing supersite Slashdot (which, by the way, bubbles over with Mac news and discussions and is well worth a visit). When you reach the front page, click on the big blue Apple logo to dig your way through to the Mac news section. There you'll get the lowdown on everything from the iToaster (see left) to Apple's attempts to sue Gwyneth Paltrow for naming her daughter Apple Martin, and not forgetting the rumours that Apple is in fact owned by Microsoft.

SlashNOT www.slashnot.com

◀ *This picture of the mythical iToaster can be found on the All-Electric InterWeb at:* www.worth1000.com

Hack a Mac

We've already showed you how to mess with the appearance of OS X (see p.105), so now it's time to think about your Mac's delightful outer shell – white and silver is just so Nineties.

If you hark back for the days when Macs came in such delicate hues as "tangerine", consider handing your Mac mini, PowerBook, iBook or iMac G5 over to a re-skinning service, such as:

ColorWare www.colorwarepc.com

Naturally, however, you'll have more fun doing it yourself. Get inspiration from the following sites, and maybe even enter the annual "Great MacMod Challenge":

Hack A Day macs.hackaday.com
MacMod www.macmod.com
AppleFritter www.applefritter.com

Got status anxiety about your old Mac G4 Cube? Why not dress it up as a top-end Power Mac:

G5 Cube Case www.conf.co.jp/new_folder/ making/cube_1.html

Or if you really hate the site of your Mac mini, why not wrap a car around it?

Classic Retro www.classicresto.com/macmini.html

And where would we be without a Lego option:

Apple Juice www.apple-juice.co.uk/lego

▲

Why aren't all iBooks produced in the style of the modified ones found at www.macmod.com? I wonder...

Mac madness

Terminal has a GSOH

```
000        Terminal — bash — 64x15
Lilly:Purity, sweetness.
Magnolia:Dignity, perseverance.
Marigold:Jealousy.
Mint:Virtue.
Orange blossom:Your purity equals your loveliness.
Orchid:Beauty, magnificence.
Pansy:Thoughts.
Peach blossom:I am your captive.
Petunia:Your presence soothes me.
Poppy:Sleep.
Rose, any color:Love.
Rose, deep red:Bashful shame.
Rose, single, pink:Simplicity.
Rose, thornless, any color:Early attachment.
Rose, white:I am worthy of you.
```

So, you thought Terminal utility was strictly for the serious Mac-head looking to squeeze that little bit extra out of his or her (probably his) machine via the use of the command line interface? Well, this techie-looking tool actually has a sensitive side. Open Terminal from **Applications/Utilities** and type:

```
cat /usr/share/misc/flowers
```

Hit **Enter**, and you'll see a poetic list of flowers, along with each of their meanings.

Not satisfied? How about a lo-fi game of Tetris? Open Terminal again, type emacs and hit **Enter**. Next press **Escape** and type **x**. Finally, type **tetris** and hit **Enter**.

System Prank

System Prank is a free download that simulates the uninstallation of Mac OS X and its replacement with Windows XP – complete with system bugs and viruses. Try it on your friend's new PowerBook (no harm will come of it).

System Prank www.titanium.free.fr/english.html

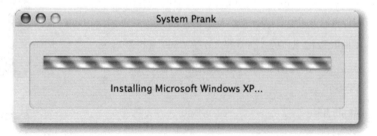

Mini vMac

Tiger may be slick and powerful, but can it match the retro charm of the OS featured on the Macintosh Plus, one of the first Mac computers to hit the market? Grab the Mini vMac emulator and decide for yourself.

Mini vMac minivmac.sourceforge.net

Apple spoofs

There are loads of spoof Apple products to be found online, and most have the letter "i" plastered at the start of their name, which makes them pretty easy to track down using Google. At times you might have trouble distinguishing the real ones from the pranks. But often it's not too difficult…

iShave www.application-systems.de/ishave
iBrew www.dropcap.co.uk/ibrew

Most spoofs are from Apple fans, but occasionally imaginary products are dispatched from across enemy lines. For example:

iToilet www.electric-chicken.co.uk/itoilet.html

The iToilet must have had a real resonance for one Jonathan Ive (see p.6 to find out why).

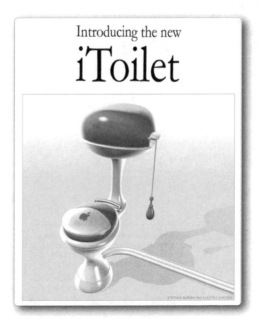

Introducing the new
iToilet

P-P-P-PowerBook

This epic tale of scams, pranks, PowerBooks and eBay will have you laughing for days. Download the PDF of the whole story from:

www.p-p-p-powerbook.com

Useless software

Our brief survey of Mac madness wouldn't be complete without a warm-hearted endorsement of the software available from:

Useless Macintosh Software Applications www.jschilling.net/software.php

Among the wonders on offer are The Lonesome Electric Chicken, who spews forth philosophical snippets of wisdom; EarthquakeX, which allows your Mac to experience fully-customizable on-screen earthquakes; Heart Monitor, which places an anatomical heart on your desktop that beats faster or slower depending on the activity of your Mac's processor; and PowerOrgasm X, which, when installed on an iBook or PowerBook, gives your Mac the climax of its life whenever the power cord is plugged into it (remember that scene from *When Harry Met Sally*?).

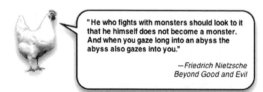

"He who fights with monsters should look to it that he himself does not become a monster. And when you gaze long into an abyss the abyss also gazes into you."

—*Friedrich Nietzsche
Beyond Good and Evil*

Index

Index

index

index

index

index